RULES OF THE MIND

RULES OF THE MIND

John R. Anderson
Carnegie Mellon University

With the collaboration of
Francis S. Bellezza, C. Franklin Boyle,
Frederick G. Conrad, Albert T. Corbett,
Jon M. Fincham, Donn Hoffman,
Nicholas Kushmerick, Christian Lebiere,
Mark K. Singley, and Quanfeng Wu

LEA LAWRENCE ERLBAUM ASSOCIATES, PUBLISHERS
1993   Hillsdale, New Jersey   Hove and London

Lawrence Erlbaum Associates, Inc., Publishers
365 Broadway
Hillsdale, New Jersey 07642

Library of Congress Cataloging-in-Publication Data

Rules of the mind / by John R. Anderson.
      p. cm.
   Includes bibliographical references and index.
   ISBN 0-8058-1199-0 (alk. paper). — ISBN 0-8058-1200-8 (pbk. :
alk. paper)
   1. Cognition.   2. Human information processing.   I. Anderson,
John R. (John Robert), 1947–
BF311.R85   1993
153—dc20   93-3217
                                                       CIP

Books published by Lawrence Erlbaum Associates are printed on acid-free
paper, and their bindings are chosen for strength and durability.

Printed in the United States of America
10 9 8 7 6 5 4 3 2 1

Contents

Preface

In 1983, I completed a description of a fairly general theory of human cognition called ACT* (Anderson, 1983a). Its most compelling feature was that it was capable of applying to a wide range of cognitive phenomena. I have spent much of the 10 years since then testing the empirical consequences of that theory. Although my colleagues and I could have focused on many different empirical phenomena, there is no question that the majority of the effort in our laboratory has gone into understanding the nature of cognitive skills. Much, but not all, of this research has been devoted to the development of intelligent computer-based tutors that teach mathematical and computer-programming skills.

The reason for the focus on cognitive skill was probably that the theory was cast as a production system, and production systems provide particularly appropriate models for understanding cognitive skills. My motivation in writing this book was to give a general overview of the data from our laboratory (particularly from our tutors), which I felt argued quite persuasively for an understanding of cognitive skill in terms of a certain kind of production-rule analysis. Although we started with the ACT* theory, I have always felt that most of the data argued for production-rule theories more generally rather than for any specific production-rule theory.

I have always found it difficult to think about things in a general way for very long, however. In the pursuit of what general notions might mean in a more specific system, one often discovers flaws in that generalized thinking, but one may also find unexpected opportunities. When I first tried to write this book, I came upon such an opportunity, which led to the abandonment of the original book and the publication of *The Adaptive Character of Thought*, in 1990. The thesis of that book was that we could understand much of human cognition directly from the assumption that it was adapted to the structure of the environment. I referred to attempts to explain behavior in these terms as *rational analyses*.

Rational analysis, as practiced in that book, was largely independent of the mechanistic details of human cognitive architecture. Concerns with such details typifies a production-system theory. When I wrote the 1990 book, I wondered if I would be returning to production-system architectures or whether I could do everything in these more abstract terms. When I tried to account for the growing data on cognitive skills, however, I found that I needed the mechanistic details of a production system. It seemed to me, though, that rational analysis could be used to create some improvements in the ACT* cognitive architecture by guiding detailed design decisions. Therefore, we developed an updated version of the ACT* architecture called ACT-R (R for rational). In retrospect, it was good that I did the rational analysis book before this one, because rational analysis paved the way for an improved version of the ACT theory.

Along the way, a set of technical developments that were relevant to the computer simulation models underlying our production-system theories came together. The first was the standardization of LISP dialects into CommonLISP, which made dissemination and distribution of the theory more feasible. Second, computational power had developed to the point where every researcher could have access to the computational power to run these simulations. Third, our understanding of implementing and using production-system models had advanced to the point where we felt we could provide a system that might be generally useful. The disk included with this book helps to fulfill this goal of disseminating the ACT-R production system.

The fact that we were planning to distribute an implementation of the theory had a profound impact on the character of this book: The complex cognitive theory espoused could be subjected to extensive investigation by the reader and this forced us to take special care in casting our claims. We will have to see what the consequences of this feature are, but I think we are on the verge of a new era in our ability to distribute data and theory. I suspect that research in our own lab is going to be strongly driven by the feedback we get from those who use this simulation system.

The upshot of all these developments is a book that attempts to achieve a number of goals: to present data on skill performance and acquisition, to describe our tutoring applications, to offer a new ACT theory, and to facilitate use of the accompanying computer simulation. Some sections of this volume pursue a number of these goals, and some pursue just one of them. I have tried to indicate the purpose of the various sections along the way so that there will be no confusion about what goal is being pursued where.

Many people and organizations contributed to the research in this book. The Cognitive Science Program of ONR (through Susan Chipman) and the Human Cognition and Perception Program of the National Science Foundation (NSF;

through Joe Young) have provided sustained funding of the empirical and theoretical research. Much of the work on tutoring was funded by the Applications of Advanced Technology Program of NSF (through Andy Molnar). The Research Scientist Award, given to me by the National Institute of Mental Health, has made it easier for me to attend to my research in an academic environment. It enabled me to take a 3-month sabbatical to Flinders University in Adelaide at the beginning of 1991 to start this book. The hospitality and facilities there were invaluable. The members of my research seminar (Al Corbett, Stuart Elliott, Jon Fincham, Dan Kimberg, Ken Koedinger, Nick Kushmerick, Chris Lebiere, Marsha Lovett, Yulin Qin, Paul Reber, Steve Ritter, Ching-Fan Sheu, Lael Schooler, Chris Schunn, Emile Servan-Schreiber, and Quanfeng Wu) have provided a vital sounding board for many of the ideas. Some of the chapters in this book acknowledge their research contributions. Nick Kushmerick and, later, Chris Lebiere were the programmers responsible for the development of the ACT-R system. The development and maintenance of such a system by, essentially, a staff of one (although Nick and Chris did overlap a few months) is most impressive. Larry Erlbaum organized an excellent set of reviewers for the book: Clayton Lewis, Stellan Ohlsson, Gary Olson, Peter Pirolli, Brian Ross, and Richard Young reviewed the entire manuscript, and Ken Koedinger and Lynne Reder provided comments on some of the chapters. The book is definitely better than it would have been because of the input from these individuals. Last, but hardly least, Helen Borek has kept track of all the revisions, references, figures, and other aspects of my professional life. Without her, I would not have been able to do it all.

This book was written during Al Newell's illness; he died as the manuscript was being completed. I was especially aware of him as I was writing, because it was he who introduced production-system theories to cognitive science. But for him, I would neither be at Carnegie Mellon nor working on ACT. This book is dedicated to him.

John R. Anderson
Pittsburgh, Pennsylvania

Production Systems and the ACT-R Theory

John R. Anderson
Carnegie Mellon University

1.1 INTRODUCTION

The work of most cognitive psychologists is driven by the same basic question:
What is happening in the human head to produce human cognition? A great frustration of our field is that as we begin to search for an answer to what seems
to be a straightforward question, we discover (a) that we may not be able to
find an answer to the question, (b) that we are not sure what would constitute
an answer, and, indeed, (c) that we are not even sure of what the question
means. The goal of this book is to describe part of the answer to that question.
Given the general uncertainty of our field, however, we must first define an
interpretation of that question and specify what would constitute an answer to
it. These are the primary goals of this first chapter.

To avoid suspense, however, I offer here the partial answer that this book
offers: Cognitive skills are realized by production rules. This is one of the most
astounding and important discoveries in psychology and may provide a base
around which to come to a general understanding of human cognition. I suspect, however, that most readers must be wondering what this statement really
ly amounts to. What does it mean to say, ''Cognitive skills are realized by
production rules''? To help define this statement and place it in perspective this
first chapter contains a brief discussion of foundational issues. Section 1.2 specifies what the theoretical status of the production system hypothesis is. Then,
Section 1.3 identifies the basic features of the production rule theories of thought.
Finally, Section 1.4 discusses the identifiability problems that haunt such
proposals and how they are dealt with in the current approach. Each of these
sections has as its goal placing the current work in proper relation to the relevant

issues in cognitive science. The sections can be brief because they refer to fuller expositions of the issues elsewhere.

1.2 FRAMEWORKS, THEORIES, AND MODELS

1.2.1 Levels of Specification

Cognitive psychology (and, indeed, psychology more generally) has had an almost fatal attraction to bold, general claims about human cognition (and human nature more generally). Here are a few examples:

1. There are two memory stores: a short-term store and a long-term store.
2. Knowledge is represented in terms of visual images and words.
3. People solve problems by means–ends analysis.
4. Syntactic knowledge and general world knowledge are encapsulated in different modules.
5. Human information processing is achieved by connectionist networks of neural-like elements.
6. Cognitive skills are realized by production rules.

Each of these assertions fails the most fundamental requirement of a scientific theory: empirical falsifiability. There are ways of construing each assertion such that it could be consistent with any empirical result. For instance, almost any form of the retention function could be made compatible with the distinction between long- and short-term memory by suitable auxiliary assumptions. Yet, these assertions are transparently not without meaning and, indeed, can be elaborated into predictions that *are* empirically falsifiable. To understand what is going on here requires reviewing the distinctions among frameworks, theories, and models (Anderson, 1983a).[1]

Frameworks are composed of the bold, general claims about cognition. They are sets of constructs that define the important aspects of cognition. The distinction between long- and short-term memory, for example, would be a framework. Frameworks, however, are insufficiently specified to enable predictions to be derived from them, but they can be elaborated, by the addition of assumptions, to make them into *theories*, and it is these theories that can generate predictions. A single framework can be elaborated into many different theories. Certainly, many theories have been built around the distinction between long- and short-term memory; Atkinson and Shiffrin's (1968) theory is, perhaps, the

---

[1]Deviating slightly from standard APA form, Anderson (without initials) refers throughout to J. R. Anderson.

most famous. The details that one must specify in going from a framework to a theory may seem unimportant relative to the ideas that define the framework, but they are absolutely essential to creating a true theory. For instance, it may not seem very important to the concept of short-term memory to assume it is a buffer with a fixed number of slots, but this was essential to the predictive structure of the Atkinson and Shiffrin theory.

Even a precise theory like Atkinson and Shiffrin's, however, is not enough to make precise predictions about a specific situation, such as a particular free recall experiment. One must make additional auxiliary assumptions to define how the theory applies to that situation. For example, within Atkinson and Shiffrin's theory, different rehearsal strategies could be assumed. The theory, with assumptions about its application to a specific situation, defines a *model* for that situation. There are many models possible within a theory, each corresponding to one way a subject could approach the situation. It is a specific model that one actually tests, although sometimes one could argue that no model derivable from the theory would be consistent with the results. It has, for example, been argued that no version of the Atkinson-Shiffrin theory could produce effects associated with depth of processing (Craik & Lockhart, 1972).

Production rules constitute a particular framework for understanding human cognition, and by now many theories have been proposed as instantiations of that framework. In 1983, I proposed a particular theory called ACT*; here I propose a variant called ACT-R.² The details that define a specific production-rule theory, though perhaps insignificant compared to the features that are common to defining production rules in general, are essential if a claim that "cognitive skills are realized by production rules" is to be empirically falsifiable.

1.2.2 Cognitive Architectures

Production systems are particularly grand theories of human cognition because they are cognitive architectures. *Cognitive architectures* are relatively complete proposals about the structure of human cognition. In this regard, they contrast with theories, which address only an aspect of cognition, such as those involving the distinction between long- and short-term memory. Production systems are not unique as cognitive architectures. Popular, more recent alternatives are the various connectionist theories. To go back to an earlier era, Hullian theory (Hull, 1952) would constitute a cognitive architecture, although the adjective *cognitive* might seem a little misplaced.

The term *cognitive architecture* was brought into psychology by Newell, from his work on computer architectures (Bell & Newell, 1971). Just as an architect

---

²The reader will note this is a step in the direction of parsimony. ACT* was pronounced act star. The current theory is pronounced act ar, deleting the consonant cluster *st*.

tries to provide a complete specification of a house (for a builder), so a computer or cognitive architecture tries to provide a complete specification of a system. There is a certain abstractness in the architect's specification, however, which leaves the concrete realization to the builder. So, too, there is an abstraction in a cognitive or computer architecture: One does not specify the exact neurons in a cognitive architecture, and one does not specify the exact computing elements in a computer architecture. This abstractness even holds for connectionist models that claim to be "neurally inspired." Their elements are in no way to be confused with real neurons.

The major assertion of this book—"Cognitive skills are realized by production rules"—is a general assertion about the architecture of human cognition. It is limited in its scope only insofar as cognitive skill does not encompass all of cognition. This book illustrates some of the scope of "cognitive skill." Along the way to making precise this general assertion, I define many more detailed assertions and present evidence for them.

A missing ingredient in the discussion so far is a specification of what constitutes a production system. The next section describes the concepts that define the production-system framework. The subsequent section addresses a fundamental indeterminacy that haunts such theoretical proposals. Although this indeterminacy is a problem for all cognitive architectures, this chapter focuses on its manifestation with respect to production systems.

1.3 PRODUCTION-SYSTEM ARCHITECTURE

The basic claim of the ACT-R theory is that a cognitive skill is composed of production rules. The best way to understand what this might mean is to consider a production-system model for a common skill, such as multi-column addition.

1.3.1 An Example Production System for Addition

Production rules are if–then or *condition–action* pairs. The *if*, or *condition*, part specifies the circumstance under which the rule will apply. The *then*, or *action*, part of the rule specifies what to do in that circumstance. Table 1.1 lists a set of five production rules that are sufficient to perform a certain amount of multi-column addition. These production rules are informally stated. The next chapter deals with the issue of how to formally specify these rules and with the sticky issue of what we claim is in the human head when we propose such a set of production rules. For now it is sufficient just to get a sense of how these production rules work. These production rules operate on addition problems such as:

    264
  + 716
  ─────

The production rules are organized around a set of goals. One goal is always active at any point in time. The first production rule, NEXT-COLUMN, focuses attention on the rightmost unprocessed column and will start by choosing the ones column.

The next production to apply is PROCESS-COLUMN. It responds to the goal of adding the column digits, but there are other elements in its condition. The second clause, "d1 and d2 are in that column," retrieves the digits. Its third clause, "d3 is the sum of d1 and d2," matches the sum of those digits. In its action, it sets the subgoal of writing out d3. The clauses in the condition of a production respond to elements that are said to be in working memory. *Working memory* refers to the knowledge that the system is currently attending to.

TABLE 1.1

Production Rules for Addition*

NEXT-COLUMN
  IF   the goal is to solve an addition problem
          and c1 is the rightmost column without an answer digit
  THEN set a subgoal to write out an answer in c1

PROCESS-COLUMN
  IF   the goal is to write out an answer in c1
          and d1 and d2 are the digits in that column
          and d3 is the sum of d1 and d2
  THEN set a subgoal to write out d3 in c1

WRITE-ANSWER-CARRY
  IF   the goal is to write out d1 in c1
          and there is an unprocessed carry in c1
          and d2 is the number after d1
  THEN change the goal to write out d2
          and mark the carry as processed

WRITE-ANSWER-LESS-THAN-TEN
  IF   the goal is to write out d1 in c1
          and there is no unprocessed carry in c1
          and d1 is less than 10
  THEN write out d1
          and the goal is satisfied

WRITE-ANSWER-GREATER-THAN-NINE
  IF   the goal is to write out d1 in c1
          and there is no unprocessed carry in c1
          and d1 is 10 or greater
          and d2 is the ones digit of d1
  THEN write out d2
          and note a carry in the next column
          and the goal is satisfied

---

*c1, d1, d2, and d3 denote variables that can take on different values for different instantiations of each production.

TABLE 1.2
Trace of Production Rules for Addition

>>>Cycle 1: NEXT-COLUMN
Focusing on the next column.
>>>Cycle 2: PROCESS-COLUMN
Adding FOUR and SIX to get TEN.
>>>Cycle 3: WRITE-ANSWER-GREATER-THAN-NINE
Setting a carry in the next column.
Writing out ZERO and going to the next column.
>>>Cycle 4: NEXT-COLUMN
Focusing on the next column.
>>>Cycle 5: PROCESS-COLUMN
Adding SIX and ONE to get SEVEN.
>>>Cycle 6: WRITE-ANSWER-CARRY
Adding 1 for the carry to SEVEN to get EIGHT.
>>>Cycle 7: WRITE-ANSWER-LESS-THAN-TEN
Writing out EIGHT and going to the next column.
>>>Cycle 8: NEXT-COLUMN
Focusing on the next column.
>>>Cycle 9: PROCESS-COLUMN
Adding TWO and SEVEN to get NINE.
>>>Cycle 10: WRITE-ANSWER-LESS-THAN-TEN
Writing out NINE and going to the next column.

The production PROCESS-COLUMN illustrates the three major types of working memory elements. The first clause, "the goal is to solve an addition problem," matches a goal element in working memory. The second clause, "d1 and d2 are the digits in that column," matches part of the external problem representation. The third clause, "d3 is the sum of d1 and d2," matches a general fact from long-term memory. Often, goal information is distinguished from other working-memory information and *working memory* is used only to refer to non-goal information.

In this problem, the sum of the ones digits is 10 and so is greater than 9. The production that will fire in this situation is WRITE-ANSWER-GREATER-THAN-NINE. It sets a carry in the next column and writes out d2, which is the difference between d1 and 10. In setting a carry in the next column, the production rule is placing in working memory some information that will be used by the next production rule. Just as all the clauses on the condition side are conceived of as testing working memory, so too, all the clauses on the action side can be considered to be adding to working memory. Table 1.2 provides a trace of the production system solving the problem. The listing shows the production rules in the order that they fire and a little protocol generated by each production rule.[3]

---

[3]The actual production rule model is available in a file called Addition in the Examples folder on the accompanying disk.

As I demonstrate in this book, we can understand and tutor skills like multicolumn addition by assuming that production rules like these are the embodiment of the skill. One sees compelling evidence for production models like the one in Table 1.1 by observing a child acquiring the skill of addition using just these sorts of rules. I discuss tutoring research that displays this power of production-rule models throughout the book.

1.3.2 Critical Features of a Production System

You should now have a sense of how production rules function. It is worth emphasizing their critical features:

- Each production rule is thought of as a *modular* piece of knowledge in that it represents a well-defined step of cognition.
- Complex cognitive processes are achieved by stringing together a sequence of such rules by appropriate setting of *goals* and other writing to *working memory*, and by reading from working memory.
- Essential to production rules are their *condition–action asymmetry*, which as seen in later chapters, is reflected in many asymmetries of human behavior.
- A final important feature of production rules is that they are *abstract* and can apply in multiple situations. Thus, the rules are not specific to adding the digits 4 and 6, for instance, but can apply to any pair of digits. This generality is achieved by use of variables in actual production-system formalism. In Table 1.1 this variable use is conveyed through terms like d1, but as shown in the next chapter, the informal specification in Table 1.1 underrepresents the variable use needed to get the correct generality for the rules.

There are a number of terms used to describe production system operation: *Pattern matching* refers to the process of determining if a production's conditions match the contents of working memory. Because multiple productions may match working memory, there arises the issue of deciding which of these will be performed. *Conflict resolution* is the term used to describe the process of determining which production rules to perform. When a production rule is performed it is said to *execute* or *fire*. The sequence of matching production rules, performing conflict resolution, and then firing a production is referred to as a *cycle*.

Corresponding to a production system is usually a computer program that actually simulates the behavior described by the production system. Writing a production-system model for a particular task usually takes the form of writing a set of production rules to perform the task. Indeed, production systems are often used as programming formalisms by people working in artificial intelligence who have no particular interest in cognitive modeling. Their status as programming languages has meant that production-system theories are precise and complete theories of particular tasks. This is a considerable virtue.

One problem with production-system theories has been that it is difficult to come to a deep understanding of a model without access to the actual running simulation, and access to other people's simulations has been hampered by a lack of access to appropriate machines and languages. This barrier has been substantially eliminated by advances in modern technology. This book comes with a disk that includes the ACT-R system and a number of the simulations described here.

1.3.3 Alternative Production Systems

Over the years, multiple production systems that instantiate the general framework have been proposed. An informative overview of these production systems can be found in Klahr, Langley, and Neches (1987). Production systems can be traced back at least to Post's (1943) proposal for rewrite systems. They also constituted an important formalism in Newell and Simon's work, which culminated with the publication of their 1972 book, *Human Problem Solving*. Their early work involved production systems as a theoretical language, without a corresponding running program. The first production system that was implemented as a computer program was one called PSG, used by Newell as the basis for his original papers on production-system models of mind (1972, 1973). Figure 1.1 (taken from Klahr et al., 1987) shows the lineage of production systems derived from this first implemented system. PSG was the inspiration for the ACTE production system, which was the basis for the cognitive theory proposed in Anderson (1976). Over the next 7 years, this evolved and matured into the ACT* production system reported in Anderson (1983a). The ACT* production system was never completely implemented as a running computer system. GRAPES (Sauers & Farrell, 1982), shown in the figure, and PUPS (Anderson & Thompson, 1989), not shown, were partial implementations of the theory relevant to the acquisition of cognitive skills. One of the advantages of this book is the computer simulation that more completely corresponds to the theoretical statements in the book.

Other lines of production systems have evolved from PSG. Particularly significant among these are the OPS production systems, which evolved out of a concern for how to do pattern matching and conflict resolution more efficiently. OPS5 (Forgy, 1981) and OPS83 (Forgy, 1984) have served as the basis for development of some expert systems in artificial intelligence. The most well known of these expert systems is R1 (McDermott, 1982), which configures computer systems. Laird, Newell, and Rosenbloom (1987) produced a dramatic new system based in OPS called Soar, and Newell (1991) advanced Soar as a unified theory of cognition. A number of comparisons to Soar appear throughout this book.

Anderson (1983a) referred to the PSG and OPS systems as *neoclassical production systems* to contrast them with the ACT production systems. Soar

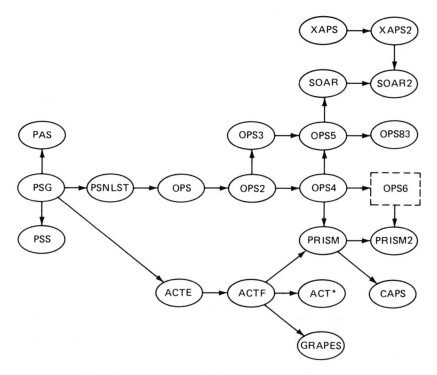

FIG. 1.1. Development of production system architectures.

certainly differs from these earlier systems in many ways and is much closer to ACT* and ACT-R, but it does preserve one important feature of the earlier systems that contrasts it with the ACT theories. This is that it represents permanent knowledge only in production rules, whereas the ACT theories propose a separate declarative representation. The next chapter discusses the significance of this procedural–declarative distinction.

1.3.4 Evidence for Production Rules

It is worth describing at the outset the general kind of evidence that indicates production rules are psychologically real, although more detailed evidence appears in later chapters. One line of evidence is simply the intuitive reasonableness of a rule set like that in Table 1.1 for describing the cognitive processes involved in a task like addition. The descriptive adequacy of a rule-based account has become apparent to most researchers in cognitive science—even those connectionists who oppose the symbol-manipulation paradigm. Thus, J. A. Anderson and Hinton (1981) acknowledged that "well-learned and regular interactions between patterns of activity can be captured as explicit rules governing manipulation of abstract symbols'' (p. 31), and Smolensky (1986) recognized that "novices are described by productions with simple conditions and actions, and experts are described by complex conditions and actions'' (p. 252).

Although the descriptive adequacy of such production rules has found ready acceptance, the critical question has been whether such rules are psychologically real. J. A. Anderson and Hinton went on to deny the plausibility of "models in which rules are added, deleted, or reordered'' (p. 31), and Smolensky asserted that "productions are just descriptive entities'' (p. 252). The critical question is what claim these rules have to psychological reality. A frequent view is that they are just descriptive approximations that obscure a deeper, underlying level where the significant psychological regularities lie. A major agenda of this book, therefore, is to show that the significant regularities in human behavior emerge at the level of production rules. It is only when a complex behavior is broken into subunits that correspond to production rules and these subunits are analyzed that we can see the detailed regularities of behavior, including the ones that connectionists are fond of. Thus, a production-rule analysis is actually critical to applying the connectionist program to complex behavior.

To establish the psychological reality of production rules, we have to commit to some theory of how production rules are executed. This is the function of the ACT-R theory that is described in the next few chapters. With that in place, I demonstrate the regularity in human performance and learning under a production-rule analysis.

In summary, the argument for the psychological reality of production rules involves two layers of evidence: One is the manifest appropriateness of rules in describing many aspects of skilled behavior. The second is the ability to predict the details of that behavior under a production-rule description.

1.4 IDENTIFIABILITY

Having explained what kind of theory ACT-R is, I come to the thorny issue of how we can know it is the correct theory. The answer might seem simple: The theory is correct if it corresponds to the available data. However, there are serious problems in using behavioral data to identify the correct theory of mind. The next subsections will explain these identifiability problems and the approach to them taken in ACT-R.

First, though, it is important to point out a tacit assumption made in the subsequent subsections. This is that the production-system framework is the right way to think about cognitive skill. The question addressed in the subsequent subsections is not how we know that there are production rules in the head, but rather, how we know ACT-R is the right production-system theory. This might well seem like we are focusing on the wrong question, but one cannot really argue for a framework because it is too poorly specified. The evidence for a framework always comes down to the success of the best theory specified within it. Thus, we have to be concerned with the details of the theory and how we know they are right. If we can get the details right, the framework will be established.

1.4.1 The Problems at the Implementation Level

For many theories, it is possible to make a distinction between an algorithm level and an implementation level (Anderson, 1987a, 1990c). That distinction is particularly well defined in the case of production systems. The *algorithm level* refers to a description of cognition in terms of the general steps of cognition. In the case of production systems, it is a description in terms of the production rules that are firing. The *implementation level* refers to a lower level description of cognition in terms of the factors that determine whether a specific production rule will fire and the speed with which it fires. The distinction is like the distinction between a high-level programming language like LISP and its machine-level implementation. Indeed, as shown in chapter 12, one can treat a production system as a programming language and simply ignore implementation issues. If we want a production system to be able to make psychological claims, however, we must be concerned with both the algorithm level and the implementation level.

As stated earlier, the details really matter when we make the claims that cognitive skills have a production-system base. Different production-system theories can differ in their details, at both the algorithm level and the implementation level. Distinguishing between different theories in terms of which production rules are actually at work (the algorithm level) is relatively unproblematic (as long as we do not get into empty debates about representation—see chapter 2). This is because the rules that are firing have such a close connection to the observed behavior. For instance, one could claim, at the algorithm level, that there was a carrying production that augmented the lower digit in an addition problem. This would be a different production system than the one in Table 1.1. It would be confirmed or disconfirmed by the observable behavior of a subject, that is, by whether the lower digit was actually augmented or not.

In contrast, there are profound difficulties in identifying what is going on at the implementation level. These difficulties arise because the theoretical claims about the implementation level are very detailed relative to the empirical data that can be used to judge the theories. These identifiability problems manifest themselves in two different ways:

1. Uniqueness. Very different proposals about what is taking place can result in the same claims about the probability and speed of production firings. These identifiability problems are rampant. For example, one might have one theory that claimed that all the production rules in Table 1.1 were matched in parallel

and another theory that claimed they were matched serially. In general, however, serial and parallel information-processing systems can be shown to be equivalent in their predictions about behavioral measures, such as processing time (Anderson, 1976; Townsend, 1974; Vosberg, 1977). Thus, behavioral data cannot distinguish between parallel and serial production matching. This is just one of the many ways that we face the fact that black boxes with very different internal structures can display identical external behavior in all respects.

2. Discovery. There is a huge space of possible implementation proposals and little guidance in finding the correct one. It sometimes seems impossible to discover one that is consistent with the data. It is like trying to find a needle in a haystack. The basic problem is that there are limitless ways to imagine the internal structure of a black box. Certainly, we have seen numerous proposals for production systems, and each has proven unsatisfactory in some regard.

One can question whether these problems really exist, and if they do whether they are peculiar to production-rule modeling. I have argued at length elsewhere (Anderson, 1976, 1987a, 1990c) that these are problems for all cognitive theorizing—not just for production systems—and it seems unnecessary to repeat the arguments. The news offered here is a way to approach these problems.

One can imagine the space of all possible cognitive theories, although infinite, as distinguishable into three ordered sets. First, there is the set of all theories. A subset of that is the set of theories consistent with the behavioral data collected so far. This subset is a tiny fraction of all theories. A much smaller subset of this subset is the set of all theories consistent with all behavioral data that could be collected. The discovery problem is that this final subset is such a tiny part of the set of theories. The uniqueness problem is that there is more than one theory in this final subset.

It needs to be emphasized that these are two independent problems. Even if we could recognize the right theory when we found it (i.e., solve the uniqueness problem), we would still have the problem of finding it. Even if we could find a theory consistent with the data (i.e., solve the discovery problem), we would face the fact that there are many equivalent theories. Thus, there are two separate problems, and they require two separate solutions. Although I cannot claim to have solved either problem completely, ACT-R reflects an approach to each problem that offers the hope of eventual solutions.

1.4.2 The Neural Approach to the Uniqueness Problem

The solution to the uniqueness problem that I have adopted is to commit to a particular style of implementation. Because cognition must be implemented in the human brain, it seems transparent that the implementation of ACT-R should be in terms of neural-like computations. Thus, the constraint used to choose among behaviorally equivalent proposals is that the mechanisms proposed correspond to what is known about neural processing. For instance, with respect to the parallel–serial issue, we know that neural computation is highly parallel. This tells us that many processes, such as memory retrieval, have to be parallel, including the matching of production rules.

The style of neural implementation assumed in ACT* and continued in ACT-R is activation based. Declarative memory structures vary in their level of activation, and this determines their availability. Also, the rate of production-rule matching is determined by the activation levels of the declarative structures the rules match. Rules compete by inhibitory processes. A major component of learning is increasing the strength of declarative structures and production rules. Thus, when we dig below the surface of an ACT theory we find a system of computation that looks much like a connectionist system. However, in ACT, these connectionist computations at the implementation level are being used to support a system that is symbolic at the algorithm level. The computer analogy is that the primitive machine operations support the symbolic processing of LISP.

We have only partially acted on our commitment to a neural-style implementation of production systems. The activation-based computations described in subsequent chapters are only a gloss of the computations a true connectionist would want to see specified in further detail. In the last chapter, I discuss some tentative ideas about further layers of elaboration.

Note, too, that the commitment to a neural-style implementation of a production system is no guarantee of a solution to the uniqueness problem. There may well be equivalent implementations consistent with what is known about neural processing. In such cases, we have to wait for more knowledge about what neural processing is like.

1.4.3 The Rational Approach to the Discovery Problem

The problem I had with the ACT* theory and other theories (even if they were neurally based) was that they do not solve the discovery problem: finding an implementation consistent with present and future data. There are an enormous number of ways to implement production systems in a neural-like system. Why believe one is more correct than another? One can try to find a theory consistent with the available data, but what reason is there to believe it will be consistent with the next empirical phenomenon? This is exactly what happened with ACT* (Anderson, 1983a). No sooner had the theory been published than results came forth that seemed inconsistent with it. Such an occurrence is hardly unique to ACT*. Of course, one can always revise the theory slightly, to make it consistent. This is what happened in Anderson (1987b), and the same thing has happened with other theories.

An infinite number of theories that are consistent with any finite body of data will make different predictions about data yet to be collected. We need some reason to believe that when we commit to one of these theories it will hold up when the new data come in. As argued elsewhere (Anderson, 1983a, 1990a), certain factors, such as parsimony, which help us choose among theories in some sciences, do not work that well in cognitive science. Biology in general and cognition in particular do not select systems on the basis of their parsimony.

It was this discovery problem that led to the rational analysis that was described in Anderson (1990a). In line with the arguments of Marr (1982), rational analysis seeks to provide some guidance in proposing the implementation details. Rational analysis was an attempt to understand cognition, based on the thesis that cognition is adapted to the structure of the environment. Anderson (1990a) was an attempt to explore this thesis with respect to the cognitive functions of memory, categorization, casual inference, and problem solving. In each case, it was argued that cognition seemed to maximize achievement of information-processing goals within the constraint of minimizing computational costs. The effort in the 1990 book was an attempt to show optimization with minimal commitment to mechanism, but rational analysis can be used to constrain the mechanisms that implement the production-system architecture. This is what happened with respect to ACT and has resulted in the new theory, ACT-R (with the R for rational).[4] The mechanisms in ACT* were tuned and slightly changed in ACT-R to yield adaptive processing under the 1990 rational analysis.

1.5 THE REST OF THE BOOK

The theory to be proposed in this book comes from the intersection of four constraints:

1. That it be consistent with the wide variety of data deemed relevant.
2. That it be expressed as a production-system architecture, which seems to capture many salient features of the performance of cognitive skill.
3. That it be implemented in terms of neural-like processes, so that it is something that might inhabit a human brain.
4. That these processes be configured to yield optimal behavior (given the statistical structure of the environment), so that we can have additional reason to believe in their correctness.

The constraints just listed are a consequence of the concern with identifiability issues. In addition to these constraints, it is worth acknowledging two other factors that influenced the shape of the theory. The first is the legacy of ACT*;

---

[4]When I wrote the 1990 book, I was not sure what the relationship between rational analysis and mechanistic theory was, although I did speculate that rational analysis could be used to guide mechanistic theory.

although the theory is not exactly ACT*, its structure bears considerable resemblance to that of ACT*. The second is the commitment to providing a runnable and usable system on the disk that accompanies this book. The need to have all of these claims embodied in one system forced a high degree of clarity and consistency in the development of the theory. I am hopeful that the accompanying simulation will do much to promote scientific communication.

As indicated earlier, there is a tension between grand claims at the framework level and the details that give reality to these claims at the theory level. This book shows this tension. Much of the book presents evidence that supports the general production-rule framework and discusses how that framework can be used, but the book also specifies the details of the ACT-R theory and the evidence for those details.

The next three chapters (2 through 4) are devoted to a detailed discussion of the theoretical assumptions of the ACT-R theory. Chapters 5 and 6 are concerned with research that supports critical aspects of the ACT-R conception of skilled performance. Chapters 7 through 10 report studies concerned with the acquisition of cognitive skill. The final chapters touch on wider issues related to production systems with production rules: Chapter 11 considers issues surrounding the use of intelligent tutors based on production systems; chapter 12 discusses how to build productions in ACT-R; and the concluding chapter, 13, reviews the assumptions of the theory and the prospects for the theory's future development.

2

Knowledge Representation

John R. Anderson
Carnegie Mellon University

2.1 KNOWLEDGE REPRESENTATION IN ACT-R

Knowledge representation is one of the thorniest issues in cognitive science. If we are to have a theory in which mental objects undergo transformations, we need to have some notation to represent these objects. The difficulty is determining what it is about a representation that amounts to a substantive theoretical claim, and what is just notation. This is a particularly grievous problem with production systems, because they take the form of a complete programming language. As a consequence, one can write systems that solve complex problems, going all the way from initial input to final output, leaving nothing that is unspecified or performed by an unanalyzed system. Programming languages, however, bring with them considerable theoretically irrelevant trappings, and it is easy to come to believe that these syntactic trappings amount to significant psychological claims.[1]

It is important to clarify which claims in the ACT-R representation are significant, and which are just notation. There are three essential theoretical commitments one makes in the ACT-R knowledge representation. One is that there are two long-term repositories of knowledge: a declarative memory and a procedural memory. The second is that the *chunk* is the basic unit of knowledge in declarative memory. The third is that the *production* is the basic unit of knowledge in procedural memory. These issues are covered in the three sections that follow.

---

[1]The problems of properly evaluating the claims of simulation models, which are acute in the case of production systems, are by no means unique to them (Frijda, 1967; Kieras, 1985; McCloskey, 1991; Neches, 1982; Ohlsson, 1988; Schneider, 1988; S. R. Young, 1985).

2.2 THE DECLARATIVE–PROCEDURAL DISTINCTION

The most fundamental distinction in ACT is the distinction between declarative and procedural knowledge. This distinction goes back to the original ACTE system (Anderson, 1976), and has remained through all the modifications. At the time of its proposal, this distinction was viewed as something of a radical suggestion,[2] one which many researchers viewed as having just been discredited in artificial intelligence (e.g., Winograd, 1975). Since 1976, however, a good deal of empirical evidence has accumulated for such a distinction in the human mind, as I review here.

Intuitively, declarative knowledge is factual knowledge that people can report or describe, whereas procedural knowledge is knowledge people can only manifest in their performance. A good example of declarative knowledge would be our knowledge that Washington, DC is the capital of the United States; a good example of procedural knowledge would be our ability to speak English.

The same abstract knowledge can have both procedural and declarative embodiments. Thus, declaratively we might have memorized the layout of the type-writer keyboard, and procedurally we may know the keyboard as part of our typing skill. Many people have lost declarative knowledge of the keyboard while remaining excellent typists. The only way they can tell where a key is on the keyboard is to imagine themselves typing the letter and seeing where their finger goes. This is an example in which the declarative knowledge seems to have atrophied. The two sources of knowledge are not mutually exclusive, however. People can and do maintain both declarative and procedural representations of the same knowledge.[3]

As noted earlier, one thing that distinguishes the ACT line of theories from the neoclassical theories and Soar is that ACT has long-term representations of both declarative and procedural knowledge, whereas these other systems have only a procedural long-term memory. The primary motivation for proposing a separate declarative memory in 1976 was to explain many of the phenomena of human memory (for a discussion see Anderson, 1983a, pp. 13–17). In particular, it is awkward, at best, to model with production rules much of the verbal learning research that is best conceived of as declarative learning. Recently, there have been some substantial efforts to model declarative learning in Soar with the mechanism of data chunking (Newell, 1991). These efforts are notable because they succeed at a difficult task, but not because of any insights they

---

[2]Perhaps calling it a reactionary suggestion would be more accurate. The idea had been around for some time, having received a notable statement by the philosopher Ryle (1949). By 1976, it had largely been discounted as a false distinction.

[3]Indeed, as I show further on, we can maintain multiple, different procedural representations of the same knowledge.

bring to the nature of declarative learning. There are numerous phenomena of verbal learning, such as associative priming, fan effects, depth of processing, configural recall, and so on (Anderson, 1983a), that data chunking does not address and that have guided the ACT theory of declarative memory. It would probably be possible to get data chunking to emulate the ACT theory, but this would amount to creating a special type of production memory that emulates declarative memory. Thus, notationally one can insist on representing declarative and procedural memory equivalently, but at the cost of clarity. The fundamental psychological claim is not that the two systems have different notations, but rather that they entail different memory processes.

2.2.1 Defining the Procedural–Declarative Distinction

Before progress can be made in discussing the declarative–procedural distinction, it is necessary to have a precise definition of the distinction. The natural tendency of experimental psychologists is to look for an *operational definition,* a set of behavioral tests that will allow them to know whether they are dealing with declarative knowledge or procedural knowledge. The most common operational definition involves verbalization. Knowledge that one is able to verbally describe or declare is considered declarative, whereas knowledge that can only be inferred from an individual's behavior is considered procedural. Although such a definition has advantages for the purposes of design and analysis of particular experiments, it does not serve very well as a general theoretical definition. There are instances of declarative knowledge that cannot be verbally communicated. For example, it is sometimes difficult to describe verbally visual knowledge that one might want to consider declarative, such as the shape of an object.[4] It also seems unreasonable to propose that nonverbal creatures do not have declarative knowledge.

The only satisfactory way to define the procedural–declarative distinction is in terms of a theoretical framework. The distinction will be defined here within a production-system framework. The distinction between declarative and procedural knowledge turns on the fundamental mode of operation of a production system. Productions function by reading information from working memory and writing information to working memory. The information in working memory is declarative knowledge, and the information in the productions is procedural knowledge. This distinction is much like that between program and data.

It follows from this relationship between procedural and declarative knowledge that declarative knowledge will tend to be describable and procedural knowl-

---

[4]One can be trained to describe pictorial information that one could not previously describe. It would make no sense to claim that acquisition of further verbal reporting skill causes a whole class of knowledge to convert its status to declarative.

edge will not.[5] To describe knowledge, some knowledge-reporting productions would have to apply that would inspect the knowledge and report it. The only knowledge that productions can inspect is the knowledge in working memory. They cannot inspect the knowledge contained in other productions. Although it would be possible to create production systems with some capacity to inspect productions, I know of only one production system, Ohlsson (1973), that has ever been created with this capacity.

It is also important to observe that all production systems cast this way, including Soar, have declarative knowledge as well as procedural knowledge. The issue that distinguishes the ACT theories from the neoclassical and Soar theories concerns the long-term status of the knowledge in working memory. In all production-system theories, there are some limitations on the capacity of working memory. In the neoclassical theories and Soar, once knowledge leaves working memory it is permanently lost, whereas in ACT the knowledge remains but is inactive. It can be reactivated for later use by a spreading activation process. The limitation on working memory capacity in ACT concerns *access* to declarative knowledge, not the *capacity* of declarative knowledge. Declarative memory contains a complete record of the past, from the last few seconds to years ago. The most recent records still tend to be active, but the older records can be made active when needed.[6]

So, the declarative–procedural distinction is built into the concept of a production system, and the only issue is the long-term status of the declarative contents of working memory. Other frameworks fundamentally blur the declarative–procedural distinction. It is not even part of most connectionist systems. Such systems are committed to a specific use of knowledge and have difficulty with deploying knowledge in novel ways. A typical connection net, coded to do addition in base 10, could not reflect on its knowledge and redeploy it to do addition in base 6.

Why should a system have both declarative and procedural knowledge? Two types of knowledge are required because one needs different knowledge structures for flexible use of knowledge than for efficient use of knowledge. Declarative representational capacity allows the system to acquire knowledge rapidly in a flexible form that is not committed to a particular use. A procedural representational capacity allows the system the ability to optimize the application of that knowledge for a specific use. It is this need for both flexibility and efficiency which motivates the declarative–procedural distinction.

---

[5]It is possible for declarative information not to be reportable because one lacks the reporting procedures. See footnote 4.

[6]Indeed, as discussed further on, the term *working memory* is only an expository convenience in the ACT theory. In principle, productions have access to all declarative knowledge, but some declarative knowledge is too inactive to retrieve. *Working memory* in ACT refers to currently available declarative knowledge.

2.2.2 Experimental Evidence
for Two Long-Term Memories

If one wants to retrieve what is thought of as declarative knowledge in a system without a separate long-term declarative memory, it is necessary to create productions that will perform this retrieval. Those productions would be of the form:

IF   Washington, DC is mentioned
THEN note that it is the capital of the U.S.A.

In contrast, this knowledge is retrieved by a spreading activation process (described in detail in chapter 3) in a system like ACT, which has a separate declarative knowledge. In such a system, this knowledge would be activated by having activation spread from Washington, DC to the fact. The two proposals behave the same at one level: First, Washington is in working memory (or active), and as a consequence, "Washington is the capital of the U.S.A." enters working memory (or becomes active). The claim of a system with only productions in long-term memory is that the same principles that govern the firing of productions govern this declarative retrieval, whereas the proposal for two separate long-term memories allows for different principles. The empirical question thus becomes whether procedural and declarative long-term memories behave the same.

A number of findings show that declarative and procedural long-term memories have different properties. The first three in the following list derive from the more flexible access to declarative knowledge. The last three derive from different acquisition and retention histories for the two types of information:

1. Reportability. As noted, procedural knowledge is not reportable, but declarative knowledge is potentially reportable. This issue of reportability of declarative knowledge is discussed further in chapter 12, in the discussion of verbal protocols.

2. Associative Priming. As discussed in Anderson (1983a), there is an associative priming process defined in declarative memory that has no correspondence in procedural memory. Thus, when one hears the word *computer*, there is priming for the word *programming* (e.g., one can read the word *programming* more rapidly), but not for one's computer programming skills (i.e., one cannot program more rapidly). Declarative priming is implemented in ACT-R through the spreading-activation mechanism.

3. Retrieval Asymmetry. As I discuss later in this chapter and throughout the book, there is an asymmetry of access to procedural knowledge that does not exist for declarative knowledge (e.g., Table 2.2 will show that learning about

LISP for purposes of coding does not generalize to using LISP for purposes of code evaluation).

4. Acquisition. As illustrated in chapter 4 and elsewhere, the origins of declarative and procedural knowledge are different. Declarative knowledge comes from direct encoding of the environment, whereas procedural knowledge must be compiled from declarative knowledge through practice. Thus, skills are often acquired by analogy to declarative representations of examples (see chapter 4).[7]

5. Retention. The retention functions for the two types of memories are independent. The most striking case of this is when people get better at using the procedural knowledge but worse at recalling the declarative knowledge. The typing example discussed earlier illustrates this.

6. Dissociation. There have been a number of recent demonstrations of dissociations of declarative and procedural memory in amnesiacs and other populations. They have received so much attention lately that I discuss them at length in the next two subsections.

This is not to say there are no features common to declarative and procedural memory. There should be, because they are both presumably implemented in neurons and should, therefore, reflect common properties of neural processing. As elaborated in chapter 4, for example, it seems that the functions describing the build-up and decay of strength are the same for the two types of memory.

Parsimony has seductive attraction in cognitive science, and theorists are often drawn to the belief that by some representational maneuver they can get two classes of phenomena out of one set of principles. This goes back, at least, to Watson's (1930) attempts to argue that memory was just verbal habit, but these efforts have so far proven themselves to be sophism. Such systems neither run nor address the empirical phenomena.

2.2.3 Dissociation of Declarative and Procedural Memory

A recent surge of research supports the separation of declarative and procedural memory. Much of it has involved looking at amnesiacs who exhibit an inability to learn new information as a function of neural damage. The widely studied patient, HM, is one such subject. HM had parts of his temporal lobes removed in an attempt to treat epilepsy. He has one of the most profound amnesias ever documented and, for over 30 years, has been unable to consciously recall new events, although he remembers things from before his operation reasonably well.

---

[7]The ACT assumption that procedural knowledge originates in declarative knowledge has been criticized. I review these criticisms at the end of the next subsection.

In other words, he has lost the ability to acquire new declarative information. Nevertheless, he has been able to acquire new skills, such as a rotary pursuit task, even though, when questioned on later learning trials, he claims not to remember ever doing the task before (Corkin, 1968).

A group of patients with similar amnesiac symptoms are Korsakoff patients, who have suffered extensive neural damage as a result of a long history of alcohol abuse and nutritional deficit. Cohen and Squire (1980) presented Korsakoff amnesiacs and normals with mirror images of words. Both groups improved equally rapidly at reading the words, but the Korsakoff patients showed substantial impairment in remembering the words they had read. Thus, they acquired the procedural skill of reading the words while failing to retain the declarative knowledge of having seen the words.

There have been numerous demonstrations of amnesiacs' learning of skills with strong perceptuomotor components, but relatively few demonstrations of their ability to learn skills that are more purely cognitive. Cohen, Eichenbaum, Deacedo, and Corkin (1985) reported teaching amnesiacs to perform in the Tower of Hanoi task, but others have failed to replicate this result (e.g., Butters, Wolfe, Martone, Gramholm, & Cermak, 1985). Hirst, Phelps, Johnson, and Volpe (1988) claimed success at teaching an amnesiac to speak French, and Milberg, Alexander, Charness, McGlinchey-Berroth, and Barrett (1988) were able to teach two amnesiacs an arithmetic algorithm.

Normal individuals sometimes appear to acquire a skill without having conscious access to the knowledge required to perform the skill. For instance, Broadbent, Fitzgerald, and Broadbent (1986) demonstrated that normal subjects could learn to operate a model transportation system without being able to articulate the rules. Amnesiacs given the same task were also able to learn it (Phelps, 1989).

In reviewing the literature on cognitive skill learning, Phelps concluded that amnesiacs are able to learn skills in cases where the skill learning does not require recalling past events and integrating them. That is, if the skill can be learned using only current declarative information and without requiring long-term declarative memory, amnesic subjects can learn it. She found that amnesiacs were able to learn Broadbent et al.'s task only if they were given concurrent access to previous trials and did not have to remember them; normal subjects did not need such assisted access to previous trials.

The research of Nissen and her associates provides further evidence for the procedural–declarative distinction. Her paradigm involves having subjects learn to press a set of buttons according to a 10-trial repeating-stimulus sequence. She separately tracks procedural learning of the sequence and declarative learning of the sequence. Her measure of procedural learning is the increase in speed with which subjects can press the button that corresponds to the next item in the sequence. Her measure of declarative learning is the ability to describe the sequence or explicitly predict it. She has shown in a number of ways that procedural and declarative learning can be disassociated:

1. Normal subjects show both declarative and procedural learning, but the two are uncorrelated (Wellington, Nissen, & Bullemer, 1989).
2. Amnesic patients show only procedural learning (Knopman & Nissen, 1987; Wellington et al., 1989).
3. Administration of scopolamine to normals impairs declarative learning but not procedural learning (Nissen, Knopman, & Schacter, 1987).

Nissen interpreted her results as showing that acquisition of procedural knowledge does not depend on declarative knowledge, in contrast to the claims of ACT. What her results really show, however, is that acquisition of procedural knowledge does not depend on *long-term* declarative learning. Indeed, when she distracted subjects from forming a declarative representation of the sequence by using a dual-task procedure, they failed to show any procedural learning (Wellington et al., 1987). Thus, it seems that active (but not necessarily long-term) declarative representations are essential for procedural learning. ACT-R requires that declarative structures be active to support procedural learning; it does not require that they be capable of being retrieved at a delay.[8]

Broadbent (1989) has similarly argued that the results from the Berry and Broadbent (1984) task contradict ACT's claim that procedural knowledge derives from declarative knowledge. They showed that subjects can learn to manipulate a rule-based system successfully but cannot consciously state the rules. It appears that, in this situation, subjects were basing their behavior on memory for specific examples and not on rules (Marescaux, Dejean, & Karnas, 1990). Similarly, the performance in the Reber task, which has long been cited as an example of implicit learning of rules, appears to originate in declarative memory for fragments of specific examples (Dulany, Carlson, & Dewey, 1984; Servan-Schreiber & Anderson, 1990). Thus, it appears that sometimes subjects are using declarative knowledge other than what the experimenter had in mind.

As one cautionary note, it is too simple to view all literature on amnesia as showing procedural long-term memory preserved. It might be more accurate to view much of it as declarative long-term storage lost. It appears that many other capacities are preserved besides procedural memory, including the priming of declarative memories established before the amnesia (Schacter, 1987).

2.2.4 Interpretation of Amnesia Results

Although the data from amnesiacs seem to support the procedural–declarative distinction of ACT-R, it is another question to determine how they are to be interpreted within the theory. One view would be that new declarative structures are lost rapidly after being formed, but this does not seem in keeping with

---

[8]Note that in many situations the requisite declarative structures are kept active in the environment.

the ACT-R theory because its model for normal functioning does not involve loss of declarative structures. Rather, what declarative structures lose with time is strength. Most amnesiacs are not totally discontinuous with normals and can recall something on delayed memory tests. This could be produced in ACT-R either by having a weaker initial encoding process or a more rapid forgetting process. In this regard, it is interesting to note that amnesiacs can be made to display the same forgetting functions as normals if they are overtrained (Huppert & Piercy, 1978). Thus, perhaps the best interpretation of amnesia in ACT-R is in terms of weak initial memory traces. The concept of trace strength is developed in the next two chapters.

As a final remark, it is certainly the case that there are theoretical interpretations of these amnesia data not based on the procedural–declarative distinction. One of the more notable alternatives is the transfer-appropriate-processing explanation of Roediger and Blaxton (1987). They argued that what are classified as declarative tasks are better considered conceptually driven tasks, and what are classified as procedural tasks are better considered as data-driven tasks. Their argument would be that the ability to acquire conceptual knowledge is impaired, whereas the more perceptual knowledge can be maintained. A major problem with this proposal is the apparent ability of the amnesic subjects to acquire relatively complex problem-solving skills that seem to defy the description of *data-driven*. Unfortunately, the empirical record on these tasks is not as clear as it is on other tasks.

2.3 THE "CHUNK" IN DECLARATIVE MEMORY

Having determined that there are two types of long-term memory, we still must decide what their characteristics are. Declarative information is represented in terms of data structures which are basically the chunks that G. A. Miller described in 1956 and which were the focus of a great deal of research in psychology until the mid-1970s (for a review, see N. F. Johnson, 1970). New declarative knowledge is added to memory (and hence long-term memory) a chunk at a time. In the language of production systems, the units in which knowledge is represented in working memory are referred to as *working-memory elements* or WMEs (pronounced wimees).[9] There are three significant features associated with a chunk, or WME, within the ACT-R theory. First, it appears that only a limited number of components can be combined in a single chunk. Second, chunks have configural properties such that different components have different roles, which would not be the case if these were just elements of a mathematical set. Third, chunks are capable of a hierarchical organization, such that

---

[9]We will retain this name although it might be clearer to try to introduce a terminological change and call them *declarative memory elements*, or dimees.

chunks can appear as components of other chunks. Subsequent subsections describe each of these properties of chunks; this is followed by some discussion of what representational notation might be appropriate for them.

It is worth saying a little about terminology here. I am using *chunk* to refer to essentially the same thing as what I called a *cognitive unit* in the book on ACT* (Anderson, 1983a). My change in terminology is just a reflection of my realization that what was essential in the concept of a cognitive unit is identical to what the term *chunk* had meant in psychology. Also, note that *chunk* as used here is very different from *chunking* as it has been used in Soar. Chunking in Soar refers to a form of procedural learning not unlike composition in ACT* (which is briefly described in chapter 4). A chunk in Miller's conception is a declarative structure.

2.3.1   The Size of Chunks—Three Elements?

A chunk is a means of organizing a set of elements into a long-term memory unit. Thus *USA* can be thought of as a chunk organizing three letters into a single unit. It is generally thought that only so many elements can be organized within a chunk. If more elements have to be combined, we need to have sub-chunks within chunks. Thus, people naturally break longer sequences up into sub-elements. For instance, telephone numbers are encoded as a prefix (the "exchange") plus a number. If subjects are asked to repeat back a set of digits, they will be observed to insert pauses indicating they have imposed a hierarchical structure on the set.

If there is a limit on the number of elements that can be organized within a chunk, the question naturally arises as to what that limit is. Broadbent (1975) argued that this number is three. He gathered together a variety of data, none of which alone is all that convincing, but in combination it begins to create a case. One of the things he did was observe the length of runs subjects would give before inserting a pause in a sequence of elements. He found that 54% of all pauses came after a pair of items, 29% after three, 9% after four, and 9% after longer sequences. This gives somewhat the appearance of a barrier after three elements.

Broadbent also cited a number of memory studies. Ryan (1969), for example, chunked a sequence of nine digits into three groups of various sizes for her subjects. She found recall to be best when the subsequences were three groups of three each. Similarly, Wickelgren (1964) found memory to be most efficient when rehearsal groups were of size three: If three were the ideal chunk size, using smaller rehearsal groups would mean more chunks would be required to encode the sequence than necessary. Using rehearsal groups larger than three would mean that the rehearsal groups would have to be broken down into sub-chunks (that would not be of optimal size three).

There have also been a number of mathematical demonstrations (e.g., Dirlam, 1972) that, under certain assumptions about the nature of memory retrieval, a chunk size of about three would lead to optimal memory performance.[10]

There are two ways to view such data and arguments. One is that there is an absolute bound on chunk size. It seems wiser, however, to view it as indicating that there is a best chunk size, that performance will deteriorate if one goes beyond it, and therefore, that the system will tend to organize itself in chunks of that size. It is interesting to carry through a limitation on chunk size and see what this would mean in a full cognitive architecture. As I illustrate in the formal representation of the addition task in Table 2.1 (in subsection 2.3.4), taking the chunk size constraint seriously can help identify flaws in one's representational assumptions that often result in too-large chunks. However, the issues of skill acquisition, which are the focus of this book, prove to be relatively insensitive to issues of chunk size limitation. So, chunk size limitations will not get any serious treatment here. The ACT-R software that accompanies this book places no constraints on chunk size, leaving it a matter of individual choice.

2.3.2 The Configural Structure of Chunks

The second feature of chunks is that their elements assume specific relational roles. This is most clearly demonstrated with strings of elements: If subjects study a set of letters in one order, it takes longer to recognize them when they are presented in a different order (e.g., Angiolillo, Bent, & Rips, 1982). The structure of elements is not always linear, however: Many chunks are spatial and have their elements encoded with respect to particular positions in space. Also, it is critical to have what are variously called *propositional*, or *semantic*, or *relational* representations, in which elements are encoded with respect to their semantic relationships.[11]

The experiment by Santa (1977) is a nice demonstration of the difference between linear and spatial representations and of the importance of configuration to the encoding of declarative information. Figure 2.1 illustrates his materials. Subjects were shown spatial arrays of either three figures or three words. They were then shown another array of elements and asked to judge if the same elements were in that array. When subjects viewed an array of figures, they were fastest when the test array presented the same figures in the same spatial locations. When they were presented with words, they were fastest when tested with a list of the elements in the left-to-right order that they would have been read in in the test array. Thus, in Fig. 2.1, the first test array is identified

---

[10]Note, however, that Servan-Schreiber (1991) argued for binary chunks.

[11]Anderson (1983a) referred to these three types of configural representations as *temporal string*, *spatial image*, and *abstract proposition*.

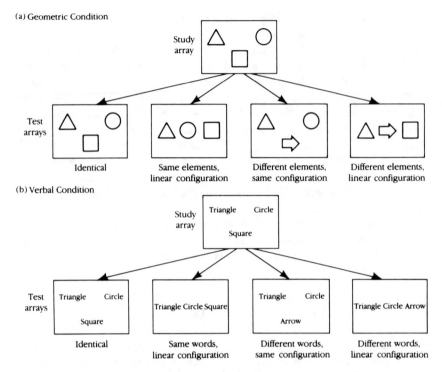

FIG. 2.1.   Illustration of Santa's (1977) experiment. Subjects studied an initial
array and then had to decide whether a test array contained the same elements.

fastest in part (a), but the second test array is fastest in part (b). It appears
that when subjects are given geometric figures, they naturally encode the elements spatially and require a spatial match. When given words, however, they
naturally encode them linearly and do best when the test array matches that
linear order. This experiment illustrates both that configuration is important in
encoding a chunk and that different configural principles apply to different chunks.

2.3.3   The Hierarchical Organization of Chunks

A third feature of chunks is that they can enter into hierarchical organizations,
such that chunks appear within chunks. A number of experiments have been
done demonstrating the existence of two levels of chunks (e.g., N. F. Johnson,
1970). For instance, the string of letters, D Y J H Q G W, might be organized
as the chunks, DY JHQ GW, which are then organized into a higher-order
chunk, which is the complete string, DYJHQGW. There have been relatively few
studies that have tried to demonstrate the existence of more than two levels

in a hierarchy, but such studies do exist. Bower, Clark, Lesgold, and Winzenz (1969) were able to show a hierarchical organization of elements (e.g., minerals) in up to four levels. Klahr, Chase, and Lovelace (1983) found evidence for a similarly complex representation of the 26 letters in the alphabet. Chase and Ericsson (1982) argued that the 80 + digit span of their memory experts also depended on a deeply nested representation. In all these cases, it is a bit difficult to get behavioral indicants to discriminate all the proposed levels, but it seems plausible that such representations are being used by the subjects.

2.3.4 A Notation for Chunks

Having settled on the significant properties of chunks, we must now concern ourselves with how to represent a chunk and its particular number of elements, configural properties, and possible positions in hierarchies. For some purposes, informal English descriptions might be adequate, but they will not be when precision is required for either theoretical statement or computer specification. In our own computer simulation work, my colleagues and I have gradually developed a "vanilla," schema-like representation like that used in many other AI applications. Table 2.1 illustrates what that representation would be like for the initial state of the addition problem discussed in chapter 1.[12]

The chunks in this representation are problem1, column0, column1, column2, and column3. Associated with each chunk are a number of slots. The first slot is the isa slot, which indicates what type of chunk it is. This identifies the configural properties of the chunk, because the type of the chunk determines what other slots there can be.[13] The first chunk in Table 2.1 is of type numberarray, and the remainder are of type column. The remaining slots in the chunk contain pointers to other working-memory elements. The first chunk in Table 2.1 has pointers to the four columns, whereas each of the column chunks has pointers to the three rows. The four columns are encoded in a list to facilitate getting the next column by the production rule NEXT-COLUMN (why this is so becomes clear in the formal encoding of the production rule in Table 2.3). The example in Table 2.1 is basically a double-linear encoding of an array (columns encoded linearly and rows encoded linearly within columns).

This schema-like system can also be used to encode spatial and propositional information. So, the study array (top box) in Fig. 2.1a could be encoded as:

---

[12]The full working-memory encoding, which includes a lot of addition-table facts, is available in the Addition file in the accompanying Examples folder.

[13]As we see in chapter 12, it is necessary to first declare what slots can appear with each chunk type.

picture 1
    isa square
    upper-left triangle1
    upper-right circle1
    lower-middle square1

triangle1
    isa triangle
    vertical top-third
    horizontal left-third

circle1
    isa circle
    vertical top-third
    horizontal right-third

square1
    isa square
    vertical bottom-third
    horizontal middle-third

TABLE 2.1
Schema Representation of the Problem:
264
+716

---

problem1
  isa numberarray
  columns (column0 column1 column2 column3)
column0
  isa column
  toprow blank
  bottomrow +
  answerrow blank
column1
  isa column
  toprow two
  bottomrow seven
  answerrow blank
column2
  isa column
  toprow six
  bottomrow one
  answerrow blank
column3
  isa column
  toprow four
  bottomrow six
  answerrow blank

---

where the terms *upper-left, upper-right,* and *lower-middle* reflect two-dimensional coordinate information to whatever degree of accuracy the system is able to maintain.

This scheme can also be used to represent propositional information. For instance, the meaning of the sentence, "The quick brown fox jumped over the lazy dogs" could be represented as:

```
event1
     isa jumping
     agent fox1
     object dog1

fox1
     isa fox
     speed quick
     color brown

dog1
     isa dog
     character lazy
     number plural
```

This representation might need substantial work in a thorough propositional system, but it serves to indicate the basic character of how such a representation would proceed.

This representation can accommodate the three key features associated with chunks: (a) Configural information is enforced by the chunk type (isa value) and associated slots; (b) chunk size limitations can be enforced by limitations on the number of associated slots; and (c) chunk hierarchies can be achieved by having the values of chunk slots be chunks themselves.

2.4 THE PRODUCTION IN PROCEDURAL MEMORY

The production rule is an encoding of knowledge that is optimized for use. Such optimization involves achieving a tradeoff between range of applicability and efficiency of application. There are four significant features associated with productions in ACT-R: their modularity, their abstract character, their goal structuring, and their condition–action asymmetry. Each can be understood as an aspect of optimizing the utility of production rules. The subsections that follow expand on what is meant by each of these features and provide evidence for them. ACT-R is not distinguished among production systems in any of these features except for the goal factoring of the production system.[14] Even in this feature,

---

[14]It is, however, distinguished from non-production system architectures by these features.

most recent production systems do have a goal structure. After considering these features, I propose a formal notation for representing productions.

2.4.1 Production Modularity

Production modularity has often been advertised as meaning that each production is a separate element that can be added and deleted, independent of any other production. This is basically true, but one should not conclude from such a statement that production rules do not interact. Changing or deleting any production in Table 1.1 produces very different behavior from the set as a whole. Solving a problem depends on the interactions among the productions involved, and the overall performance is only as good as the weakest production involved in the solution. Part of the strength of rule-based models is that they can account for many types of erroneous behavior by deletion of and changes in production rules. For instance, a common error in children's multi-column subtraction is that they have a rule that tells them to subtract the smaller number from the larger number, whether or not it is in the top row (Brown & VanLehn, 1980). This can be represented by a different production rule than the correct one.[15]

One might wonder why a cognitive skill should be broken up into rule-like units. Why not just encode the whole skill as one undifferentiated procedure? The major motivations are economy of representation and range of transfer. The five production rules in Table 1.1 can combine in various sequences to handle a wide range of addition problems. If one tried to solve the problem in large units, it would be necessary to encode special case rules for each type of addition problem (number of columns and pattern of carries). Thus, production rules tend to carve up a task at its natural joints, forming one rule for each natural unit. This explains why task analysis, which studies the structure of problems in a domain, plays such a major role in production-rule modeling.

The essential claim about modularity is that production rules are the units of the skill, which means that they are the units in which the skill is acquired, and they define the grain size at which the skill is performed. Skills are acquired in production-sized units, and any transformations of a skill occur as changes in production units. This means that a skill grows by acquiring new productions and by strengthening existing productions. This assertion often leads to the expectation that we should be able to see a step-by-step improvement in overall skill performance, but this expectation is frequently frustrated by the interactions that can occur among productions. Consider skill acquisition in the domain of learning to program in LISP, a topic that has been studied intensively in our laboratory. Figure 2.2 traces students' performance over the first six LISP problems in chapter 3 of Anderson, Corbett, and Reiser (1987). Because these problems vary in size, the measures reported are time and accuracy per unit

---

[15]For alternative production-rule accounts, see R. M. Young and O'Shea (1981) and Langley and and Ohlsson (1984).

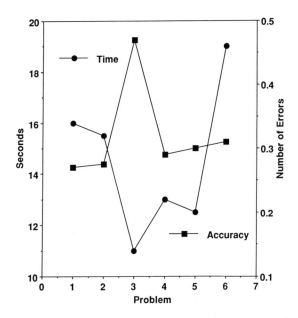

FIG. 2.2. Unsystematic learning in LISP: Latency and accuracy as a function
of problem number.

of code. Note that there does not appear to be any systematic learning trend
as a function of number of problems. It is common in observing skill acquisition
for surface behavior to show a frustrating lack of learning.

The reason for this is that different problems involve different production
rules, and some of the later problems involve many new productions and fewer
old ones, whereas others offer few new and relatively more old ones. The LISP
tutor (see chapter 7 of this volume, and Anderson, Conrad, & Corbett, 1989)
decomposes this learning performance into separate measures of performance
on specific production rules. Thus, rather than plotting performance as a function of number of problems, performance can be plotted as a function of number
of opportunities for practice of a specific rule that is involved in producing a unit
of LISP code.

One unit of code in the first problem might be generated by a production
rule that was already practiced twice. It would, therefore, be considered as the
third production opportunity, whereas in Fig. 2.2 it would be plotted as part
of the first problem. Similarly, another unit of code might be generated in the
third problem by a production rule that is firing for the first time. It would be
considered as the first production opportunity, although it would have been plotted in Fig. 2.2 as part of the third problem.

Figure 2.3 plots performance as a function of production opportunity. What
was chaos in Fig. 2.2 is here transformed into systematic learning trends. It
is data of this sort, more of which is reported throughout the book, that is evi-

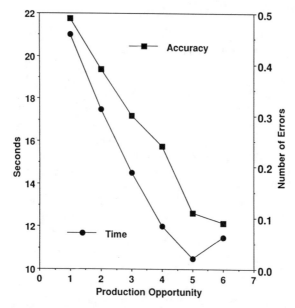

FIG. 2.3. Systematic learning in LISP: Latency and accuracy as a function of number of opportunities to practice the production.

dence for the modularity (and reality) of productions. It serves to indicate that knowledge is acquired in production units and that growth in knowledge needs to be defined in terms of production rules. Productions are the units of procedural knowledge. Kieras and Boviar (1986) have similarly shown that apparently unsystematic learning across problems can be explained in terms of the systematic learning of underlying productions.

It also turns out that the course of learning of each individual production rule is independent. In a factor analysis of performance of specific rules, Anderson et al. (1989) found that the only dependencies were based on general subject ability factors, not on overlapping or related content of the rules (for more details, see chapter 7). Thus, it does appear that the production rule is the unit that captures the systematic variation in skill learning. This is in contradiction to claims (e.g., Rumelhart & McClelland, 1986) that learning can only be defined in terms of more molecular, neural-like elements. Undoubtedly, learning takes place at the neural level, but it appears that this learning is coordinated to achieve well-defined learning at the rule level.

We see in Fig. 2.3 the first of many pieces of evidence for what I regard as the most significant results of this work. This is that the acquisition and performance of a complex piece of behavior can be understood as the concatenation of the acquisition and performance of each of its underlying production rules. This contradicts the claims that skill acquisition can only be understood in terms of smaller units (e.g., neural elements) or larger units (e.g., schemas). Production rules are the right grain size for understanding skill acquisition. We will be too busy with the details in subsequent chapters to remark much upon this fact but it is truly remarkable. More than anything else, it justifies the principal assertion of the first chapter: that cognitive skills are realized by production rules.

2.4.2 Production Abstraction and Goal Structuring

Production rules are often compared with the stimulus–response bonds from an earlier era in psychology. A stimulus–response bond encoded the contingency that, if a certain stimulus was present (e.g., a red light), then a certain response would be emitted (e.g., a peck on a key). A production rule has just this structure with its condition and action. Production rules, however, offer certain generalities and restrictions over stimulus–response bonds, which give them their power. Production-rule abstraction and goal structuring capture two of the essential ways in which production rules differ from stimulus–response bonds.

Abstraction refers to the generality of production rules. Production rules do not require that a specific stimulus be present; the rules will apply in any stimulus condition that satisfies the pattern specification of the condition. Thus, an important issue is just what patterns one allows to be specified in the condition side of a production. A theory of this would allow us to specify exactly how knowledge will transfer. This is the topic of chapter 9.

Basically, what one can specify in an ACT-R production is an interconnected set of knowledge chunks. What is critical is the configuration and not the exact chunks. Thus, PROCESS-COLUMN in Table 1.1 does not depend on the exact numbers but only on the fact that two digits are in the column of focus and that they have a specific sum. As I show in the formal specification of the production rules, this generality is achieved by variabilizing each chunk. Thus, the variable is the critical element in achieving production-rule generality. Oddly, it is proper treatment of variables that is causing some of the greatest difficulties for connectionist theories of mind (Smolensky, 1990).

There is, however, a restriction on the application of a production rule that does not have a counterpart in a stimulus–response bond. Production-rule conditions not only make reference to certain external situations but also specify certain *goal conditions*. Different production rules can fire in response to the same external situation depending on the internal goal. For instance, given different goals a system can choose to add or subtract the same array of numbers. An ability to respond differently to the same stimulus condition is critical to the adaptativeness of the system.

Evidence for these two properties of production rules can also be found in the domain of learning how to program in LISP. A good test case concerns the coding of variable names. In writing a computer program, one has to create a variety of variable names (e.g., *counter*, *base*, *salary*, etc.) and place them at different points in the program. The skill of coding variables could not be represented by a stimulus–response rule calling for the same action whenever a specific stimulus situation occurs. Thus, the coding of a variable name is an example of an abstract, non-stimulus–response skill. On the other hand, one can code variables for different purposes in LISP. In our LISP curriculum one starts out by coding variables as global variables to hold values, then uses them for parameters of a function, and finally employs them as local variables to hold temporary results. In the expert model for LISP programming, there are three separate productions for coding variables in response to these three goals.

Figure 2.4 illustrates the course of performance on these variable-coding productions in terms of number of errors per production. (The maximum number in the LISP tutor is three.) First we plot the average performance in Lesson 1, where these are global variables. They are introduced in Lesson 2 as parameters and continue in that role throughout Lessons 3 and 4. The figure shows their performance over Lesson 2 and their average performance in Lesson 4. Finally, it plots average performance in Lesson 5, where they are first introduced as local variables. At each point where a new use is introduced, there is a big increase in error rate. Within Lesson 2 there is a constant improvement with repeated use for the same purpose. There is continued improvement over lessons as is indicated by the performance in Lesson 4. Thus, even though it

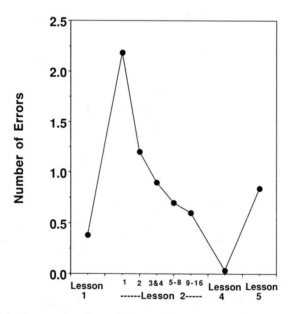

FIG. 2.4. Accuracy in coding variables at various points in the LISP curriculum.

is not the same stimulus–response pair, there is constant improvement as long as the goal stays constant. When the goal changes, performance deteriorates because a new production rule must be learned. Thus, productions, with their variable abstraction and goal-factoring, seem to capture the range of generalization of a skill.

2.4.3 Condition–Action Asymmetry

Production rules contrast with other formalisms, such as schema representations,[16] in that production rules make a distinction between condition and action. A rule will work if its condition matches and will perform its action. It is not possible to have the rule reverse itself and go from action to condition. It is this commitment to direction of action that gives the production rule its efficiency. There are, however, circumstances in which such reversal is logically possible, and many people have the intuition that we should be able to reverse our knowledge. For example, many people believe we should be able to deploy the same knowledge in language generation as in language comprehension. Although we have not researched this issue in the area of natural language, in the area of problem solving we have consistently supported the condition–action asymmetry and found evidence against this belief in the symmetrical use of knowledge.[17]

A good case in point comes, again, from the domain of learning to program in LISP. Kessler (1988) compared learning to write LISP code versus learning to evaluate it. Some subjects were told to write a function that rotates a list one to the right, such as:

(defun rotater (lis) (append (last lis) (reverse (cdr (reverse lis)))))[18]

In the other condition, subjects might be given this code and asked to step through how the code would apply to a list (a b c d). Thus, subjects were either asked to go from the desired behavior of the function to the code for the function or vice versa. The experiment involved crossing three conditions of the

---

[16]I refer here not to the passive data schema structures used for chunks in ACT-R, but to the active schemas found in the work of Abelson (1981), Schank and Abelson (1977), Bobrow and Winograd (1977), Rumelhart and Ortony (1976), and the more recent neural network equivalents in, for example, Rumelhart, Smolensky, McClelland, and Hinton (1986).

[17]For a brief consideration of the relevant evidence in the domain of language, see Singley and Anderson (1989, pp. 139–140).

[18]It is not important that the operation of this function be understood to appreciate the point in text, but for those who care: Reverse reverses a list and cdr removes the first element. Thus, (reverse (cdr (reverse lis))) reverses a list, removes the former last element, and reverses it back again. Thus, if lis were (a b c d) this would return (a b c). Last returns a list of the last element and append appends two lists together. Thus, if lis were (a b c d), the whole code would append (d) and (a b c) to yield (d a b c).

TABLE 2.2
Effect of Prior Experience on Ability to Code and to Evaluate Code*

	Target Task	
Prior Experience	Coding Time per Problem (Errors)	Evaluation Time per Problem (Errors)
Coding	163 sec. (2.0)	358 sec. (8.6)
Evaluation	304 sec. (4.3)	231 sec. (5.1)
Nothing	412 sec. (4.9)	376 sec. (7.2)

*Data from Kessler (1988).

initial experience with two transfer tasks. Subjects were given no prior experience, prior experience in generating such code, or prior experience in evaluating such code. They were then transferred to one of two conditions for the transfer task: generating more code or evaluating more code. Table 2.2 shows their performance on the transfer task as a function of their prior experience. Subjects were much faster and more accurate if their transfer task matched their training task. When the target task was coding, subjects with prior experience evaluating code seemed to be at some advantage over those in the control condition, but it is not a statistically significant difference. When the target task was evaluation, subjects with prior experience coding showed no advantage over control subjects.

There *is* an asymmetry in the use of knowledge. This basic result with respect to LISP has been replicated a number of times (McKendree & Anderson, 1987; Pennington & Nicolich, 1991). As I discuss in chapter 9, the prediction of ACT-R is not that there will be no transfer from one use of knowledge to another. Productions for each use arise from a common declarative representation, so practicing the knowledge in one way offers the opportunity to practice that declarative representation and so enhance the other use. Pennington and Nicolich (1991) were able to get significantly better performance in a transfer condition than in a control condition, but there are strong limitations on the amount of transfer, and strong asymmetries result from the fact that different uses of the same knowledge cannot be implemented by the same production rules.

2.4.4 A Notation for Productions

Having now specified the features that distinguish productions, we need to decide on the notation for specifying them. In addition to the features enumerated, a strong constraint is that they have to read from and write to working memory. Thus, the formalism that specifies the chunks in working memory forms the foundation for the formalism that specifies the production rules. We just need to add notation to indicate variables, goals, conditions, and actions.

Table 2.3 shows the formal specification of the production rules in Table 1.1.

TABLE 2.3
ACT-R Production Rules for Addition

NEXT-COLUMN
```
=goal>
  isa addition-problem
  object =array
=array>
  isa numberarray
  columns ($ =column2 $)
=column2>
  isa column
  - bottomrow +
  answerrow blank
  -(=array>
  columns ($ =column2 =column1 $)
=column1>
  isa column
  answerrow blank)
==>
=subgoal>
  isa write-answer
  column =column2
!push! =subgoal
```

PROCESS-COLUMN
```
=goal>
  isa write-answer
  column =column
  object nil
=column>
  isa column
  toprow =num1
  bottomrow =num2
=fact>
  isa addition-fact
  addend1 =num1
  addend2 =num2
  sum =sum
==>
=goal>
  object =sum
```

(Continued)

TABLE 2.3
(Continued)

WRITE-ANSWER-CARRY
  =goal>
    isa write-answer
    column =column
    object =num
  =column>
    isa column
    note carry
  =fact>
    isa addition-fact
    addend1 =num
    addend2 one
    sum =new
==>
  =goal>
    object =new
  =column>
    note nil

WRITE-ANSWER-GREATER-THAN-NINE
  =goal>
    isa write-answer
    column =column
    object =num
  =fact>
    isa addition-fact
    addend1 ten
    addend2 =new
    sum =num
  =column>
    isa column
    – note carry
  =problem>
    isa numberarray
    columns ($ =column1 =column $)
  =column1>
    isa column
==>
  =column1>
    note carry
  =goal>
    object =new
  =column>
    answerrow =new
  !pop!

(Continued)

TABLE 2.3
(Continued)

WRITE-ANSWER-LESS-THAN-NINE
```
    = goal >
      isa write-answer
      column  = column
      object  = num
    = num >
      isa number*
    = column >
      isa column
      - note carry
      - ( = fact >
      isa addition-fact
      addend1 ten
      addend2  = new
      sum  = num)
    == >
    = column >
      answerrow  = num
    !pop!
```

This is essentially the actual code for the production rules and what is found on the accompanying disk.[19] A production rule begins with a specification of a series of working memory chunks which define its condition. The condition is separated by an arrow from the action of the production. The first working-memory chunk, denoted = goal, is the goal that the production refers to. Following it are a series of working-memory elements. All of these working-memory elements are variabilized. Values of various slots, except the isa slot, can be variabilized. Variables are denoted by the prefix =, a frequent convention in production systems, although not the convention used in previous ACT systems. The > symbol in Table 2.3 separates the chunk name from its slots.

PROCESS-COLUMN is probably the easiest production rule to follow in the table. It applies when the goal is set to write out an answer in the column, but the answer is not yet calculated (i.e., the value of the object slot is nil). The pattern:

```
= column >
    isa column
    toprow  = num1
    bottomrow  = num2
```

---

[19]The complete code is in the Addition file in the Examples folder. This contains a few more parentheses and LISP function calls than what is shown in Table 2.3.

retrieves the digits in the column and binds them to =num1 and =num2. The
pattern:

```
= fact >
    isa addition-fact
    addend1 = num1
    addend2 = num2
    sum = sum
```

retrieves their sum and binds this to =sum. The action side of this production
just fills in the object slot of the goal with the sum of =num1 and =num2.

The first production NEXT-COLUMN in Table 2.3 illustrates the true complexity of production rules when they are implemented in ACT-R. Basically,
it retrieves the rightmost unanswered column. The pattern:

```
= array >
    isa numberarray
    columns ($ = column2 $)
= column2
    isa column
-   bottomrow +
    answerrow blank
```

matches a column, =column2, with a blank answer. The construct ($ =column2
$) matches an arbitrary column in the list of columns with the $ being string
variables that match anything to the left or right. The test "− bottomrow +"
checks that we have not come to the end of the problem as signalled by the
plus sign. To determine that this is the leftmost such column, a test is needed
to guarantee that the column to the right does not also have a blank answer.
This is done by negating (indicated by a minus sign in the NEXT-COLUMN)
the following pattern, which represents a situation where the column to the right
is blank:

```
= array >
    columns ($ = column2 = column1 $)
= column1 >
    isa column
    answerrow blank
```

The action of the production sets a subgoal to write an answer in the column
and pushes it by !push! command. This subgoal is popped by the !pop! actions
of WRITE-ANSWER-LESS-THAN-TEN and WRITE-ANSWER-GREATER-
THAN-NINE. ACT-R assumes a last-in-first-out (LIFO) goal stack, which

remembers subgoals and reactivates subgoals, such that when a subgoal is satisfied (popped), the next most recent subgoal will become active. For instance, the production system in Table 2.3 focuses on the subgoal of doing a column; when that is satisfied, it returns to the main goal of solving the addition problem. The next chapter and chapter 6 elaborate on the meaning of such goal actions and the evidence for them.

The production NEXT-COLUMN reveals the reason that columns are represented in an unbounded list rather than some hierarchical chunk structure with limited size for each chunk. The pattern ($ = column2 $) retrieves a column anywhere and ($ = column2 = column1 $) finds the preceding column. These patterns are insensitive to the serial positions of the columns. This is psychologically unrealistic, as people probably are influenced by the serial structure of the columns. In a second way, this production rule is unrealistic in that it models a situation in which all of the column structure is represented in working memory. It would be more reasonable to assume some scheme for moving focus across an external addition array and just encoding a column or two at any one time. This illustrates the point made earlier that when we find ourselves violating limits on chunk size, it is a sign that there are some unreasonable representational assumptions at work. These assumptions may be convenient approximations for some purposes, but they can be disastrous if they mask the psychological processes of interest.

Such machine-runnable code specifications do not appear again until chapter 12. For the purposes of this book, I use more readable English specifications like those in Table 1.1. At one research meeting, I had people rate the specifications in Tables 1.1 and 2.3 for clarity. On a 10-point scale where 1 was *totally obscure* and 10 was *totally transparent*, Table 1.1 received an average rating of 8.6 and Table 2.3 an average rating of 4.3. Because this was a group relatively sophisticated about actual production systems, the 4.3 probably overestimated the average clarity of Table 2.3. The reason one needs such formal specifications at all is that there is no guarantee that the English production set in Table 1.1 actually corresponds to something that would work. Indeed, in writing such formal production-rule models, it is not unusual to discover flaws in one's original conception of the skill. Problems of vagueness, contradiction, and incompleteness that arise in natural language statements may only become apparent when productions are converted to code.

2.5 CONCLUSIONS

A chapter on representation has to come early in a book on cognitive architecture because one needs to establish a notation for describing the elements of cognition. The actual theoretical claims of this notation are relatively few, but they are important. Even where an important concept is being advanced, such as the procedural–declarative distinction, it is not the case that the representational accompaniment (declarative chunks vs. procedural productions) is absolutely necessary. As briefly noted, one could get a system without the distinction to mimic a system with the distinction, if at the cost of clarity. So, even here the representational assumptions are just notation to make important theoretical points transparent. The theoretical points lie more in the processes that are defined on the notation. These processes are set forth for the case of ACT-R in the next two chapters. These next two chapters therefore assume, at times, a somewhat more technical character.

3

Performance

John R. Anderson
Carnegie Mellon University

3.1 GENERAL ISSUES

3.1.1 Conflict Resolution

The previous chapter specified the knowledge representation schemes in the ACT-R theory. We must still specify how this knowledge gets transformed into behavior. In computer science terms, this is like finding an interpreter for a programming language. It might seem quite simple to determine what to do in a production system—one must find out what production matches the declarative information in working memory and fire it. The problem is that multiple productions can match the information in working memory. Indeed, the same production can sometimes match in multiple ways. Each way a production can match is referred to as an *instantiation*. The problem is to decide which instantiation(s) to fire. *Conflict resolution* is the term given to the process by which a production system decides which of the possible matching productions will fire.

Figure 3.1 illustrates a common puzzle known as the eight puzzle, which is used in the study of problem solving. It consists of eight movable tiles and one blank space, organized on a 3 × 3 grid. By moving a tile into the empty space, one can move tiles around the puzzle. The puzzle is presented as starting from a particular configuration, such as the one illustrated in Fig. 3.1a, with the goal of moving the tiles to achieve another configuration, such as the one illustrated in Fig. 3.1b. In a production-rule model for performing this task, one

2	1	6
4	•	8
7	5	3

into

1	2	3
8	•	4
7	6	5

FIG. 3.1. The eight puzzle. The problem is to convert the first array into the second.

would have separate production rules that would call for moving left, right, up, and down. All these would match in Fig. 3.1a. How does one decide which to apply?[1]

The traditional solution—represented in OPS (see McDermott & Forgy, 1978) and in earlier versions of ACT—was first to calculate all possible production instantiations and then to try to apply various conflict resolution principles to select among the rules. These included:

1. The principle of refractoriness. The same production-rule instantiation should not be executed multiple times.
2. The principle of recency. Production rules that match to data that entered working memory recently are preferred over those that match older material.
3. The principle of specificity. Production rules that contain more tests in their conditions are preferred over those that have fewer.
4. The principle of strength. Stronger productions are preferred over weaker ones, where the strength of a production is typically determined by the number of successful applications of that production in the past.

These seemed to be good rules of thumb, but it is hard to see why they should be hard and fast. They are not, for example, particularly useful in choosing among moves for the eight puzzle. In practice, one often has to specially craft production rules in order to make sure conflict resolution works the way it should. One response to the lack of motivation of these principles, which is taken up in Soar, is to eliminate all automatic conflict-resolution principles and have all decisions about what to do be a matter of explicit computation at the production-rule level.

3.1.2 The ACT-R Scheme for Conflict Resolution

The approach in ACT-R has been to try to design a conflict-resolution system that would explicitly try to minimize computational cost while still retrieving the production rule most likely to lead to the best result. Computational resources (activation) are assigned to matching production-rule instantiations according to

---

[1]There is a file called 8 puzzle in the Examples folder on the disk for performing this task. There is more discussion of this file in Section 12.5.1.

which instantiations seem more likely. This means that instantiations are generated in a rough order of plausibility, such that the first production instantiations
generated are likely to be the best. Each production is evaluated when it is instantiated. The production rule selected is the first one that appears to give
a satisfactory result or that, in Simon's (1955) terminology, *satisfices*. The remainder of this chapter expands on how resources are assigned to matching
production-rule instantiations, how production-rule instantiations are evaluated, and how we determine that an instantiation satisfices.

For purposes of analysis, it is sometimes convenient to speak of the conflict-
resolution processes as taking place sequentially, so that one production instantiation is generated at a time, but that is an expository convenience. The assumption in ACT-R is that all production instantiations are being matched in
parallel. The matching of some instantiations will be completed before others
because some conditions are less complex and because some instantiations
receive more resources. This will then produce a serial ordering of production
instantiations in terms of when their computation is completed.

The basic idea behind this scheme comes from my work on rational analysis
(Anderson, 1990a), which indicated that certain aspects of cognition seemed
to be designed to optimize the information processing of the system. In the current context, with goals explicitly mentioned in the production rules, *optimization* means maximizing the probability of achieving these goals while minimizing
the cost of doing so or, to put it more precisely, maximizing the expected *utility*, where this is defined as expected gain minus expected cost.

There is no necessary reason to suppose that conflict resolution works in
this optimal fashion. The fact that other aspects of cognition appear to operate
optimally (Anderson, 1990a) gives credence to the possibility, but this is a conjecture, which is judged by how well it does in accounting for the data. Anderson (1990a, chapter 5) provided some evidence for optimal conflict resolution
in the domain of problem solving. Subsequent chapters of this book provide further evidence for this conjecture.

3.2 PATTERN MATCHING

In all implementations of production systems, pattern matching turns out to be
the computationally expensive part of executing productions. Thus, it seems
reasonable to suppose that matching of a production's condition to form an instantiation will be what determines how long it will be before the production
instantiation is available for evaluation. It was part of the ACT* proposal that
pattern matching was the critical component in production latency. That assumption continues in ACT-R, although the particular proposal in ACT-R is conceptually simpler and has its basis in the rational analysis of cognition.

The critical observation is that matching a production rule involves matching a series of chunks from working memory to the condition elements of a production. Consider the production PROCESS-COLUMN from Table 1.1:

PROCESS-COLUMN
    IF   the goal is to write out an answer in c1
            and d1 and d2 are the digits in that column
            and d3 is the sum of d1 and d2
    THEN set a subgoal to write out d3 in c1

Time to match this production should be the sum of the times to match the three clauses in the condition of the production:

T_1 (time to match the goal description)
$+ T_2$ (time to match the column description)
$+ T_3$ (time to retrieve and match the addition fact)

Subsequent subsections will consider the various factors that go into determining the time it takes to match a chunk. These factors include the special role of goal chunks, the role of data activation, and the role of production strength.

3.2.1 Goal Structures

The rate at which goal chunks are matched is determined by their level of activation, just as the matching of any other chunk. To understand the activation of goals, it is necessary to recognize that there is a hierarchy of goals, starting with various primitive goals involving basic needs and drives. The behavior of any subject in the laboratory, however, is not directly in response to such basic goals but rather in response to subgoals. Thus, a subject may be trying to solve a Tower of Hanoi problem in order to satisfy a subject participation requirement in order to pass a psychology course in order to get a college degree in order to get a job in order to earn social respect. The subject might well have lost track of this chain of goals in the laboratory. From our perspective as cognitive psychologists, all this does not matter. We take it as a given that the subject is responding to the goal of solving the Tower of Hanoi problem and ignore the motivational issues that led him or her to that goal. Provided we are correct in our assumption that this is the operative subgoal, we can proceed with our cognitive analysis, oblivious to issues of higher motivation.

To model this hierarchy of goals, ACT-R has a goal stack, where a series of goals are placed. Productions that can match to any goal on the stack are allowed to fire. If a goal is satisfied (popped) all goals below it on the stack are popped. Only the last (i.e., the topmost) goal placed on a goal stack is made a source of activation. This causes the system to focus largely on that goal. Goals below the top goal are active to the degree that they receive activation from the top goal and from other sources of activation. The next subsection discusses calculation of activation.[2]

The hierarchies in goal stacks are not some perverse importation of computer programming into cognitive modeling. Rather, they are a direct reflection of the dependency structure in the task environment. When a goal is placed on the stack above another (e.g., the goal of getting gas in the car is placed on top of the goal of taking a trip) this is because one depends on the other. One focuses on the top goal in the stack because this is what one is likely to make progress on. Goal stacks are a rational adaptation to the structure of the environment.

The hierarchical goal structures, even under a specific goal like solving the Tower of Hanoi, can be complex, and a person may well lose track of the intermediate steps that led to the current goal. Often these steps can be reconstructed as needed. For instance, a student may forget why he or she is performing a particular multiplication in the midst of an algebra problem but, on rereading the problem, the reason can usually be reconstructed. Forgetting of goals can be modeled by loss of activation, just as can forgetting of any other declarative structure.[3]

To what degree might the existence of complex hierarchical goal structures be a relatively unique primate or, more specifically, human trait? There is evidence that the prefrontal cortex is heavily involved in the kind of planning and problem solving that involves complex goal structures (Goldberg & Bilder, 1987), and the prefrontal cortex becomes substantially larger as one moves along the phylogenetic scale toward *homo sapiens*. Although we try not to speak of species as "higher" or "lower" on such a scale, such reference seems to have real meaning in the case of novel planning and problem solving. This was much of the content of Köhler's (1927) classic phylogenetic comparisons: Only his primates were capable of complex subgoaling; his lower organisms could not subgoal going around even a single obstacle.

Tool use, often considered an especially human activity, definitely requires substantial hierarchical planning. The decision to design a tool is already a significant subgoal (a means to an end), and the construction of a tool can involve complex coordination of subgoals under that. Neither hierarchical planning nor novel tool use are uniquely human accomplishments, and they are found to various degrees in other primates. Still, one has to be impressed by their flowering in the human species. It may also be the case that natural language, with its strong hierarchical structures, calls upon the same capacities that seem especially strong in humans. In Anderson (1983a), I made the argument that language use was a special case of problem solving.

---

[2]Although ACT-R does not implement dual (or multiple) processing, this could be accomplished by having multiple goal stacks.

[3]The ACT-R implementation, however, does not model forgetting of goals.

It should be noted that the postulation of a goal structure is a major feature of many symbolist positions, which puts them in sharp contrast with most connectionist positions. This is not to say that connectionist models cannot be built for hierarchical problem solving, but it does suggest that hierarchical problem solving is the kind of task that justifies the symbolist position. To date, there have been no insightful connectionist models of problem solving. Chapter 6 provides some data showing the effects of goal structures on the microstructure of cognition.

3.2.2 Data Activation

As in ACT* (Anderson, 1983a), the rate at which a production matches in ACT-R is a function of the level of activation of the declarative structures to which it matches. The metaphor used in discussing ACT* was that activation was the energy that runs the pattern-matching machinery. As reviewed in Anderson (1984), most spreading-activation theories embody the assumption that structures that are more active receive more favorable processing. There was always something vaguely adaptive about this arrangement, but it was never thought through why it was adaptive. A consequence of this lack of rational analysis is that previous proposals (in particular, ACT*) had flaws in their assumptions, as exposed in Anderson (1990a). In contrast, ACT-R enjoys the guidance of a rational analysis in its proposals for the role of activation in cognition.

Level of activation of a declarative chunk should reflect an estimate of the probability that the chunk will match to a production in the next cycle. It makes sense to give more resources to a chunk that is more likely to be matched. In this way, one can maintain a large declarative data base of knowledge and not have performance degrade because of searches through that data base for critical information.

The activation of a chunk reflects its log odds of matching some production. That is, if P_i is the probability of a chunk i matching some production, its activation A_i is $\log P_i/(1 - P_i)$. There are two principal reasons for using log odds:

1. It is more reasonable to think of activation as summing, in line with its neural interpretation. It is natural to think of calculations on probabilities as multiplying, and calculations on log odds as adding.
2. Log odds has an advantage over log probability because it can take on both positive and negative values. This maps onto the current conceptualization of neural activation as rising above or below base levels.

Anderson (1990a) argued that the activation of a memory structure should be the sum of the base level of activation for that memory element plus the activation that spreads to it from elements in the current context. The formula proposed is:

$$A_i = B_i + \sum_j S_{ji} \tag{3.1}$$

where B_i is the base-level activation (or strength) of the structure, and S_{ji} are the strengths of association to i from elements j in the current context.[4] These base-level activations and strengths can be negative as well as positive. Positive strengths of association denote associated items, whereas negative strengths denote dissociated items. The level of activation of a data element, A_i, can be interpreted as the log posterior odds that it is relevant to the current context. The base-level activation, B_i, reflects the log prior odds and S_{ji} reflects log likelihood ratios that an item i is relevant, given that j is in the context.[5] Their calculation is discussed in the next chapter, on learning.

ACT-R uses a slightly elaborated version of the formula:

$$A_i = B_i + \sum_j W_j S_{ji} \tag{3.2}$$

where W_j reflects the salience or validity of element j and can vary from 0 to 1. It can be conceived of as the amount of activation that the element j is emitting. Critical to the application of Equation 3.2 is the definition of what is meant by the "contextual elements over which the summation is taking place" (the js in Equation 3.2). These sources of activation are defined as the elements in the current goal chunk and the elements currently being processed in the perceptual field. An important instance of the latter category can be words currently being rehearsed.

It should be noted that Equation 3.2 describes an activation process that is different from the spreading activation process in ACT* (Anderson, 1983a). Activation goes from one element j to another element i but no further, whereas in ACT*, it would continue to spread beyond i. Anderson (1990a) argued that all the critical information should be contained in these direct links, eliminating the need to spread activation across multiple links. (Consult that paper for a discussion of the evidence for this activation process relative to the evidence for ACT*'s spreading activation process.[6]) Many phenomena of memory can

---

[4]This computation is quite similar to that performed in the SAM memory model (Gillund & Shiffrin, 1984).

[5]The Bayesian formula for calculating the odds of hypothesis A, given evidence E is:

$$\frac{P(H|E)}{P(\bar{H}|E)} = \frac{P(H)}{P(\bar{H})} \times \frac{P(E|H)}{P(E|\bar{H})}$$

$P(H|E)/P(\bar{H}|E)$ is called the *posterior odds*, $P(H)/P(\bar{H})$ is called the *prior odds*, and $P(E|H)/P(E|\bar{H})$ is called the *likelihood ratio*. The hypothesis, H, in this case is that i is a memory chunk that is needed, and the evidence, E, is that chunk j appears in the context.

[6]On the other hand, this assumption requires storing associations among all the elements in working memory. If there are n elements, n^2 associations are required. This can be very costly in terms of storage space, which can be a real limitation in the implementation on the accompanying disk. A multi-link spread process can be seen as motivated to get the effect of a direct-link system with fewer associations. In the accompanying implementation, we enable the user to cut down on the storage costs by having association strengths default to zero and by not representing zero-strength associations.

be understood in terms of memory making most available that information which is likely to be needed, given the momentary context and past history. These phenomena include fan effects, priming effects, and effects of frequency in memory. ACT-R inherits the ability to account for all of these. They are not discussed in this book because of its focus on skill performance and skill acquisition. Chapter 12, however, does present a simulation of a simple fan experiment.

One of the interesting consequences of this theory of data activation is the altered notion of *working memory* in ACT-R, as compared with that employed in most production systems. Effectively, all of declarative memory *is* working memory, and data activation determines which chunks are considered before which others. Elements are effectively not in working memory if they are so inactive that they fail to match to some production before a production fires; this is, then, a highly relative and production-specific conception of working memory. It is often convenient to speak of a working memory as having some fixed set of items, but this is just an approximation for expository purposes.

3.2.3 Production-Rule Strength

Production rules gather strength as they prove useful. Strength is thought of as a measure of the log odds that some instantiation of the production will fire. The next chapter has more to say about the *process* of strength accumulation; in this chapter I discuss the *effects* of production-rule strength. The basic assumption is that the probability and speed of application of a production will vary with its strength. The experimental world is full of demonstrations of improvement in speed and reliability of skilled performance with practice. Moreover, the form of this improvement is generally thought to satisfy a power function (Newell & Rosenbloom, 1981). Figure 3.2 illustrates this with some data from Neves and Anderson (1981), who examined the relationship between practice at a geometry-like task and speed of performing the task. Here, time to do the proof is plotted as a function of number of proofs. Such data reflect the amalgamation of a large number of productions used to perform the task, but the same relationship holds at the level of individual productions, as well (Anderson et al., 1989; this volume, chapter 7). Chapter 4, on learning, expands further on the nature of this improvement and the reasons for it.

3.2.4 Time to Match a Production

The two previous subsections gave separate analyses of the odds that a chunk i will match to some production that fires and the odds that some instantiation of a production p will fire. This subsection relates these factors to the time it should take to match a chunk i to a production p.

The appendix to this chapter presents a rational analysis of how production

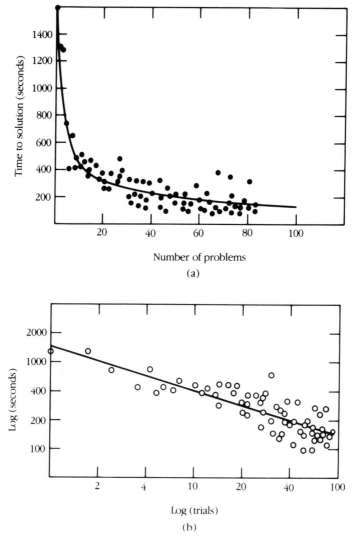

FIG. 3.2. Time (RT) to generate proofs in a geometry-like proof system as a function of the number of proofs (P) already done: (a) function on a normal scale, $RT = 1410P^{-55}$; (b) function on a log-log scale. From Neves and Anderson (1981), with permission.

strength and chunk activation should combine to determine the time to match a chunk to a production. The underlying assumption in that analysis is that there is a contention among various productions for retrieval of chunks from long-term memory, and that priority to retrieve more active chunks should be given to stronger productions. Because chunk activation reflects the odds that the chunk will match to a production, and production strength reflects the odds that the production will fire, this scheme of prioritizing minimizes the expected time to identify the production that will fire. The exact time to match a chunk to a production depends on its standing relative to the competition. The appendix develops the following formula for the expected time to match chunk i to production p:

$$T_{ip} = Be^{-b(A_i + S_p)} \qquad (3.3)$$

where T_{ip} is the time to match, A_i is the activation of chunk i, S_p is the strength of production p, and b and B are constants. The time to calculate a production instantiation, T_p, is the sum of a sequence of such matches, one for each chunk, so it follows that:

$$T_p = \sum_i Be^{-b(A_i + S_p)} \qquad (3.4)$$

Equation 3.4 is the central equation to understanding the timing properties of the ACT-R system. It identifies the time to match a production as a sum of the times to match individual chunks. This scheme for generating production instantiations will be sensitive to the strength of production, the complexity (number of chunks to be matched) in the condition, and the level of activation of the matching data chunks. All three factors have been shown to influence speed of performance of a cognitive task (for a review, see Anderson, 1983a). The equation implies that production-rule strength and activation have multiplicative effects on latency. Pirolli and Anderson (1985) and Anderson et al. (1989) described data indicating strength and activation interact multiplicatively in determining time. Further data in support of this are reported in chapters 5, 7, and 8.

The model for pattern matching is a parallel one in which all instantiations are pursued simultaneously, with the time for completing their calculation described by Equation 3.4. This will tend to deliver more plausible instantiations first, because it favors more probable productions matching to more probable (i.e., active) data structures. Nevertheless, a less plausible instantiation with a simple condition to match might come in before a more plausible instantiation with a complex condition to match. Thus, the model delivers instantiations in an order roughly determined by their plausibility divided by their complexity.

Although the pattern matching of production instantiations is parallel, within a production the chunks get matched serially, leading to the sum rule in Equation 3.4. This is a major departure from the ACT* conception of pattern matching, but is required by the logic of pattern matching in ACT-R. Consider the matching of production PROCESS-COLUMN. Its formal ACT-R specification (see Table 2.3) is:

```
=goal>
    isa write-answer
    column  =column
    object nil
=column>
    isa column
    toprow  =num1
    bottomrow  =num2
=fact>
    isa addition-fact
    addend1  =num1
    addend2  =num2
    sum  =sum
==>
    =goal>
        object  =sum
```

Initially, the goal =goal will be a source of activation reflecting the fact that it is relevant to matching the production. Thus, it will be matched quickly. Conditional on its being matched, the identity of =column will be determined. It is assumed that such already-bound chunks, like =column, can themselves be quickly matched. The way their rapid matching is implemented in Equation 3.3 (or 3.4) is to represent their activation at a maximum. The element that will take a long time to match in PROCESS-COLUMN is =fact, because it is not a source of activation nor has it been bound earlier in the match. The assumption is that =num1 and =num2 are sources of activation, because they are in the current column. The level of activation of =fact and hence its speed of matching will depend on the activation it receives from these two sources.[7]

This example illustrates the three situations that are possible with respect to working-memory activation:

1. The chunk is a source of activation. It is maximally associated to itself and so will be highly active and will match quickly. This situation applies for =goal.

---

[7]When the addition example on the disk is loaded, such activation-based computations are not evoked, but you can see such activation-based computation by turning on the flags for "Rational Stuff" and "Default IA Equations." To see chunk-by-chunk computations, also turn on the "Activation Trace" flag. The current addition example does not make =num1 and =num2 sources of activation. They can be made so by adding them as activation sources in the production NEXT-COLUMN (where they are referred to as =toprow and =bottomrow) and removing them as activation sources in PROCESS-COLUMN. See Section 12.3.2 for information on adding and deleting activation sources.

2. The chunk has already been identified as part of a previously matched chunk. In this case it is treated as a source of activation and so is quickly matched as in 1. This situation applies for = column.
3. Neither 1 nor 2 holds, in which case its match will depend on the activation it receives from various other sources.[8] This situation applies for = fact.

Because of 2, the order in which chunks are listed in a production condition matters. Faster matching will be obtained if chunks are introduced only after they have been matched as parts of other chunks. This is not always possible, however, and some chunks will have to be retrieved by indirect matching, as in 3.

3.2.5 Summary

Figure 3.3 illustrates the process of production selection. It illustrates the matching of seven productions. Time moves to the right. The solid bars denote matching of chunks in a production. Several chunks are part of a production condition, so there are several bars, the length of each reflecting how long the match took. The arrow at the end reflects when the match of the last chunk was completed; the number it points to reflects the evaluation of that production. The vertical bar to the right reflects when a decision was made to fire the best production uncovered so far, namely P3. Note that the matching of P6 and P7 had not been completed by this point. This figure is intended to illustrate how the matching of each production progresses serially, chunk by chunk, while all instantiations are being pursued in parallel. It is also meant to illustrate how all this pattern matching terminates with the selection of the production to fire.

3.3 PRODUCTION EVALUATION

The previous section specified how individual production instantiations are matched. As noted, these instantiations are made available in the approximate order of plausibility. The task of deciding which one to select remains. This requires a computation of the expected value of a production instantiation. To reduce decision time, the system only considers the most plausible productions and stops when it determines that the time to wait for further production instantiations to come in is not worth the expected improvement. When the system stops, it fires the best production that it has found so far.

---

[8]To enable such chunks to match, the "Enable Indirect Matches" flag must be set in the simulation even if you do not have the activation-based computation turned on (see Footnote 7).

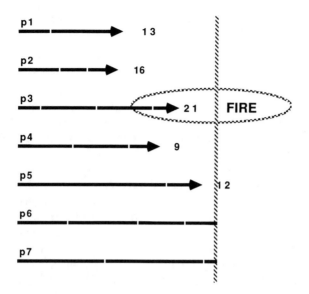

FIG. 3.3. Illustration of the computations involved in selecting a production.

In contrast to the typical production-system models that one writes to simulate a single task on a computer (where there are relatively few instantiations), it is assumed that in the human situation there are a great many instantiations. This is partly because of the richness of human knowledge and behavioral potential, which means that, at any point in time, there are a great many things we could do. Thus, it is not reasonable to consider exhaustively all potential productions.

Also, in contrast with typical production-system models, it is assumed that it is not a matter of certainty which production rule should fire. All that can be done is to estimate the expected payoff of each rule, and choose the one that is greatest. This makes the process of identifying the best production quite analogous to Bayesian decision making.

The process by which productions are evaluated is taken whole cloth from the prescription developed for the rational analysis in Anderson (1990a). There it was assumed that one can associate with each production instantiation a probability, P, that it will successfully lead to the goal and expected cost, C, of achieving that goal by this means. One can also assign a value, G, to the goal. The value of the production instantiation, then, is the expected gain minus the expected cost, or $PG - C$. According to the theory, one keeps evaluating production instantiations until the expected improvement over the current best instantiation does not justify expending effort in matching further instantiations. Basically, in Simon's (1955) terms, one satisfices by selecting the best so far without any guarantee that it is the global best. In this section, I consider, in more detail, the process by which P and C are estimated and this satisficing process.

3.3.1 Estimating the Probability of Success and Cost

Each production produces some transformation of the problem, presumably on a path toward the goal. If it does not achieve the goal, other productions will have to complete the steps to the goal. In many experimental tasks this situation is somewhat degenerate, in that a single production achieves the goal, but there are many other situations, like the eight-puzzle example, where a particular production only provides a step toward the goal. Anderson (1990a) offered a more thorough rational analysis of how to approach this situation. This chapter describes a somewhat simplified version of that.

The probability of success is related to two underlying probabilities. One is the probability that the chosen production will have its intended effect; the second is the probability that one can get from where that production left off to the goal. In some cases, productions are more or less guaranteed to have their intended effect. For instance, if a production just writes something into working memory, then presumably it gets into working memory. On the other hand, a production that calls for some external action, such as flipping a switch to turn on a light, may or may not succeed, depending on such things as whether the switch is connected to the light and how reliably the switch functions. Let q be the probability that the production will have its intended effect and r be the probability that one will get from there to a complete solution. If your goal was to read the fine print on some medical instructions, and the first production in achieving this goal was switching on the light, q would be the probability you would succeed in switching the light on, and r would be the probability that you would succeed in reading the instructions if the light were switched on. P, the probability that the production will lead to success, can then be given as:

$$P = qr/(1 - (1 - q)f) \qquad (3.5)$$

where f represents the deterioration in prospects if the production fails (fP is the probability that the goal can be achieved even if the production fails to produce its intended effect).[9]

A similar analysis can be performed of the cost, C. Let a be the cost associated with performing the production. (Every production has some cost associated with the cognitive effort it represents, but a production that calls for some external action can potentially have a much larger cost.) Let b be the cost of further actions after this production. As derived in Anderson (1990a), the total cost, C, can be represented as:

$$C = a + b \qquad (3.6)$$

Now the question becomes one of how to estimate the quantities q, r, a,

---

[9]For a derivation, see Anderson (1990a). We set $f = 1/2$ in our applications.

and b.[10] The probability q and the cost a can be estimated from the production itself: One can keep statistics about how often the production succeeds and about its cost. (The next chapter discusses how these statistics are used to estimate q and a as part of the ACT-R learning process.) The quantities r and b are more problematic because they refer to yet unknown actions. The solution in Anderson (1990a) for estimating these quantities was to base their estimates on how similar the state produced by the production was to the goal and how much effort had been spent so far. The basic assumption was that when the difference between the resultant state and the goal was greater, there would be a greater expected effort to reach the goal and a lower probability of success. In addition, the more effort already expended, the more likely that the goal could not be achieved and so, the lower the probability.

Anderson (1990a) developed an analysis of how to estimate the probability r as a function of difference and effort. Figure 3.4a shows the relationship derived. Similarly, Fig. 3.4b shows the relationship between difference and expected cost b. They are the functions that are used in the simulation.

The appendix to this chapter provides an accounting of the derivation of the functions in Fig. 3.4. Critical in that derivation are two quantities, r^* and b^*. The probability r^* is the mean probability over occasions that a successful execution of the production will be followed by successful achievement of the goal; b^* is the mean cost over occasions of further effort after firing of the production. What the functions in Fig. 3.4 do is to allow the system to adjust these "priors" depending on the particular circumstance.

Figure 3.5 summarizes the relationships that go into evaluating a production. The production's evaluation is sensitive to the quantity $PG - C$. P is determined by q and r, whereas C is determined by a and b. The estimate of r is sensitive to the effort so far, the difference from the goal, and the underlying parameters, r^* and b^*. The estimate of b is just sensitive to the difference and b^*.

There is a fair amount of mathematics that goes into the calculations in Fig. 3.5. It prescribes what the mechanisms should do to properly evaluate the production rules. It is not a description of the evaluation process. Presumably, at the neural level, features of the situation, such as effort and difference, are directly mapped into an evaluation of the production instantiations.

As developed in Anderson (1990a), this theory, with its emphasis on difference reduction, produces the hillclimbing behavior seen in so many subjects' problem-solving behavior. Combined with operator subgoaling capacity, it will also produce means–ends analysis. Thus, these production utility calculations are directly responsible for some of the most salient characteristics of human problem solving.

---

[10]It is worth noting the difference between these parameters and strength. Production strength estimates the probability that a production *will* fire. These estimate its value *should* it fire.

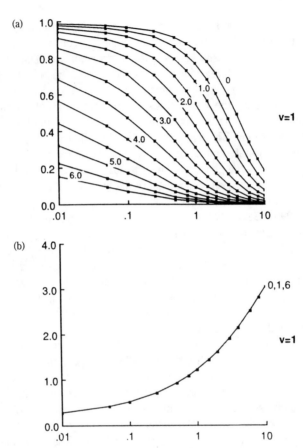

FIG. 3.4.   (a) Probability of success as a function of similarity to goal (abscissa) and amount of past effort (different functions); (b) expected further effort as a function of similarity to goal.

3.3.2 Satisficing

The net effect of production evaluation is to assign an expected value $PG - C$ to each production instantiation. Instantiations are evaluated as they become available. The question becomes when to cease evaluating instantiations and accept the current best. This is the issue of satisficing, as introduced by Simon (1955). I repeat here the formalization of the concept of satisficing given in Anderson (1990a).

Figure 3.6 illustrates the situation on a scale where possible values of a production instantiation (calculated as $PG - C$) vary from G to negative values. Let B_t be the value of the best instantiation uncovered by time t. One continues

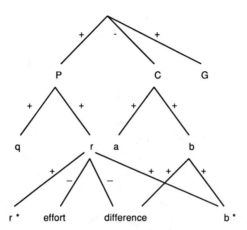

FIG. 3.5. The relationship among the quantities used in evaluating a production. The relationships are signed as positive or negative.

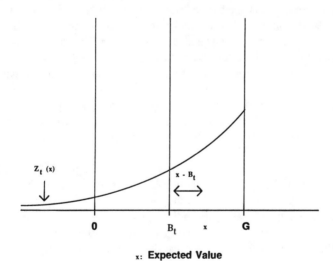

FIG. 3.6. An illustration of the calculation of the expected gain associated with considering another production instantiation.

to wait for more instantiations only if there is a sufficiently good chance that the next instantiation will be sufficiently better than B_t. Before generating the next instantiation, we cannot know how good it will be. All we can have is an expectation of a certain goodness of the next instantiation. Let $Z_t(x)$ be a distribution of possible goodness values of the instantiation. It is indexed by t to allow for the possibility that later instantiations are less likely to be as good as earlier instantiations, given their ordering by plausibility. The following expresses the expected improvement, I_t, over B_t if we consider the next instantiation:

$$I_t = \int_{B_t}^{G} (x - B_t)\, Z_t(x)dx \qquad (3.7)$$

This equation considers all cases in which the next instantiation has a better value than B_t and multiplies the amount of improvement, $(x - B_t)$, by the probability of improvement, $Z_t(x)$. ACT-R stops considering instantiations when this expected gain is less than the cost associated with the time to compute the next instantiation, which is treated as a fixed threshold. Anderson (1990a) proposed a theory of the distribution of $Z_t(x)$ and how it decreased with t. It contains the details that serve as the basis for the implementation of ACT-R.[11]

Again, the mathematics associated with this figure prescribe what the mechanisms should do to behave optimally. There is no claim that these equations are actually calculated. In this case, at the neural level, the various instantiations possibly compete in an inhibitory, winner-take-all contest. That is, the more highly an instantiation is evaluated, the more it inhibits other instantiations.

Note that one can adjust one's speed–accuracy tradeoff by adjusting the value, G, of the goal. Because the value of any move is defined as $PG - C$, by increasing G, one increases the range of potential gain. Thus, the theory naturally produces a speed–accuracy tradeoff by increasing G, the payoff. One can also imagine implementing speed–accuracy tradeoffs by forcing the system to respond at various points, even if it has not fully considered all the production rules it would. This would correspond to the deadline method for generating speed–accuracy tradeoffs (A. V. Reed, 1973).

In the typical speed–accuracy tradeoff, subjects can improve their accuracy at the expense of their speed, or vice versa. However, as noted by Pachella (1974), certain experimental manipulations produce a reverse speed–accuracy relationship. In testing a number of conditions varying in difficulty, one typically finds the conditions with lower accuracy have slower times. This is also predicted by the theory. A more difficult condition is modeled by having lower-valued production instantiations (as measured by $PG - C$) for that condition. This means that the current best will not be very good, so there is more gain expected from waiting longer. When one finally does terminate, it will have been after

---

[11]In Anderson (1990a), n, the number of operators considered so far, was used in place of t, time. The formula from that source has been updated by replacing n by t: We are now measuring elapsed time and not number of operators considered so far.

having chosen a production of lower expected value and consequently, worse average performance. So, basically, in conditions of decreased quality, there will be more search (producing longer times) to find a production of lower mean quality (producing worse performance as measured by accuracy).

3.4 SUMMARY

This completes the ACT-R theory of how selection of a production rule is controlled by:

1. The goal that is currently active.
2. The past history of use of various declarative chunks.
3. The elements in the current context.
4. The complexity of the rule.
5. The past frequency of use of the production rule.
6. The past history of success of the production rule.
7. The amount of effort put into solving the problem so far.
8. The similarity between the goal state and the state resulting from applying the production rule.
9. What other options for behavior are available.

This is a complex set of factors, and I regard it as a considerable accomplishment to place them in a coherent framework that is consistent with the relevant data. It is to the joint credit of the rational analysis and the discipline of implementing a computer simulation that we were able to arrive at a coherent rendition of these factors.

The analysis here focuses on predicting both which productions will be selected and how long it will take for them to fire. These are two essential ingredients of a theory of skill performance, but there is one factor missing: a complete analysis of errors of performance. The current theory can account for random errors of omission in that certain production instantiations might be overlooked, and systematic errors of omission, in the form of buggy production rules, but it cannot explain slips, or unsystematic errors of commission. This would require extending the current theory to incorporate partial matching. Such a possibility is discussed briefly in chapter 13.

APPENDIX: DERIVATION OF EQUATION 3.3

There are three critical steps in the derivation of Equation 3.3. One is a proposal for how the odds that a chunk will match a *specific* production that fires relates to both the odds that a chunk will match *some* production that fires and the odds that the production will fire. The second part of this analysis concerns how these odds should relate to match time. The third step involves combining the previous two to get Equation 3.3.

Step 1: Analysis of Odds

Let O_{ip} be the odds that the chunk i matched to production p will lead to the instantiation that fires, let O_i be the odds that chunk i will be part of the instantiation that fires, and let O_p be the odds that an instantiation of p will fire. Then, the critical assumption is that O_{ip} is proportional to the product of O_i and O_p:

$$O_{ip} \sim O_i \cdot O_p$$

This first assumption seems approximately right, although its exact truth would depend on specifics of just what combinations of productions, p, and chunks, i, can match. (Note that then $A_i = \log O_i$ and $S_p = \log O_p$.)

Step 2: Relationship of Odds to Match Time

Anderson and Schooler (1991) presented an analysis of why time to retrieve a memory trace might be a power function of odds. This can be extended to explain why time to match a chunk to the production condition is a function of the odds of that chunk–condition combination. The term *chunk instantiation* is used here to refer to a chunk–condition combination.

The basic assumption is that, at any point in time, the system is trying to retrieve a large number of chunk instantiations as part of creating various production instantiations. There is contention, however, among these retrievals, and the system will retrieve the most probable first. The time to retrieve a chunk instantiation will depend on how many more-probable chunk instantiations there are. In other words, the time will depend on the position of the chunk instantiation in the distribution of odds for all chunk instantiations. The reasonable assumption is that there will be a mass of odds near zero with a tail of a fewer and fewer high odds; that is, the distribution of instantiations will be J-shaped or highly skewed. Thus, the expectation is that most instantiations will have near-zero odds, and a rapidly diminishing few will have higher odds. Odds is the right scale because one can define a probability density with a mass near zero and a tail that goes out to infinity.

A great many things show such J-shaped distributions, including distributions of scientists by number of publications, words by frequency, and firms by size. Ijiri and Simon (1977) presented the following density as characterizing such distributions:

$$f(x) = Ax^{-k} \tag{3.8}$$

where f is the frequency of an item of measure x (e.g., word frequency, firm size, or odds), and A and k are constants. If instantiations are examined in order of odds or probability, then the time to examine an instantiation with odds O_{ip} will be proportional to the number of instantiations greater than O_{ip}. This can be calculated as:

$$\int_{O_{ip}}^{\infty} ax^{-k}dx = BO_{ip}{}^{b} \tag{3.9}$$

where $B = a/(k - 1)$ and $b = k - 1$. Thus, time is related to odds as a power function with exponent b. One implication of this analysis is that power functions in odds imply power functions in time, although not necessarily with the same exponent. In Anderson and Schooler (1991) this was critical to explaining power functions for learning and forgetting in terms of similar power functions describing probability of occurrence in the environment.

Step 3: Derivation of Equation 3.3

We have:

$$T_{ip} = B\, O_{ip}{}^{-b}$$
$$O_{ip} = O_i\, O_p$$
$$O_i = e^{A_i}$$
$$O_p = e^{S_p}$$

Combining these yields:

$$T_{ip} = Be^{-b(A_i + S_p)} \tag{3.3}$$

APPENDIX: DERIVATION OF THE FUNCTIONS IN FIGURE 3.4

The basic assumptions are as follows:

1. There is some probability, r^*, of the problem being solvable should the production fire.

2. Conditional on the problem being solvable, there is a gamma distribution, $G(x|v,b^*)$, of amount of effort expended to solve the problem. The mean of this gamma distribution is vb^* with variance vb^{*2}. If $v = 1$, the distribution takes the form of a heavily skewed exponential. As v gets large, the distribution becomes more normal. In the applications in this book, $v = 1$.

Then there are the following conditional probabilities:

3. If one is trying to solve an unsolvable problem, there is an exponential

distribution of differences between the current state and the goal state. The mean of this distribution is α. Note that an exponential distribution is the standard noninformative Bayesian prior for a dimension that varies from zero to infinity (Berger, 1985).

4. If one is solving a solvable problem, there is also an exponential distribution of differences with mean $c\beta$, where c is the amount of effort still required to solve the problem. This has the reasonable consequence of making the mean difference proportional to c.

From these assumptions, it is possible to derive r and b:

Let $P(F)$ be the prior probability of the goal not being solvable.

$$P(F) = 1 - r^* \tag{3.10}$$

Let $\pi(S,x)$ be the prior probability for a success with cost x.

$$\pi(S,x) = r^*G(x|v,b^*) \tag{3.11}$$

where $G(x|v,b^*)$ is the gamma distribution with parameters v and b^*:

$$G(x|v,b^*) = \frac{x^{v-1}e^{-x/b^*}}{b^{*v}\Gamma(v)} \tag{3.12}$$

where $\Gamma(v) = (v-1)!$ Let $\pi(D|F)$ be the probability density describing the distribution of differences, D, in a failure state. It is assumed that this is the Bayesian noninformative exponential:

$$\pi(D|F) = e^{-D/\alpha} / \alpha \tag{3.13}$$

Let $\pi(D|S,c)$ be the probability density of differences, D, in a success state with cost, c, yet to spend. Assuming a Bayesian noninformative exponential with mean proportional to the cost, c.

$$\pi(D|S,c) = e^{-D/c\beta} / c\beta \tag{3.14}$$

Then, the posterior probability of a failure is given by:

$$P(F|D,E) = \frac{P(F)\pi(D|F)}{P(F)\pi(D|F) + \int_0^\infty \pi(S,x+E)\,\pi(D|S,x)dx} \tag{3.15}$$

Similarly, the posterior density of a success with cost, c, is given by:

$$\pi(S,c|D,E) = \frac{\pi(S,c+E)\pi(D|S,c)}{P(F)\pi(D|F) + \int_0^\infty \pi(S,x+E)\pi(D|S,x)dx} \qquad (3.16)$$

Now, the desired quantities, r and b, can be calculated:

$$r = 1 - P(F|D,E) \qquad (3.17)$$

$$b = \int_0^\infty x\pi(S,x|D,E)dx \ / \ r \qquad (3.18)^{[12]}$$

The parameters that control this estimation are v and b^*, which describe the gamma distribution of costs in success states; α and β, which describe the distribution of differences in failure and success states; and r^*, which describes the probability of success. Because $v = 1$, the mean of the gamma distribution is simply b^*. The metric of difference is arbitrary, so β can be set to 1, which means that there is a mean difference of 1 when we are 1 unit away from the goal. The parameter, α, is set to 5, which means that, on the average, the current state is 5 units from the goal if the goal is unreachable. The parameters r^* and b^* are set by a learning process that is described in the next chapter.

---

[12]Equations 3.15 through 3.18 do not have closed-form solutions and are solved by numeric integration techniques.

4

Learning

John R. Anderson
Carnegie Mellon University

4.1 OVERVIEW

The preceding chapter described how the units of knowledge in declarative and procedural memory get converted into action as a function of their strengths, base-level activations, probabilities, and costs. We must still explain how the knowledge got there and acquired those parameters. Such considerations are at the heart of a theory of skill acquisition. This chapter will describe the ACT-R theory of skill acquisition which is an update of the ACT theory of skill acquisition, as set forth in Anderson (1982, 1987b, 1989c). According to ACT-R (and ACT*), all knowledge starts out in declarative form. Therefore, the first section of this chapter begins by discussing how knowledge gets stored in this form. Declarative knowledge is necessarily inert by itself, so the second section describes how such declarative knowledge gets interpreted to produce behavior. The third section then discusses how such interpretive application of knowledge becomes compiled into production form. The fourth section describes how this knowledge is tuned once it is in production form.

A major theme of this chapter is the relationship between acquisition of new knowledge at the symbolic level and tuning of this knowledge at a subsymbolic level. In ACT-R, when discrete events happen—when we learn the name of a new colleague or a new rule for solving a calculus problem—a new chunk or production rule has to be created. This is symbolic learning. Determining when we will next need to use that chunk or rule is another issue. *Tuning* refers to a statistical estimation process by which we learn to predict the utility of the knowledge in a particular context. Human intelligence comes from both having the right knowledge and making it available at the right time.

4.2 DECLARATIVE STORAGE

There are essentially two ways declarative knowledge can be created in ACT-R (or, indeed, in any of the ACT theories): Declarative knowledge structures can be created as the encoding of external events, or they can be created in the action side of a production.

Anderson (1983a) speculated that there was only a probability that a declarative structure would be made permanent when it was created. This was motivated to fit data concerning probabilistic all-or-none learning (Anderson, 1981). There is no such probability parameter in the current simulation, however. In the context of the ACT-R simulation, it seems bizarre to encode an item in declarative memory and then rip it out after a little while. Data indicating probabilistic learning may be understood as indicating there is some probability that the subject will encode the item in such a way that it can be retrieved given the prompt at test. The strongest form of such an encoding bias would be for subjects just not to attend to a particular item, as does happen in many verbal learning experiments. If the item is not attended to it can hardly be recalled later on. There are other ways to get recall failure besides failure to register the item at all. For instance, the item may be too weakly encoded, or may be encoded in a different sense at study than at test, or may be encoded in a different context at study than at test. Human memory research has found so many ways to get recall failure that it hardly seems necessary to postulate a further probability of not making permanent a declarative structure once it is formed.

Simply having a declarative structure stored does not guarantee that it will be retrieved to match to the condition of a production. Retrieval of a declarative chunk is governed by its level of activation, which was given by Equation 3.2 of the previous chapter:

$$A_i = B_i + \sum_j W_j S_{ji} \qquad (3.2)$$

where the summation is over the chunks, j, that are in the current context. Learning takes place on B_i, the base level of activation of i, and on the S_{ji}, the strengths of association. The design of these learning processes in ACT-R has been strongly guided by the rational analysis of memory in Anderson (1990a). Basically, A_i is the log posterior odds that the structure will be used[1] in the current context, and the learning processes are supposed to give a best estimate of that quantity. B_i are the log prior odds, and S_{ji} are logs of the likelihood ratios. The subsections that follow discuss separately learning of the B_i values and the S_{ji} values.

Before getting into the mathematical details of these learning processes, however, it is worthwhile to be explicit about what these learning processes

---

[1]In the context of ACT-R, *used* gets operationalized as *matched to a production that fires*.

are trying to achieve. They are intended to provide estimates of these odds that are as accurate as is possible. Learning of base-level activations and associative strengths is essentially a matter of Bayesian statistical inference. As we gather experience with where and how memories are used, we increase our ability to identify when they will be used again.

4.2.1 Learning Base-Level Activations[2]

The B_i are supposed to be estimates of the log odds that a chunk will be used. Anderson and Schooler (1991) reported a set of systematic relationships that hold in the environment between past uses of an item and the odds that it will be needed now. If an item has been used t time units ago, its odds of being used now are:

$$\text{Odds} = at^{-d} \tag{4.1}$$

where a is a constant, t is the time since the chunk was used, and d is an exponent, usually between 0 and 1. If an item has been used n times in the past at times $t_1, t_2, \ldots, t_n$ ago, then its odds of being used now proves to be a sum of the odds that derive from the individual presentations:[3]

$$\text{Odds} = \sum_{j=1}^{n} at_j^{-d} \tag{4.2}$$

The following formula then gives the base-level activation, B_i, which should reflect log odds:

$$B_i = \log \left(\sum_{j=1}^{n} t_j^{-d} \right) + B \tag{4.3}$$

where $B = \log a$.

As developed in Anderson and Schooler (1991), not only does Equation 4.3 describe the environmental data on how probability of reuse varies with pattern of past use, but it also captures most of the behavioral data on how availability in human memory varies with pattern of past use. It predicts that memory will increase as a power function of practice and decrease as a power function of delay, both of which appear to be behavioral laws.[4]

---

[2]Learning of base-level activations in the ACT-R simulation only occurs if the flag for "Base-Level Learning" is turned on.

[3]The discussion in Anderson and Schooler (1991) included an analysis of spacing effects, which is omitted here for simplicity, but ACT-R could be expanded to include the Anderson and Schooler spacing analysis.

[4]Anderson (1982) showed that if the n presentations in Equation 4.2 are evenly spaced, this quantity is closely approximated by $\dfrac{anL^{-d}}{1 - d}$ where L is the life of the unit, that is, the time since its creation. This approximation can be obtained in the simulation by turning the "Optimize Learning" flag on.

Figures 4.1 and 4.2 illustrate these relationships. Figure 4.1 displays a variety of retention functions; Fig. 4.2 displays a variety of practice functions. The retention curves include various measures of retention as a function of log delay; the practice curves display data as a function of log amount of practice. Figures 4.1a and 4.2a display the theoretical quantity B_i calculated according to Equation 4.3, with $d = .5$ and $B = 0$. This appears as a straight line, trivially, in Fig. 4.1a, and not so trivially in Fig. 4.2a.

As noted, B_i can be taken as an estimate of the log odds that an item will

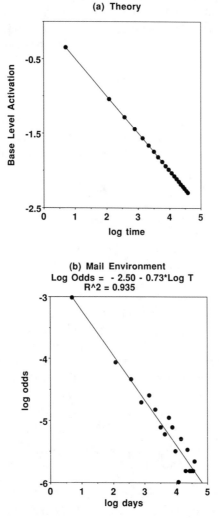

FIG. 4.1.   Retention functions: (a) Predicted by theory, (b) observed in the environment, (c) observed in retrieval time, (d) displayed in long-term potentiation.

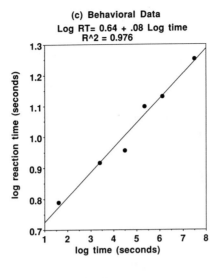

(c) Behavioral Data
Log RT= 0.64 + .08 Log time
R^2 = 0.976

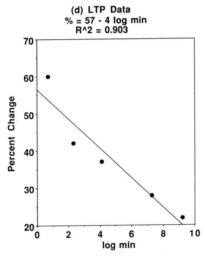

(d) LTP Data
% = 57 - 4 log min
R^2 = 0.903

FIG. 4.1. Continued.

be needed. Figures 4.1b and 4.2b display some data from Schooler and Anderson on the timing of electronic mail messages sent to me. Figure 4.1b shows the odds that I will receive a message from someone on a particular day as a function of how many days it has been since the last message was received from that person; Fig. 4.2b looks at this odds as a function of the total number of days I have received mail from that person in the last 100 days. These figures plot log odds as a function of log delay (Fig. 4.1b) or log practice (Fig. 4.2b). Note that the linear functions for these environmental relationships are like the linear functions for the theory in Figs. 4.1a and 4.2a. This confirms that these

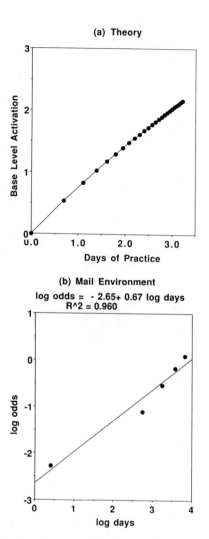

FIG. 4.2. Practice functions: (a) Predicted by theory, (b) observed in the environment, (c) observed in retrieval time, (d) displayed in long-term potentiation.

theoretical functions do, in fact, estimate log odds. The functions in Figs. 4.1b and 4.2b do not have similar slopes and intercepts, as do the functions in Figs. 4.1a and 4.2a, but the parameters for the functions in Figs. 4.1a and 4.2a could be adjusted to get a correspondence.

Figures 4.1c and 4.2c look at the relationship between log retrieval time and two independent variables, drawn from behavioral data: Fig. 4.1c is taken from Anderson and Paulson (1977), on sentence recognition, and Fig. 4.2c is from Pirolli and Anderson (1985), on sentence recognition. The appendix to chapter 3 showed that a linear function in log odds with respect to the environment

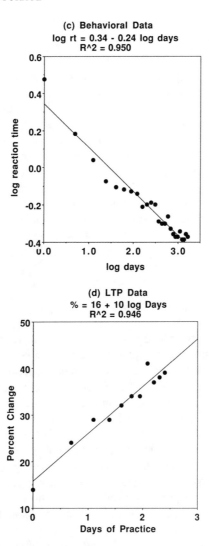

(c) Behavioral Data
log rt = 0.34 - 0.24 log days
R^2 = 0.950

(d) LTP Data
% = 16 + 10 log Days
R^2 = 0.946

FIG. 4.2. Continued.

implied a linear function in log time with respect to behavior. The behavioral measures in Figs. 4.1c and 4.2c, as predicted, do mirror the results in the environment (Figs. 4.1b and 4.2b). These linear behavioral functions in log scales would convert into power functions in the original scales. Thus, the functions in Figs. 4.1c and 4.2c are examples of the power law of forgetting (Wixted & Ebbesen, 1991) and the power law of practice (Newell & Rosenbloom, 1981).

Finally, Figs. 4.1d and 4.2d present some data on long-term potentiation (LTP), which is thought to be one measure of long-term learning. With high-frequency stimulation of the hippocampus, neurons undergo a long-lasting increase in their responsiveness to further stimulation. The data in Fig. 4.1d, from Barnes (1979), shows how LTP decreases with delay; the data in Fig. 4.2d, from Barnes and McNaughton (1980), shows the increase with practice. Thus, the LTP data replicate the theoretical, environmental, and behavioral functions.

Note that the functions in Figs. 4.1a and 4.2a, which reflect theory, and those in Figs. 4.1d and 4.2d, which reflect LTP, both plot the dependent measures on untransformed scales, whereas Figs. 4.1b and c and 4.2b and c, which reflect environmental and behavioral functions, both plot odds and latency on log scales. Recall from chapter 3 that the prediction was that activation should reflect *log odds*, and that latency should be a power function of odds. Thus, a linear relationship in log odds should be reflected as a linear relationship in activation and log latency. So, the choice of scales in all the figures are just what the theory prescribes. The fact that they all come out as linear functions in these scales is quite astounding. In particular, it suggests that LTP could be one neural component of the activation behind B_i.

4.2.2 Learning Associative Strengths[5]

S_{ji} is, in essence, a strength of association. It is supposed to estimate a log likelihood ratio measure of how much the presence of j in the context increases the probability that i is needed. To define S_{ji} more precisely requires some notation. Let C_j represent the event that j is in the context, and N_i represent the event that i is needed. Then for Equation 3.2 to calculate log posterior odds, S_{ji} should be an estimate of the log likelihood ratio $\log (P(C_j|N_i)/P(C_j|\overline{N_i}))$, where $P(C_j|N_i)$ is the probability that j is present in the context given chunk i is needed, and $P(C_j|\overline{N_i})$ is the probability that j is present given i is not needed. It is sometimes useful to approximate the probability ratio by $R_{ji} = P(C_j|N_i)/P(C_j)$ $= P(N_i|C_j)/P(N_i)$, which is a measure of how more or less probable i is in the context of j than it is in its base probability. The approximation can be justified by the observation that conditionalizing the presence of j on the absence of needing just one chunk, i, can little change $P(C_j|\overline{N_i})$ from $P(C_j)$, because there are so many chunks. Adopting this approximation for analytic convenience, we now discuss how to calculate R_{ji}. Remember that $S_{ji} = \log (R_{ji})$.

On the creation of a new chunk, the R_{ji} have to be set to default strengths, R^*_{ji}, which reflect guesses as to what the strengths of association should be. The value of R^*_{ji} will depend on whether j and i are connected in declarative memory. They are considered to be connected if j appears as an element in chunk i, or vice versa. Otherwise they are considered unconnected. If they are unconnected, $S_{ji} = 0$ (or $R^*_{ji} = 1$), which reflects the assumption that i is neither

---

[5]Learning of associative strengths only occurs in the ACT-R simulation if the flag for "Associative Learning" is turned on.

more nor less likely in the presence of j than its base probability. In the case that they are connected,

$$R^*_{ji} = 1/n \ / \ 1/m = m/n \tag{4.4}$$

where n is the number of things j is connected to, and m is the number of facts in the data base. This reflects the view that $P(N_i|C_j) = 1/n$, or that all chunks connected to j are equally likely when j is present; and that $P(N_i) = 1/m$, or that all facts in data base are equally likely. Both assumptions are approximations, but they will do for purposes of initial settings.

With experience, one gathers evidence of what the proportions are. $P_e(N_i|C_j)$ is empirically defined as $F(N_i \ \& \ C_j)/F(C_j)$, where $F(N_i \ \& \ C_j)$ is the number of times i is needed when j is present in any context, and $F(C_j)$ is the number of times j is present in the context. Similarly $P_e(N_i)$ is empirically defined as $F(N_i)/F$, where $F(N_i)$ is the number of times i is needed, and F is the number of opportunities (productions matched) since i was created. R_{ji} is estimated as a weighted combination of the prior estimate, R^*_{ji}, and the empirical ratio, $E_{ji} = P_e(N_i|C_j)/P_e(N_i)$. The typical Bayesian solution to such estimation problems is to take a weighted average of the prior value (weighted by some constant a) and the empirical value (weighted by the number of observations, $F(C_j)$):

$$R_{ji} = \frac{a \ R^*_{ji} + F(C_j) \ E_{ji}}{a + F(C_j)} \tag{4.5}$$

Equation 4.5 implies the fan effect, which has played a major role in other ACT theories. (For a review, see Anderson, 1983c.) The *fan effect* refers to the fact that the speed of access from a cue, j, to a trace, i, decreases as the number of memories associated to j increases. So, a typical fan experiment might manipulate the number of facts (is) a subject studies about a fictitious person (the j) and observe decreased speed in recognizing any fact. The number of facts will affect n in Equation 4.4 and so lower R^*_{ji}. Similarly, as more facts about a person are learned, the less probable any particular one will be when the person appears. This will lower $P_e(N_i|C_j)$ and, so, E_{ji}. Note, also, that past research (e.g., Anderson, 1983a) has shown that, with practice, the critical variable that influences R^*_{ji} does become $P_e(N_i|C_j)$ and not the actual number of facts. This shift to the empirical proportion is what is predicted by the Bayesian combination rule in Equation 4.5.

In addition to predicting the fan effect, it turns out that Equation 4.5 implies priming effects, whereby associatively related primes speed up access to target information. Indeed, as reviewed in Anderson and Milson (1989), a wide range of memory phenomena are predicted by this rational analysis of memory. ACT-R, embodying that rational analysis, inherits these predictive successes.

4.2.3 Origins of Declarative Knowledge

Before proceeding to a discussion of procedural learning, it is worth acknowledging an important issue that this discussion of declarative learning has not addressed. The development here has been concerned with matters like the strength of encoding of the knowledge, but has ignored the issue of how that knowledge came to encode the content it did. When we hear a string of words, it is a major task to place an interpretation on these words. When we study an example in mathematics, it is important how we interpret that example. When we see a scene, it is a matter of inference that we see a dog and a cat and that one is chasing the other. Much of cognitive psychology can be construed as the study of how declarative knowledge gets its content, and this is being ignored here.

I have had a sketch of a solution to this problem in the ACT theory since Anderson (1976), but filling in the details of that sketch would be a major undertaking. The sketch is that the perceptual system delivers some relatively primitive representation of the input, which is then processed through acquired interpretive processes. This sketch is the standard one assumed in the information-processing approach to cognitive psychology. In Anderson (1983a), I argued that these interpretive processes were just additional production rules acquired like other rules. I am less convinced that this is true for all the processes, although it certainly must be true for some.[6]

Throughout this book I make what are informal but plausible assumptions about the initial encoding of this declarative knowledge. These assumptions are crucial, because all subsequent processing is in response to what is initially put into the system.

4.3 INTERPRETIVE APPLICATION OF DECLARATIVE KNOWLEDGE

4.3.1 Learning From Examples

If an individual is at a point where an existing production will produce the correct next step, then things can proceed as described in the previous chapter on perception of production rules. That is, the subject can order the one or more possible productions by plausibility and select among them according to their expected values. When no appropriate production comes to mind, when one is at an impasse for which there is no adequate knowledge, what can be done?

---

[6]Anderson (1990a) contained a rational analysis of categorical and causal inference processes that are important parts of these interpretive processes. It does not seem that the rational analysis of these components can profitably be rendered in production rules.

Our observation is that subjects try to look for some example, from their past, of a behavior that helped in an analogous situation. They try to solve the problem by analogy to that example. This is called *interpretive problem solving*, because it involves interpreting a declarative record of a previous problem-solving episode (either their own problem solving or someone else's).[7]

It should be possible to evoke interpretive problem solving by analogy even when there are applicable productions.[8] Problem solving by production should always be in competition with problem solving by analogy. Problem solving by analogy to an example should be judged in the same way as any regular production. One can consider the interpretive route to reflect essentially a meta-production, with its own strength and probability. Its plausibility should be judged according to its strength and the level of activation of the data structures that it interprets. It should be evaluated according to expected cost and probability calculated just as they are for any other production. Thus, it should be possible for the interpretive application of knowledge to beat out routinized productions. This is a critical feature if one is to have a system that can change its ways given the intention to do so.[9]

4.3.2 The ACT-R Analogy Mechanism

Figure 4.3 illustrates the overall conception of problem solving by analogy to a prior example. When one solves a problem by analogy to an example, the example is understood as both a goal and a response that achieved the goal. The current problem is represented as a goal without a response. Analogy involves first mapping the example goal onto the current goal, and then applying that mapping to the example response to derive a response for the current situation. It may be the case that the previous example had preconditions stored on its successful operation. Any unsatisfied preconditions have to be subgoaled and satisfied before one can use the analogous operator. Analogy is also used in mapping the preconditions from the example to the current situation.

It remains to define the mapping and application processes in Fig. 4.3, which define the essence of problem solving by analogy. The mapping process involves finding a correspondence between the goal and the result of the example. Both the goal and the result are defined by schema-like chunks. To take a simple

---

[7]As VanLehn (1990) or Newell (1991), this analysis sees impasses as critical to learning although the ACT-R response to such impasses is rather different.

[8]However, in the accompanying simulation, analogy is only evoked at such impasses.

[9]Intentions in ACT-R would be represented as declarative structures encoding an example of the intended behavior. By making these structures highly active, analogy to the examples can beat strong productions.

PROBLEM SOLVING BY ANALOGY

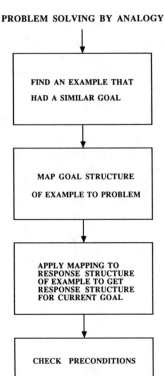

FIG. 4.3. An attempt to create an
analogous problem-solving operator.

example, suppose the result that we are trying to get is to add 712 and 91 in
LISP. This may be encoded:[10]

goal1
    isa lisp-operation
    type addition
    arg1 712
    arg2 91

One might have an example where typing (* 2 3) caused 2 and 3 to be multiplied
in LISP. The result of this example would be encoded:

example1
    isa lisp-operation
    type multiplication
    arg1 2
    arg2 3
    achieved-by response1

---

[10]This example is illustrated in the "Lisp Analogy" file in the Examples folder on the accompanying disk.

where response1 is what caused this LISP operation to happen.[11] It is encoded as:

```
response1
    isa lisp-call
    first *
    second 2
    third 3
```

To perform a mapping, the result chunk and the goal chunk must be of the same type. In addition, all the elements of the result chunk must map onto elements of the goal chunk. For one element to map onto another, it also must be of the same type. For instance, in mapping goal1 onto example1, multiplication can map onto addition because both are arithmetic operations, and 2 can map onto 712 and 3 onto 91 because they are both numbers. The types of these elements would be stored on their isa slots.

Once the mapping is achieved, it is necessary to apply it to the example response. The response (in this case, response1) can be retrieved from the achieved-by link. One applies the mapping by creating a chunk structure of the same kind as the example and replacing elements from the example by the terms they are mapped onto in the goal. Using this rule we would create the following structure:

```
response2
    isa lisp-call
    first ?????
    second 712
    third 91
```

where we have completely specified the new response except that we do not know what the new first element is. This is because the mapping between example1 and goal1 did not involve a correspondence for *. At this point we have to do some relational elaboration of the first term. We might have the following embellishment of multiplication:

```
multiplication
    isa arithmetic-operation
    implemented-by *
```

In this elaboration we find *. Because we know multiplication maps onto addition, this can be mapped onto the following description of addition:

---

[11]In Anderson (1990a), these relationships were explicitly treated as causal. On some occasions calling them *causal* seems a bit anomalous. Thus, we have retreated to the more neutral *achieved-by* predicate.

addition
    isa arithmetic-operation
    implemented-by +

Now we find that + is the symbol that corresponds to * and it can be used to fill in the missing slot of response2.

4.3.3 Analogy in Perspective

This is basically the theory of problem solving by analogy, which was first articulated as part of the PUPS production system (Anderson & Thompson, 1989, and analyzed in Anderson, 1990a). It consists of essentially two parts. The first is the extraction of a mapping and application of the mapping, which defines the range of generalization. The second is the process of relational elaboration, which occurs when direct mapping is not enough. These two processes are quite simple but, as Anderson and Thompson showed, are capable of simulating quite complex problem-solving episodes. As reviewed in Anderson and Thompson, the PUPS theory of analogy is similar to a number of other models of analogy that have been advanced (e.g., Carbonell, 1985; Gentner, 1983; Thagard, Holyoak, Nelson, & Gochfeld, 1990; Winston, Binford, Katz, & Lowry, 1983). The major contribution of our work is to place these ideas within a production-system framework (which identifies its role in a more general theory of cognition) and to perform a rational analysis of the justification for problem solving by analogy. The behavioral evidence cited for these other theories is largely consistent with ACT-R's use of analogy.

This is a particularly simple analogy process, and by itself will not extend to many cases of problem solving by analogy. For instance, the example just described would only allow for mapping among two-argument arithmetic functions. It would not enable one to infer how to use nonarithmetic functions in LISP or how to deal with ones with more or less than two arguments. The process of finding a mapping between two examples can be a major problem-solving task in itself. Anderson and Thompson (1989) explored this to some degree in the PUPS system, under the topic of "knowledge refinement," but it remains a major open issue in ACT-R just how to model the full scope of the analogy process. All that is implemented in the simulation is what is described here.

Anderson (1990a, chapter 4) performed an analysis of why analogy was a rational thing to do. It basically came down to the assumption that causal structures that apply to one member of a category have a high probability of applying to other members of a category. This is why the isa slots are checked in the implementation of analogy in ACT-R. Note that this also means that ACT-R is unlikely to implement the across-domain analogies that are popular in some descriptions of analogy but are so difficult to get to occur spontaneously in the laboratory. Gick and Holyoak (1980, 1983), for example, found subjects very resistant to using an analogy of a general attacking a fortress as a model for a doctor attacking a tumor with radiation. This hesitancy is probably justified, because it seems unlikely, a priori, that a general's plan would transfer to radiation therapy (even if, a posteriori, it turns out to be a good analogy in this case).

Another issue concerns where the examples for analogy come from. In many cases, people are directly presented with examples for purposes of learning. Much research in psychology, however, has focused on cases when the analogy must be retrieved from memory. Retrieval of examples for analogy is determined by their level of activation just as is retrieval of other declarative structures. Because of this, ACT-R predicts the oft-obtained result that subjects tend to be reminded of examples that contain elements from the current problem (e.g., Ratterman & Gentner, 1987; Ross, 1989).

4.3.4 Sternberg's Analogy Task and Relational Elaborations[12]

Much of the ACT-R theory of analogy is concerned with a detailed analysis of how analogies are computed. Sternberg and Gardner (1983) carried out one of the more extensive studies relevant to this computational process. It is worthwhile to consider their data in terms of the ACT-R theory.

Figure 4.4 illustrates the type of analogy problem used by Sternberg and Gardner. Subjects were given three schematic drawings of people, A, B, and C. They were asked to identify the person D who was in the relationship to C that B was to A. The person's goal can be represented as:

```
goalc
    isa test-mapping
    size short
    weight thin
    color dark
    sex male
```

and the example as

```
examplea
    isa test-mapping
    size tall
    weight thin
    color dark
    sex male
    achieved-by targetb
```

---

[12]This example is illustrated in the Sternberg file in the Examples folder on the accompanying disk. It receives more discussion in Section 12.4.3.

A   B   C   D

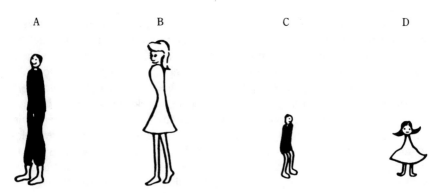

FIG. 4.4.   Example of Sternberg and Gardner's materials. Subjects must judge
if person D is in the same relationship to C as person B is to A.

targetb
    isa person
    size tall
    weight thin
    color light
    sex female

The mapping between goal and example gives the following correspondences:

tall   → short
thin   → thin
dark → dark
male → male

Using these mappings, ACT-R produces the following description of the
answer:

answer
    isa person
    size short
    weight thin
    color ?????
    sex ?????

where ????? denotes elements that cannot be filled in because there are no mappings for light and female in the targets. They will have to be filled in by relational elaborations. In this example, the subject might use the fact that light
and female are the opposite of dark and male to infer light and female are the
correct values in the answer. A more detailed discussion of this example appears in chapter 12; an expanded model appears on the accompanying disk.

Each of these relational elaborations that fills in an unmapped slot involves a recursive call to the analogy mechanism to expand the description of the unmapped element. One would naturally predict then, that the number of elements requiring relational elaboration should be a major determinant of the time to compute an analogy. Empirically, it turns out that the number of relational elaborations appears to be the principal "cost" in the research in human analogy. Sternberg and Gardner (1983) estimated .28 seconds for each difference between *a* and *b* that requires such an elaboration. It does seem, then, that ACT-R captures what is difficult in computing an analogy.

4.4 COMPILATION INTO PRODUCTION FORM

I must stress that the behaviors calculated by analogy are inductive inferences. To return to the LISP example, just because (* 2 3) calculated the product of 2 and 3 does not mean that (+ 712 91) had to calculate the sum of 712 and 91. It is an inductive inference that it will. Mediating this inference is a generalization to the effect that, by creating a list in LISP consisting of a symbol denoting an arithmetic operator followed by two numbers, we will get that operator performed on those numbers. The generalization is that this will hold no matter what the numbers or what the operators. This generalization could be represented as a production rule:

```
= goal
    isa lisp-operation
    type  = operation
    arg1  = arg1
    arg2  = arg2
= operation
    isa arithmetic-operation
    implemented-by  = symbol1
= = >
= subgoal
    isa lisp-call
    first  = symbol1
    second  = arg1
    third  = arg2
```

This production says, if the goal is to achieve a LISP operation on two arguments and there is an arithmetic symbol that corresponds to the argument, then set a subgoal to type a lisp-call consisting of that symbol and the arguments.

This may or may not be a valid inference. Anderson (1990a, chapter 4) can be consulted for an analysis of how one assigns a probability to this inference.

What is apparent is that, if the inference works in the new situation involving *, 712, and 91, its probability of being valid in subsequent situations is much higher. This suggests that one might want to store the inference as a production rule rather than calculate it again. Calculation of such inferences is computationally expensive because it involves searching for an appropriate generalization, and relational elaboration is particularly expensive. Furthermore, we are not guaranteed that it can even be repeated because it requires retrieval of the right example, which may no longer be sufficiently active.

On the other hand, creating a production rule may be an expensive investment. Basically, a production rule is a compiled procedure for pattern matching that requires setting up its own control structure. It probably involves allocating storage space to hold variable bindings. It is definitely a matter of speculation how productions might be achieved neurally (e.g., Smolensky, 1990; Touretzky & Hinton, 1988; this volume, chapter 13), but it seems probable that they demand considerable resources. This suggests that one would only want to create a production rule when there is good evidence that it will be reused.

These are the basic considerations that must be weighed in a rational analysis of the knowledge compilation process in ACT. On one hand, one wants to avoid the cost and uncertainty of the analogy process. On the other hand, one does not want to expend resources needlessly unless the production rule is going to be used with some frequency.

If the system chooses to create a production rule, it should fashion one that is the equivalent of the computation that was involved in the interpretive application of the declarative knowledge. This is done by determining what declarative chunks were used in the mapping and relational elaboration. In the example these were:

    example1
        isa lisp-operation
        type multiplication
        arg1 2
        arg2 3

which was involved in the original mapping and

    multiplication
        isa arithmetic-operation
        implemented-by *

which was involved in the relational elaboration. These become the conditions of the new production, with variables replacing the symbols (multiplication, 2, and 3) in the mapping plus any symbols involved in relational elaboration (in this case, *). The action side of the production rule is a description of the response in this example, with variables where constants were mapped (2, 3, and *).

Note that such a production rule can be created after a single example. This opens up the possibility that compilation could be a one-trial learning phenomenon. The system may want to wait for evidence of repeated use, however, before investing in a production rule. Also, even after a rule is created, it does not follow that all subsequent information processing will be taken over by this production rule. Recall that problem solving by analogy should be in competition with problem solving by production rule. A production rule, when first created, might be relatively weak and do poorly in competition with analogy to a highly active example. Thus, the switch to production-rule performance might be gradual. Some of our earlier work with the tutors (e.g., Anderson et al., 1989) suggested one-trial learning, but more recent research (e.g., Anderson & Fincham, 1992) indicates a more gradual knowledge compilation process.

4.4.1 Composition Processes?

ACT* allowed for the possibility of *production-rule composition*, which has some things in common with chunking in Soar. The basic idea was that if a number of productions fired to achieve a goal, one could form a new production that would serve as a macro operator and summarize the computation of the set of productions. In algebra, for example, if there is one production to add constants to both sides, as in the transformation:

$$x - 3 = 4 \rightarrow x - 3 + 3 = 4 + 3$$

and another production to delete $-3 + 3$, as in the transformation:

$$x - 3 + 3 = 4 + 3 \rightarrow x = 4 + 3$$

one could produce a production that would move the constant to the other side directly, as in the transformation:

$$x - 3 = 4 \rightarrow x = 4 + 3$$

There is no such composition process implemented in ACT-R, although there is good evidence that subjects can acquire such multistep productions (e.g., McKendree & Anderson, 1987). The effect of such composition can be obtained by compiling an analogy to an example that illustrates the multistep transformation. One could, for example, observe the effect of multiple transformations in the example just described, and use that end state as input to a new analogy.

A prediction that follows from this view is that one gets the effects of composition from compiling examples rather than from operating on production traces. The unit of organization in the example is the object, whereas the unit of organization in the process is the goal. This distinction can be seen in geometry, where a diagram naturally decomposes into a set of geometric objects, whereas a proof decomposes into a set of subgoals. The inferences brought together as goals in geometry are different from the inferences brought together by objects. Koedinger and Anderson (1990) presented evidence that inferences in geometry are chunked by what objects they apply to and not by what goals they serve.

4.4.2 Analogy Compilation: The Sole Mechanism for Production Creation?

The only way new productions can be created in ACT-R is by compiling the analogy process. That is, new productions can only enter by analogy to an example. This means that it is not possible for the system to receive example-free instructions and follow those directly. We have noticed, for instance, that when subjects receive new instructions, they interpret these instructions in terms of an example provided with the instruction or imagine some example and use the example to guide their behavior.

So, for instance, consider what the learner might do with the following derivative rule in calculus:

$$\frac{dy}{dx} = nx^{n-1} \text{ if } y = x^n$$

when asked to find a derivative for

$$y = x^3$$

The learner will be observed to map the problem into the rule template assigning 3 to n and proceed forward from there. The learner's behavior would be no different had the example been:

$$\frac{dy}{dx} = 6x^5 \text{ if } y = x^6$$

except that the template avoids any ambiguity that might exist about where the 5 came from.

Analogy to examples can have its difficulties, though. It is not always clear how to interpret an example, and learning by this route can be adversely affected by mistaken inferences. I suspect that the reason why one must learn by example rather than instruction is that little direct instruction was available in learning situations in our evolutionary history. If our ancestors learned a skill, there were two possibilities for its acquisition. One was that they had to learn it by discovery, either because no one possessed that skill or, more likely, because they did not have access to such a person. In such a case there would be no instruction, and they would be forced to learn by induction from what works.

The second possibility was that they had access to a teacher who could perform the skill. Given the noninspectability of procedural knowledge, however, that teacher would not have been able to tell them what it was that he or she knew. What the teacher *could* do was to perform an example of the skill for them and enjoin them to do likewise. This is the essence of learning by apprenticeship, a topic that has received some attention lately (e.g., Collins, Brown, & Newman, 1989). Most instruction still takes this form. A teacher who is good will choose the examples wisely and provide useful elaborations, but will not tell the student what to do in detail. It is the student who must determine this. Many people have the belief that, in schools, basic skills like subtraction are taught by direct instruction. When one looks at the content of the instruction and contrasts this with the procedures the student must acquire, however, it is clear that the student is faced with inducing what is needed from carefully crafted examples that have evolved over time as those optimal for analogical learning (VanLehn, 1990).

Consider the following sequence of instructions for moving text, from the Macintosh manual:

1. Select by dragging across the text.
2. Choose cut from the edit menu.
3. Select the insertion point by clicking where you want the text to go.
4. Choose paste from the edit menu.

Such instructions do not really tell the learner how to perform the task but rather specify a series of subgoals. The learner must already know how to achieve each subgoal. Following such instruction does not directly create an internal procedure (i.e., a set of productions) for moving text. Following these instructions (either actually or just mentally) creates an example, from which the procedure can be learned by later analogy.

4.5 PRODUCTION-RULE TUNING

A number of parameters associated with a production rule determine its firing: the strength parameter, which helps determine the computation of a production-rule instantiation, and the probability and cost parameters, which help determine the evaluation of a production instantiation. There are two probability parameters, q and r, associated with the production, and two cost parameters, a and b. The parameter q reflects the probability the production will produce its intended effect, and a is the cost of executing the production. The parameter

r reflects the probability that the goal will be achieved if the production has its intended effect, and b is the estimated further cost until the goal is achieved. The parameters q and a are quantities directly stored with the production, but r and b require estimation from state similarity and effort, according to Fig. 3.4. These estimation functions are parameterized by a mean probability over situations, r^*, and a mean cost over situations, b^*. Each production has its own parameters for r^* and b^*. ACT-R's learning mechanisms are concerned with estimating q, r^*, a, and b^* for each production from experience with that production.

4.5.1 Production Strength[13]

Production strength, s, is supposed to be an estimate of the log odds that a production will fire. It increases by the same computation as does the growth of chunk strength:

$$s = \log \left(\sum_{j=1}^{n} t_j^{-d} \right) + B \qquad (4.6)$$

where the summation is over the various times, t_j, that have passed since the production was used. It is Equation 4.6 that governs the decrease in time to fire a production with practice because strength determines match time (Equation 3.4). It is responsible for a power-law function relating time to amount of practice. Thus, procedural speed-up and declarative speed-up follow the same functional form. This helps explain why many complex tasks, like doing proofs in geometry, which undoubtedly involve a declarative and procedural mixture, show a composite speed-up that is very much like a power function (this volume, Fig. 3.2; Neves & Anderson, 1981).

Note that production strength estimates the likelihood of the rule, not how useful it will be. In the earlier ACT*, these two considerations were conflated into a single strength measure at the cost of considerable confusion. ACT-R achieves greater clarity by separating the measure of production rule success from that of frequency of use.

4.5.2 Production-Rule Success and Cost[14]

One of the parameters that govern evaluation of production rules is q, which reflects the probability that the production rule will achieve its intended effect. Using the standard Bayesian method for estimating this quantity (see

---

[13]Learning of production strengths in the ACT-R simulation only occurs if the "Strength Learning" flag is turned on.

[14]Learning of costs and probabilities only occurs in the ACT-R simulation if the "Parameters Learning" flag is turned on.

Berger, 1985, for estimation of a beta distribution):

$$q = (\alpha + m)/(\alpha + \beta + m + n) \qquad (4.7)$$

where m is the number of times the production rule leads to success, n is the number of times it leads to failures, and α and β are parameters describing prior probability of success, where prior probability is $\alpha/(\alpha + \beta)$. This formula gives a weighted average of the prior probability $\alpha/(\alpha + \beta)$ and the empirical proportion $m/(m + n)$. As $m + n$ increases, it becomes dominated by the empirical proportion.

A similar formula describes the estimation of r^* (the mean probability of eventual success should this production succeed), except that m and n now refer to whether the goal is eventually achieved, given the production was successful, and not whether the production rule had its intended effect. The next chapter shows in a navigation task that the human system can adjust its estimates of these success parameters.

The parameter a describes the distribution of effort spent executing the production rule. Assuming that it describes the mean of an exponential distribution of completion times, then the standard Bayesian estimate for a is:

$$a = (b + \sum_{i}^{n} e_i)/(v + n) \qquad (4.8)$$

where the summation is over the efforts, e_i, spent in executing the production rule, n is the number of such efforts, and b and v are parameters of the prior distribution, such that the prior mean is b/v. This formula gives a weighted average of a prior estimate b/v and empirical average of past efforts $\sum e_i/n$.

A similar formula describes the estimation of b^* (the mean cost of effort after this production), except that the efforts going into $\sum e_i$ are further costs after the production executes. The next chapter also discusses evidence that such parameters are learned by the production system.

4.6 LEARNING: A FINAL COMMENT ABOUT COMPUTATION

The learning mechanisms described in this chapter involve a mixture of the learning of new symbolic structures and the statistical tuning of parameters associated with these structures. The statistical learning processes require doing extensive computations every time a chunk or production is used. This can create considerable slowing in the implementation, and we allow the users to turn these learning processes off if their application is not really focused on such learning. The brain, however, should be capable of supporting such computations, because they can occur in parallel. Indeed, I suspect these learning processes could be implemented by slight variations on familiar neural learning algorithms.

Navigation and Conflict Resolution

John R. Anderson, Nicholas Kushmerick, and
Christian Lebiere
Carnegie Mellon University

5.1 INTRODUCTION

This chapter marks the beginning of the empirical section of the book. The next six chapters are concerned largely with reporting new empirical support for the ACT-R theory. ACT-R inherits a lot of the empirical support of ACT*. In particular, the declarative memory component of ACT-R accounts for the many memory phenomena described in Anderson (1983a) in basically the same way as in ACT*. The theory is somewhat different, however, having used Anderson and Milson's (1989) rational analysis of memory to guide its model of the spreading activation process. Thus, the memory theory both inherits the successes of the rational analysis and acquires a new dimension of justification.

Chapters 5 and 6 present empirical evidence for two aspects of the ACT-R performance theory. This chapter looks at conflict resolution, which is dealt with in a substantially different way than it was in the ACT* theory. The next chapter considers the role of goal structures, which is more precisely defined in ACT-R than in ACT*. Chapters 7 through 10 then examine the main target of the ACT-R theory: skill acquisition.

Conflict resolution is the process that decides which production rule will fire. Conflict resolution is performed in a relatively unique manner in ACT-R. Unlike most production systems, ACT-R does not have an initial stage in which all the production instantiations are calculated, followed by an identification of the best instantiation. Rather, production instantiations are evaluated as they are generated, and the generation of further candidates is terminated as soon as one is found that satisfices. The order in which production instantiations are generated and their evaluation are both dominated by probabilistic considerations. This activation-based pattern matching favors production instantiations that are more probable. The actual evaluation of an instantiation involves the calculation of an expected utility. This probabilistic treatment of evaluation is very different from typical treatments of problem-solving situations.

Anderson (1990a) argued that typical experimental studies of human problem solving looked at situations that were much more deterministic and regular than true human problem-solving situations. Among these nonrepresentative domains are puzzles, such as the Tower of Hanoi, and formal, academic topics, such as mathematics problem solving. In such domains, there is no uncertainty associated with the outcome of an action. There is also no interesting variation in cost of the different actions. These have been fine paradigms for understanding certain aspects of human problem solving, but they have led to the neglect of other aspects. In particular, these paradigms ignore how human problem solving deals with uncertainty and considerations of cost and probability of success. Also in Anderson (1990a), I suggested that the paradigmatic example of such issues in human experience is route finding in navigation, in which different routes are associated with varying levels of success, with a range of distances to traverse, and with a variety of potential obstacles.

5.2 NAVIGATION

We started thinking of navigating in the city of Pittsburgh and of how we might create an experimental analogue of that task. Pittsburgh, with its maze of non-parallel roads and three-dimensional structure, is a relatively challenging environment for navigation.[1] For reasons of experimental tractability, we did not really want to put people in cars and send them touring around Pittsburgh. Instead, we asked subjects how they would get from one location in Pittsburgh to the next, with questions like, "How would you drive from the Squirrel Hill Giant Eagle to Three Rivers Stadium?"

There were two salient features of their solution processes. One was that they always planned forward from the start location to the goal, although logically they could have planned backward, too. Second, they planned in terms of routes: "I would take Murray to the Parkway and take the Parkway to Three Rivers Stadium." We were not very satisfied with these protocols: They were very sketchy and seemed to ignore some of the important issues in making such a trip. It seemed to us that different subjects were taking in varying degrees their task to be satisfying the experimenter and not planning the trip. Also, such plans always worked because subjects did not have to face the real uncertainties and costs of navigation.

---

[1]The city has numerous ravines, and it is quite possible to take a road that is 50 or more feet above where you want to go.

With the information from these planning protocols, we designed a task that had more of the character of navigating in Pittsburgh for someone new to the environment. It does, however, reflect a kind of navigation problem that is relatively uncommon in most people's experience. Our reasons for choosing this task were (a) that it preserved what we felt were essential features of real navigation, (b) that it exposed the assumptions of our theory of conflict resolution to test, and (c) that it was experimentally tractable.

Figure 5.1 illustrates the sequence of screen images that subjects might see as they performed this task on the Macintosh. Part (a) is the initial screen image. The screen was approximately 24 cm × 33 cm. The subject was placed at a certain location on the map, indicated by a grey dot; the goal was to reach another location, indicated by a black dot. Emanating from the subject's location were various routes. Dots along these routes indicated possible stopping locations. Thus, subjects could see what destinations they could get to directly from their current location. This preserved the forward planning of routes, which seemed to be an essential feature of the planning protocols. A subject could choose some location to move to by clicking on that location, which made a simulated car slowly drive to that location. The rate of traversal was quite slow (approximately 4 sec to traverse 1 cm), in order to create a real cost associated with the process of navigation.

When the subject reached the new location, that location would turn grey, and the subject would see the routes emanating from that location and the places reachable from there. In this example, the subject chose to move directly upward in Fig. 5.1a. Figure 5.1b shows the routes and locations presented to the subject on reaching that new location. Figures 5.1c and d follow the subject as she found her way to the goal. The routes and locations are all part of a single large map, which is revealed in Fig. 5.2.[2]

In this study, we only exposed to subjects the routes from their current location because we wanted to follow in real time the process by which they combined routes. If the total map had been available, subjects could have mentally planned the trip and then executed it all. This methodology can be seen as analogous to the word-by-word presentation strategy for studying the dynamic processes of reading (e.g., Aaronson & Scarborough, 1977).

At any point in time, a subject had the option of parking his or her car and simply walking directly to the goal. The speed of walking was excruciatingly slow (approximately 40 sec to traverse 1 cm), and subjects would only want to take this option when they were very close to their goal. On some maps, they had to take this option, as there was no car route that took them all the way to the goal.

---

[2]This map is not like most of the maps subjects solved, in that it involved a misleading path that subjects had to back out of.

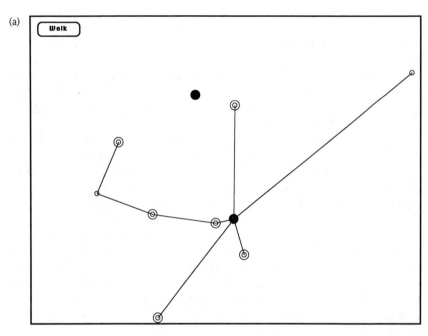

(a)

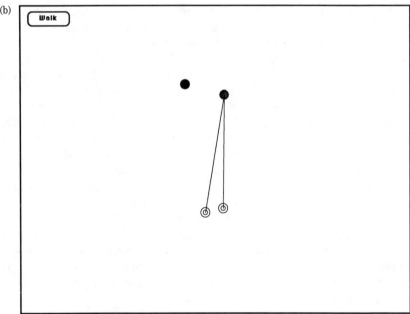

(b)

FIG. 5.1 a–d.   The various states observed by a student trying to navigate the map in Fig. 5.2.

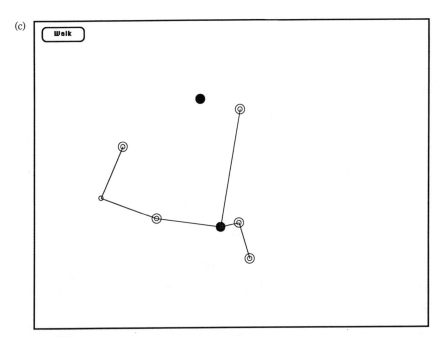

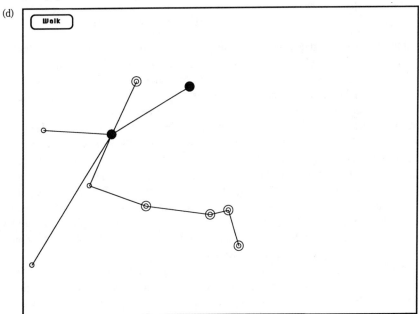

FIG. 5.1 a–d.   Continued

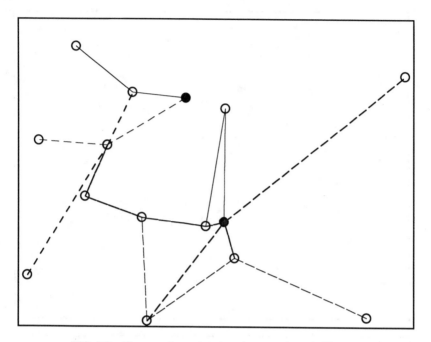

FIG. 5.2.   The map the student is trying to navigate in Fig. 5.1.

These maps offer a combination of known cost and uncertain cost. The subject knows how long it will take to get to the point he or she picks but, unless that is the goal, there is some uncertainty about how much further cost there will be.

Chase's (1982) study of taxicab drivers in Pittsburgh is relevant to this question of human route finding. His major concern, however, was subjects' spatial model of Pittsburgh, not their route planning. B. Hayes-Roth and F. Hayes-Roth (1979) studied planning errands in a town. Their situation was much more complex than ours, because their subjects had to juggle a great many errands and their relative priorities, and much of their subjects' behavior can be seen as a response to managing that information. On the other hand, there was no well-defined sense of success, as there was in our experiment. Although these past efforts have been quite successful at studying what they set out to study, they do not really provide evidence addressed to the moment-by-moment conflict resolution involved in problem solving.

We have performed two experiments looking at subjects' problem solving with these "progressive" maps. The first experiment used relatively simple maps, like the one illustrated in Figs. 5.1 and 5.2. The second experiment introduced a number of additional complications to further test the theory. These are discussed after we present a theoretical analysis appropriate to the simpler maps and the results from the first experiment.

TABLE 5.1
Productions Involved in the Navigation Task

COMBINE-ROUTES
IF   the goal is to find a route from
location1 to location2
and there is a route to location3
and location3 is closer to location2
THEN take the route to location3
and plan further from there.

DIRECT-ROUTE
IF   the goal is to find a route from
location1 to location2
and there is a route from
location1 to location2
THEN take that route.

WALK
IF   the goal is to find a route from
location1 to location2
THEN walk.

GIVE-UP
IF   the goal is to find a route from
location1 to location2
and you are getting nowhere
THEN give up.

5.3 THE THEORETICAL ANALYSIS

Table 5.1 gives the English version of production rules used in the simulation of the model. They are not the actual ACT-R production rules; for current purposes, so much detail is unnecessary.[3] The first production rule chooses to move to some intermediate location between the current location and the goal; the second production recognizes when there is a route that goes all the way to the goal; the third production rule chooses to walk; and the fourth production rule chooses to give up.[4] Note that, at any point in time, a number of production rules may be instantiated and, in the case of the first production rule, in-

---

[3]The productions and maps for the first experiment are available in Map Experiment 1 and for the second experiment in Map Experiment 2 in the Examples folder on the accompanying disk. You can get a pretty thorough trace of conflict resolution by setting the flags for Matches Trace, Conflict Resolution Trace, and Conflict Set Trace.

[4]The third production rule reflects an option available to subjects in just the first experiment, whereas the fourth production rule reflects an option available only in the second experiment.

stantiated in multiple ways. This is the classical conflict-resolution situation of having to choose among multiple alternatives.

Specifying how this production rule model applies requires specifying both the factors that determine the temporal sequence in which instantiations are calculated and how a particular instantiation is chosen. These two topics are taken up in the next two subsections.

5.3.1 Calculation of Production Instantiations

One factor relevant to determining when a production instantiation will be calculated is the level of activation of the data structures to which it matches. In this experiment the various data structures were the routes and locations. These elements would be active to the extent that they were associated with the foci of attention: the current location and the goal. We decided that strength of association should reflect Euclidean distance. It seemed that, everything else being equal, elements should be more strongly associated if they are physically closer. We had done an earlier simulation of navigating in Pittsburgh for which we had collected actual ratings of similarity between the various pairs of locations in the city. We found these were correlated with Euclidean distance (r = .46), but there were many exceptions reflecting semantic factors (e.g., two shopping locations). Because there were no semantic factors operative for our arbitrary maps, we just used Euclidean distance.

We then needed some way to scale Euclidean distances into strengths of associations. We thought it reasonable that strength should decay exponentially with distance. Therefore, we calculated transformations of these distances according to the formula $t(i, j) = e^{-d(i, j)}$, where $d(i, j)$ is the distance between i and j. If i and j are two locations, this is just the Euclidean distance. If either are routes, we calculate the shortest Euclidean distance between them. We also wanted to create quantities that would be distributed around zero because strength reflects log likelihood ratios, and the average log likelihood ratio should be zero. Therefore, we converted the $t(i, j)$s into z-scores calculated per map from the mean of the $t(i, j)$s for that map and their variance. These exact transformations are somewhat arbitrary, but they are not critical. What is critical is that strengths of association reflect Euclidean distance. This means that production rules will tend to be ordered according to Euclidean distance.

Equation 3.4 made time to match a production a sum of the times to match each of its condition chunks. These times are, in effect, multiplied by factors that reflect the strength of the productions. The WALK production was assigned a strength of −4, COMBINE-ROUTES 0, and DIRECT-ROUTES 6. These strengths tended to dominate the process and determine the order in which the productions were matched. The multiple possible instantiations of the COMBINE-ROUTES production would be matched in an order that reflected the activations of the route and the intermediate location, which in turn reflected their distances from the current location, and the goal. Thus, the proposal largely comes down to the claim that direct routes are considered first, and walking last, with intermediate locations in between to be considered in an order that is a function of their Euclidean distances from the source and the goal.

5.3.2 Production Evaluation

Recall from chapter 3 that the value associated with each production instantiation is $PG - C$ where P is an estimate of probability of success, G is the value of the goal, and C is an estimate of the cost of the goal. C is the sum of a and b (Equation 3.6), where a is the cost associated with the production and b is an estimate of future cost. The a parameter was set to $d/\text{rate}a$ where d was the distance to be traversed and $\text{rate}a$ was the estimated rate of travel. The parameter b was estimated from the Euclidean distance that had yet to be traversed. The Euclidean distance from the intermediate state was scaled such that the average interpoint distance on the map was 1. This distance estimate was used to get a traversal estimate from Fig. 3.3b. This was then converted into estimated future time by multiplying it by the parameter b^*, which is an estimate of average future effort. Thus, in this application, C was a sum of route distance plus a Bayesian estimate of future route distance based on Euclidean distance from the intermediate state to the goal.

The estimation of P depends on q and r (Equation 3.5), where q is the probability that the production will succeed, and r is the probability of eventual success given that the production succeeds. The probability r was estimated using scaled distance and amount of effort according to Fig. 3.3a. Again, this transformation depends on r^*, which is average probability of success.

Thus, to evaluate a production, we needed to associate with each production the parameters $\text{rate}a$, b^*, q, and r^*. Rather than arbitrarily assigning these parameters, we decided to use the ACT-R learning mechanisms (discussed in more detail with respect to Experiment 2) to establish values for these parameters by running the simulation over all the maps. These parameters were then fixed and used in the simulation of Experiment 1. They are given in Table 5.2.

The final parameter to be specified was the point at which the model would stop evaluating productions. This depended on when I_t in Equation 3.7 was not greater than a threshold, x. This, in turn, depended on the value of the goal

TABLE 5.2
Values of Parameters for Experiment 1

Production	Strength	ratea	b^*	q	r^*
WALK	−4	.03 cm per second	not used	.97	.94
DIRECT-ROUTES	0	.25 cm per second	not used	.99	.96
COMBINE-ROUTES	6	.25 cm per second	4.39^a	1.00	.99

[a]This is equivalent to approximately 22 cm, which would take approximately 88 sec to drive.

and the threshold. G was set to be 30 units of utility and x was set to be .3.[5] With the parameters set as specified, the model tended to consider about 4.1 production instantiations out of an average 6.6 in the conflict set in Experiment 1, which I now describe.

5.4 EXPERIMENT 1:
BASIC RESULTS IN NAVIGATION

This first experiment was designed to get some basic data on how subjects perform navigation across a set of maps intended to be largely natural and not involve tricks such as the one in Fig. 5.1. However, a few examples like Fig. 5.1 were included to find out what subjects would do in unusual situations. A total of 24 maps were created; they were divided into two sets of 12 each. Fifteen subjects solved each set.

5.4.1 Method

Subjects. Subjects were 30 undergraduates at Carnegie Mellon University (CMU) who were recruited for an experiment advertised as taking about half an hour. They chose to receive either one hour's credit toward a human subject requirement or $5.

Materials. We created 12 maps consisting of 15 randomly chosen points and 12 maps with 30 points. We connected these points informally, yielding about 10 routes for the 15-point maps and 20 routes for the 30-point maps. Each route connected 3 or 4 points. Of each set of 12, 6 were chosen to be relatively "normal" maps, in which one could get from source to goal following a roughly natural

---

[5]One unit of cost was worth 20 sec of travel time. Because cost and the value of the goal were set in terms of the same units, this means we assumed the subject thought the goal was worth $30 \times 20 = 600$ sec of effort.

TABLE 5.3
Summary of Behavior in Experiment 1:
Average Number of Moves and Units of Distance
(Simulation Averages in Parentheses)

	SIMPLE (15-point)	COMPLEX (30-point)
EASY	3.80 moves (3.83)	4.87 moves (5.33)
	28.2 cm (28.4)	25.1 cm (26.8)
LONG	3.77 moves (3.50)	4.00 moves (4.00)
	33.4 cm (34.7)	26.3 cm (30.8)
WALK	3.87 moves (4.00)	6.4 moves (7.00)
	31.6 cm (31.4)	20.8 cm (21.0)
BACK UP	3.57 moves (3.00)	7.37 moves (6.50)
	25.5 cm (18.0)	42.7 cm (37.5)

strategy of choosing sub-routes that led progressively closer to the goal. Two maps in each set had a misleading dead end from which one had to back out (as in Fig. 5.1). These were called Backup maps. Two had no route that went all the way to the goal: One could only get close to the goal, and would then have to choose to walk. These were called Walk maps. The final 2 offered subjects the choice at one point of taking a long, roundabout path that led directly to the goal or an indirect route to an intermediate location close to the goal. These were called Long maps.[6]

Procedure. Subjects performed the experiment on a Mac II computer with a two-page black-and-white monitor. The map took up approximately 24 cm by 33 cm. A subject indicated a move by clicking on the location he or she wanted to go to. A vehicle (a dot) would then move to that position at a rate of 4 sec per cm. When the vehicle reached the new destination, the display changed, so that the subject could see all the routes that passed through that location. The walk or quit options could be selected by clicking buttons on the screen with a mouse. If a subject chose to walk, the dot's speed slowed down to 40 sec per cm but it went directly to the final goal. The 12 maps were presented in a different random order to each subject.

5.4.2 Global Results

Table 5.3 presents an overall characterization of performance on the problems in terms of the average number of moves made to solve each type of map and the distance traversed in arriving at the goal. As displayed in Table 5.3, the

---

[6]The disk simulation Map Experiment 1 has 2 of the 24 maps. The map in Fig. 5.2 can be run directly and set up by typing (load-e-f-b). A 30-point map that requires walking can be loaded by typing (load-d-e-w).

data are relatively uninformative about what the subjects were actually doing in solving the maps, because it fails to relate the data to any theoretical interpretation, so we ran the ACT-R model on the same maps that the subjects saw. The ACT-R model is capable of solving the same maps the subjects solved, but does it solve the maps in the same way as our human subjects? We address these questions at two levels of analysis. One is a more gross analysis, to determine whether the model is solving the problems in the same general way as the human subjects. The second is a more microscopic analysis, to determine whether the processing that is occurring at each step corresponds to the processing implied by the ACT-R analysis of conflict resolution.

5.4.3 Macroscopic Analysis

One type of macroscopic correspondence can be measured by comparing the data from the human subjects and the model on the eight categories of maps in Table 5.3. There is good correspondence with respect to both number of moves (r = .94) and distance traversed (r = .83).

A more specific question is whether the model experiences the same difficulties across individual maps as do the subjects, using this measure of number of moves. Figure 5.3 provides one attempt to answer that question. It displays the correlation, .83, between the average number of moves for subjects and the number of moves for the model. This might seem relatively good, but you

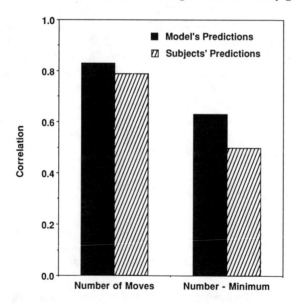

FIG. 5.3. The model's ability to predict subjects' behavior and the subjects' ability to predict subjects' behavior.

TABLE 5.4
Percent of Model's Solutions Corresponding to Different
Categories of Subjects' Solutions and
Similar Percentages Calculated Over All Subjects

	Model	Human
Most Common Solution	58%	62%
Other Solution	38%	30%
Unique Solution	4%	8%

must bear in mind that a certain amount of correlation is built in, due to the logical structure of the task. Some maps just take longer than others. Therefore, we looked at the difference between the observed number of moves (mean in the case of subjects), and the minimum number of moves needed if one took the optimal path. This difference reflects, in some sense, what is due to "psychology" and not problem structure. The correlation between these difference measures is thus reduced to .63. This is a more modest result, although it is statistically still quite significant ($p < .01$).

How good a correlation is .63, given the noise in the data? A relevant comparison is how well a particular subject does in predicting the average data. The average correlation between individual subjects and the performance of the remaining subjects is .5. Thus, the model is at least as good a predictor of subjects' behavior as is any individual subject.

Table 5.4 presents a different way of looking at the agreement between subjects and model. It classifies the model's total solution path as (a) the most popular path across subjects, (b) one of the other paths, or (c) a path used by no other subjects. Similarly, it classifies for each subject whether his or her paths were (a) the most popular across other subjects, (b) another path used by some other subjects, or (c) a path used by no other subject. Clearly, the model picked the majority solution as much as the subjects did, and chose a unique solution about as frequently as the subjects did. Once again, its correspondence to subject behavior is about the same as that of the average subject.

At a macroscopic level of analysis, the model's behavior seems undistinguishable from that of the human subjects. Both of these efforts (Fig. 5.3 and Table 5.4) to get a global measure of match, however, are dissatisfying. A decision by the subject or the model to make one move rather than another can lead them to different parts of the map, from which their behaviors will diverge radically. Thus, the match–mismatch statistics do not get at the trial-by-trial decision making. As a remedy to such a global measure, one sometimes finds problem-solving models judged by their ability to simulate a single subject's problem-solving steps.[7] The substantial variability in the data, however, sug-

---

[7]However, it is actually rare to find reports of cases where details of a running simulation are put in careful correspondence to the details of individual subjects. This issue is discussed in greater detail in chapter 12.

gests that such evaluations will not be particularly informative. A measure is needed that both follows the particular problem-solving courses of specific subjects and which provides aggregate measures of how well the model is doing at predicting all subjects.

There are two dimensions of analysis here. One is whether one deals with accounting for the data of a single subject or the group's data. The other is the grain size at which one examines the data: decision-by-decision or using entire solutions. Typically, these have been confounded: detailed analyses of single subjects or global analyses of groups of subjects. What is needed is a methodology that can follow a group of subjects, each on a decision-by-decision basis. Such a methodology would provide both detail and generality. *Model-tracing*, described in the next subsection, is such a methodology.

5.4.4 Microscopic Analysis

An analysis is needed that considers each choice point in the problem solution and compares the move the subject made with the move that the model made. The problem is that the model and the subject often diverge, eliminating the potential for further comparisons. To deal with this problem we adapted the model-tracing methodology from our tutoring work (Anderson, Boyle, Corbett, & Lewis, 1990). The basic idea is that there is some production instantiation at each choice point that will match what the subject does. What we do is to allow the model to proceed with its conflict resolution and see what move it will make. If its move matches that of the subject, we fire that production. Otherwise, we find the highest instantiation in the conflict set that will generate the same move as the subject and force the model to fire that production instantiation. This guarantees that the model will always be on the same path of solution as the subject, so the decision making of the model can be compared at each choice point with that of the subject.[8]

Figure 5.4 shows how often the model and the subjects agreed at the level of this choice-by-choice comparison. The basic idea here is that the production system places an ordering on the instantiations it generates, from best to worst (and it will choose the best if it considers it). The abscissa in Fig. 5.4 gives the production rules ordered by their evaluation. The figure plots the proportion of all subject choices that match the production instantiation in that position. A match to the first production instantiation means that the model and the subject agree on what to do at that position. As can be seen, the model predicts the subject's choice about 67% of the time. When the model mispredicts, the subject's choice usually matches the second or third best production. Thus, the

---

[8]This idea of resetting the model's behavior to correspond to the subject's can be traced back at least to Feldman (1963), who called this *conditional analysis*.

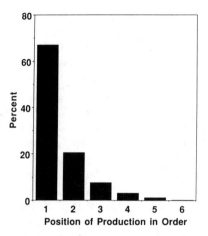

FIG. 5.4. The proportion of subjects' moves matching production rules at various points in the plausibility ordering.

model is close even when it does not exactly predict the subject's behavior.

Figure 5.5 is another attempt to measure just how far off the model is when it mispredicts the subject's behavior. As described in chapter 3, ACT-R associates a $PG - C$ evaluation with each production. The ordinate of Fig. 5.5 gives the difference between the model's evaluation of the production the subject chooses and the model's evaluation of the best production. The abscissa gives the rank ordering of the subject's production (ordered according to the model's evaluations of the productions). The difference is also plotted between the best

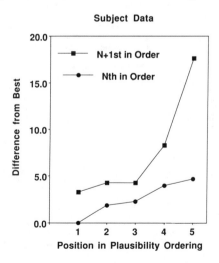

FIG. 5.5. The difference in evaluation between (a) subject's move and best move and (b) one worse than subject's move and best move.

and one worse than the subject's choice. As can be seen, the difference between the best and the subject's choice is relatively small when compared to the difference between the subject's choice and just one worse in the ordering. Also, the average difference between the nth and the best is less when the subject chooses the nth than when the subject chooses the $n + 1$st. Thus, when the subject's choice does not match the model, there tends to be only a small difference between the subject's choice and the model's choice.

We next added normally distributed noise to the evaluation with a mean of 0 and a standard deviation of 2. We compared this model's behavior with the behavior of the model given deterministic evaluation. It matched the deterministic model about 70% of the time. (The standard deviation was chosen so as to give this match.) Figure 5.6 shows an analysis of the noisy model comparable to the analysis in Fig. 5.5 of the subject choices. It plots the difference in evaluation between the production that the noisy model adopted and the best one chosen by the model without noise. The choices of the noisy model tend to hover close to the best, with one worse having a considerably worse evaluation.

Figure 5.7 provides another attempt to measure how well the noisy model corresponds to the behavior of the subjects. We calculated, by Monte Carlo simulation, the probability that the noisy model would choose each of the 9,408 instantiations generated at all 1,318 choice points encountered by the subjects. We then classified these instantiations into 10 decile categories for each .10 units of probability. That is, an instantiation is classified in decile category i if it would be chosen between $.10(i - 1)$ and $.10i$ proportion of the time. We then calculated the average proportion of times the model would choose instantiations in each decile and the average proportion of times the subjects chose that in-

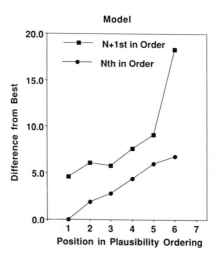

FIG. 5.6. The difference in evaluation between (a) noisy model's move and best move and (b) one worse than noisy model's move and best move.

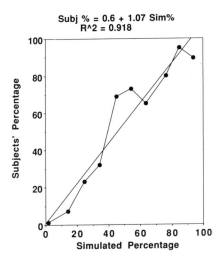

FIG. 5.7. The relationship between the probability with which the noisy model chose an instantiation, and the probability with which subjects chose that instantiation.

stantiation. The results are displayed in Fig. 5.7. As can be seen, the correspondence is quite good. The correlation is .958, and the best fitting equation is one that basically makes the subjects' probability the same as the model's probability.

To summarize the analyses in Figs. 5.4 through 5.7, it seems that, at the level of specific choices, the model does a good job of accounting for subject behavior. When it mispredicts, the subjects' choice is close to the best move that it predicts. If a little noise is added to the evaluation process, the model shows similar deviations from best performance.

5.4.5 Analysis of Latencies

The preceding analyses were meant to establish that the model comes to conclusions similar to those of the subjects. We now address the question of whether it comes to these conclusions by similar means. ACT-R uses a satisficing procedure to determine what to do. It evaluates productions as they are matched until it is satisfied it has found a good enough production. It then executes that production. How long it waits to respond is determined by the satisficing logic described by Equation 3.7, which in turn is determined by the evaluation of the best production considered so far.

Figure 5.8 plots subjects' response latency as a function of the model's latency before it makes its decision. Where the model's latency is between 0 and 1.5, all choice points were aggregated and plotted as 1.0 on the abscissa. The human subjects' average latency in this case is 2.51 sec; this is the value for the

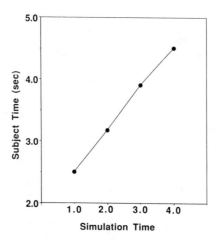

FIG. 5.8.   The mean time to make a move as a function of the number of productions considered by the model.

ordinate. Similarly, points were plotted for the intervals 1.5 to 2.5, 2.5 to 3.5, and > 3.5. As you can see, there is a near-linear relationship between model time and human time (R^2 = .998). The time the model spends considering productions is strongly influenced by the value of the best production such that, if it is very good, few productions will be considered. It is also determined by the position of the best in the order, which is determined by the activation levels. The sooner the best is discovered, the sooner the system will tend to quit. On the other hand, the correlation between total number of instantiations (i.e., number of choices) and latency is not significant. Indeed, this correlation is negative (r = −.16). Thus, the critical factor is time to choose the instantiation, not number of choices. The subject times (T_s) can be predicted from the model times (T_m) by the equation T_s = 1.84 + 1.34 T_m, implying that 1.84 sec were involved in executing the decision (not modeled) and each of the model's time units corresponds to 1.34 sec.

5.4.6   Conclusions From Experiment 1

The macroscopic analysis indicated that the rules used by the model approximated the rules subjects used. The microscopic analysis was more focused on the concern of this chapter: conflict resolution among the rules. Subjects appeared to be choosing among moves in a way that correlated with expected value (Figs. 5.4 through 5.7) and selecting moves in a way that is correlated with the model's satisficing process (Fig. 5.8).

5.5 EXPERIMENT 2: STRATEGY CHANGE IN NAVIGATION

The results of the first experiment certainly supported the ACT-R theory of conflict resolution, but we thought we could design a better navigation task to expose the cost and probability computations that were supposed to be underlying the conflict resolution. In the second navigation task, therefore, we added the following four complications to the maps:

1. One quarter of all maps were just not solvable. (We took away the walk option and added the give-up option.) Moreover, every second that passed while driving around the map there was a .5% chance (1 in 200) of the car breaking down. This meant that it was in the subjects' best interest to try to identify unsolvable maps, give up, and move on to the next map.

2. Half of the roads were marked as fast and half as slow. The rate of progress on the fast roads was three times that on the slow roads. This meant that distance was not the only variable relevant to evaluating the cost of an operator. The two speeds were 2 sec per cm or 6 sec per cm.

3. One quarter of both fast and slow roads were marked as having construction. If the subject chose to try to traverse such a road anyway, there was a 50% chance that there would be a barrier midway and the subject would have to drive back to where he or she began and try again.[9] Thus, there was a probability that an operator would not succeed.

4. All maps were of the more complex 30-point variety. This resulted in an increased number of options per move and an increased number of production instantiations.

These manipulations are relevant to three of the parameters in the model. The first manipulation is relevant to an estimation of r^*, the probability that one will succeed if the operator succeeds. The second manipulation is relevant to the estimation of a, the cost of the operator. The third manipulation is relevant to the estimation of q, the probability that the operator will succeed.

In addition to making the maps more complicated, we wanted to test the degree to which subjects could learn to tune their strategies and whether we could model these with the parameter-tuning mechanisms of ACT-R. Therefore, the 10 subjects that participated were tested over 6 days. Each day they were given 45 minutes to solve as many maps as they could. As added motivation they were also paid per map solved. The formula for pay was $2/day + $.50/map solved. Subjects earned from $46.50 to $61.00.

---

[9]If a path failed once because of construction, it would continue to fail on repeated tries. Similarly, a construction route once successful would always be successful.

5.5.1 Global Results

Of major concern in this experiment was what strategies the subjects were employing and whether their strategies varied with practice. Figure 5.9 provides one set of data relevant to these issues. It plots the mean number of maps the subjects solved, the mean number on which they experienced a breakdown, and the mean number on which they gave up. Subjects' improvement is reflected by the increasing number of solutions on successive days. What increased even more rapidly, however, was the number of give-ups. The subjects were apparently improving performance by increasingly identifying and rejecting troublesome maps and giving up on them faster. This is supported by a decrease in number of moves per map, which started out at 4.4 on Day 1 and decreased to 3.1 by Day 6. The increased propensity to give up cannot account for all of the subjects' improvement, however: Subjects averaged 129 moves in the 45 minutes on Day 1 but 171 on Day 6. Thus, they were also taking less time per move.

With practice, subjects chose their moves more quickly (decreasing from about 2.5 sec per move on Day 1 to 1.5 sec per move on Day 6). Because the majority of their time was spent actually traveling along routes, this could not have produced the magnitude of improvement. About 20 of the extra 40 moves were give-ups, which are cheap in time. Figure 5.10 illustrates the source of the rest of the improvement. It plots the percentage of moves that are give-ups, that involve construction, or that involve a slow path. (The latter two categories are not mutually exclusive.) There is an increase in the tendency to give up,

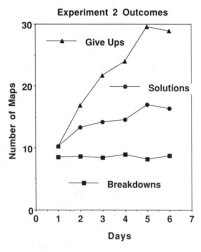

FIG. 5.9. The mean number of maps resulting in different outcomes as a function of practice.

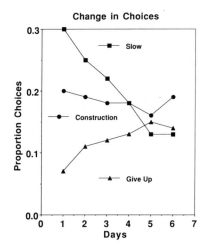

FIG. 5.10.   The proportion of various types of choices as a function of practice.

but the greater change is in the decrease in the number of slow moves. Subjects cut in half their choices of routes that take three times as long to traverse.

It is an interesting question whether subjects' learning is converging on an optimal strategy in terms of maximizing the number of maps completed. We address this question when we come to the microscopic analysis. First, however, we have to say something about the model that we placed in correspondence with this data.

5.5.2 The Production-System Model

The production rules used to model this task are derivatives of the production rules that were used for the first experiment, but there are some modifications. First, because we removed the walk option, there is no longer a WALK production. Second, having added a give-up option, we enabled the GIVE-UP production. Third, the COMBINE-ROUTES and DIRECT-ROUTES productions were split into four rules each, to represent the four possible combinations of fast and slow paths, construction and no construction. This allowed us to represent different parameters for each of these four situations.

Altogether there were nine productions—the eight route productions and one for giving up. We allowed learning on four critical parameters for the route productions:

a: This was the cost of the production, if it was successful. It took the form of a time parameter a^*, which could be multiplied by the route distance to get a total time. Initially, there was no difference for the fast and slow productions, with both set at 4 sec per cm.

b^*: This was the parameter that scales future costs. It was set to an initial value of 2.[10]

q: This was the probability of success of a production. Initially, there was no difference between the productions involving construction and those not, with both having a probability of success of .75.

r^*: This was the average probability of eventual success, should the production succeed. It was initially set at .9 for all productions.

The learning rules used were those described in the previous chapter. For the cost parameters, a and b^*, the learning rule was

$$a = (b + \sum_{i}^{n} e_i)/(v + n) \qquad (4.8)$$

where $\sum e$ is the sum of the observed times, and n is the number of such observations. The variables, b and v, are parameters reflecting the model's priors, such that the mean prior time is b/v. The initial values of the prior parameters for a were $b = 40$ and $v = 10$, to give an initial value of 4 seconds to traverse a centimeter. The initial values for b^* were $b = 80$ and $v = 40$, giving a value of 2.

For the probabilities, q and r^*, the learning rule was:

$$\text{prob} = \frac{\alpha + m}{\alpha + \beta + m + n} \qquad (4.7)$$

where α and β are parameters, such that the prior probability is $\alpha/(\alpha + \beta)$, and m and n are the number of successes and failures, respectively. In the case of the probability q, m is defined as the number of times the production is successful and n is the number of times it fails. The initial values of the prior parameters were $\alpha = 60$ and $\beta = 20$, to give the initial probability of .75. In the case of the probability r^*, m was defined as the number of times the production was followed by success, and n was defined as the number of times it was followed by breakdowns, with give-ups not counted. The initial values of the prior parameters were set at $\alpha = 45$ and $\beta = 5$, for an initial probability of .90.

Figure 5.11 shows the changes in the probability parameters q and r^* over days; Fig. 5.12 shows the resulting changes in the rate parameter, a. The scale for future costs, b^*, does not change appreciably with learning. Figure 5.13 shows the resulting changes in predicted moves over the 6 days. When compared with Fig. 5.10, it shows a somewhat similar trend. The behavior of

---

[10]The conversion factor is about 20 sec per unit. Thus, the mean expected further effort was 40 sec.

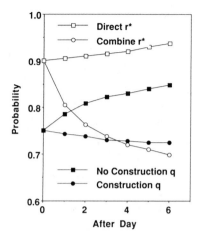

FIG. 5.11.   Changes in probability parameters r and q of the model as a function of exposure.

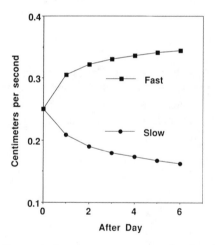

FIG. 5.12.   Changes in the rate parameter a as a function of experience.

the model is slightly more optimal than the subjects. When left to solve the same maps as the subjects, it solved an average of 20.1 maps on Day 6, whereas the subjects averaged 17.4.[11] As far as we know, the model's final behavior reflects optimal problem solving. That is to say, no subject did better, nor have we been able to find some setting of this model (or another model) that does better.

_____

[11]In figuring out how long the model took to solve maps, we made it traverse real maps and face real time and hazards. We also added to each move a time to reflect production selection.

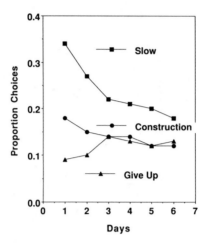

FIG. 5.13.   Changes in the proportion of various types of choices in the model as a function of experience. Compare with Fig. 5.10.

5.5.3 Microscopic Analyses

Figure 5.14 shows how well the model does at predicting specific moves. It is comparable to Fig. 5.4, although here the model's first choice corresponds to the subjects' move slightly less often. This reflects the greater number of moves available to the subject (i.e., more paths, more locations). Similarly, Fig. 5.15 is comparable to Fig. 5.8, showing the relationship between the

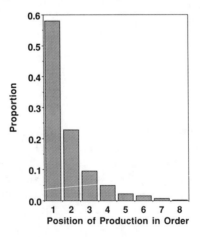

FIG. 5.14.   The proportion of subjects' moves matching production rules at various points in the plausibility ordering.

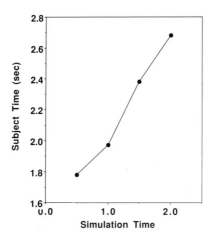

FIG. 5.15. The mean time to make a move as a function of the number of productions considered by the model.

model's latency and the subjects' latency. Once again, there is a near linear relationship (R^2 = .982). The model times and the subject times are a good bit faster than those in Fig. 5.8, reflecting the higher average level of practice.

The function in Fig. 5.15 does hide one phenomenon, however: Both the model and the subjects increased their speed as the experiment progressed. Figure 5.16 illustrates the comparable speed-up. The model's speed-up is due to the strengthening of the production rules.

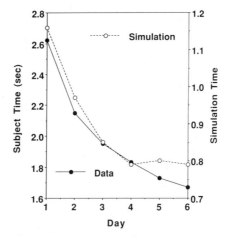

FIG. 5.16. The mean latency of subjects and model as a function of number of days in the experiment.

5.6 CONCLUSIONS

The data from these experiments are remarkably consistent with the ACT-R production-rule theory. This success largely reflects on the conflict resolution processes in that theory. To review:

1. Subjects' latencies support the theory of production matching:
   a. The general correlation between the number of productions considered and latency (Figs. 5.8 and 5.15) supports the role of activation in determining what instantiations are considered.
   b. The speed-up over days (Fig. 5.16) supports the theory of strength growth and the role of strength in calculating production-rule instantiations.
2. Subjects' choices support the theory of production-rule evaluation:
   a. The tendency of the model to agree with the subjects (Figs. 5.4 and 5.14) indicates they are responding to the same factors. The deviations can be attributed to noise in the evaluation process (Figs. 5.5 through 5.7).
   b. Both the subjects and the model are responsive to their experience with parameters and can appropriately tune their choices (Figs. 5.10 and 5.13).

Undoubtedly, ACT-R is not the only model that could be advanced to account for these data. Nonetheless, it appears to be the right sort of model. Although subjects are clearly quite rule-like in their behavior, their choices among rules has a softness and adaptiveness that cannot be captured in most production-rule theories.

The time per production, as illustrated in Figs. 5.8 and 5.15, ranged from less than 1 sec to more than 4 sec. Clearly, more has to be involved in these times than the execution of a single production, as the subject encodes the changed board and executes a move. Still, these figures suggest that execution times for individual productions are sometimes on the order of a second or more. Data in later chapters support similar numbers for time for a production to fire. These are very long times compared to production-rule times in a theory like Soar (Newell, 1991), where individual productions are supposed to be taking place on the order of every 10 msec.

This may be the most fundamental difference between ACT and Soar: that they choose to use productions to model cognition at very different grain sizes. In the ACT conception, production rules model the significant transitions in cognitive state. A single production rule in ACT-R corresponds, approximately, to the elaborate-decision cycle in Soar, during which productions fire prolifically to decide what to do next. What is modeled by this lowest level of production firing in Soar, which effectively accomplishes conflict resolution, is a level of processing that is best modeled in nonsymbolic terms. We suspect that the equations we gave in chapters 3 and 4 to describe these processes have ultimately connectionist implementations. Thus, ACT and Soar have quite different conceptions about what in cognition can be modeled symbolically.

6

The Tower of Hanoi and Goal Structures

John R. Anderson, Nicholas Kushmerick, and
Christian Lebiere
Carnegie Mellon University

6.1 INTRODUCTION

One of the important features of ACT-R (and ACT* before it) is the special role in organizing problem solving that it gives to goals. Cognitive scientists differ sharply in how they view goal structures. On one hand, for those who object to the computer metaphor, nothing can be more distasteful than the proposal that a goal stack controls behavior. Therefore, it is important that we ask whether we can find empirical evidence for the role of goal structures. On the other hand, for those who work in problem-solving research, the idea of displaying empirical evidence for goal structures seems a bit peculiar. Many feel that they would not be able to make sense of their data without such a construct. It would be like trying to do physics without a concept of time. Nevertheless, it is worth reflecting on just what assumptions we are making about goal structures and whether we can marshal evidence for these assumptions.

The critical idea in ACT-R's use of goals is that one can have a stack of subgoals that are dependent on one another. Thus, to use Newell and Simon's (1972) example, one can be trying to contact a garage in order to repair a car in order to be able to take a child to a preschool. These various goals would be ordered on a stack, with contacting the garage on top of the stack. This is a last-in-first-out (LIFO) stack, where the last subgoal one has put on the stack is the goal one is currently focused on. When one satisfies that goal, the next most immediate goal becomes the focus. In computer science terminology, one *pushes* goals on the stack and *pops* them from the stack. The goal stack becomes an important mechanism for remembering one's intentions in problem solving.

Some problem-solving tasks are solved without a significant subgoal structure. The navigation task in the previous chapter had that property. These kinds of problems can be viewed as being solved by hillclimbing rather than by means-ends analysis. However, as argued in chapter 3, goal structures are important to much of human problem solving. They are an essential part of tool use, are critical in much of academic problem solving, and may underlie the hierarchical structure of language.

The Tower of Hanoi task is an excellent one for studying use of a subgoal structure. One might view it as the laboratory preparation of choice for studying goals. It is unquestionably artificial, but it is an artifact that throws almost everything else away and, so, exposes the goal structure.

Consider the five-disk version of the classic Tower of Hanoi problem in Fig. 6.1. The subject's task is to move the five disks from Peg A to Peg C. The constraints on the movement are (a) that only one disk can be moved at a time, (b) that only the top disk on a peg can be moved, and (c) that a larger disk cannot be placed on a smaller disk. Simon (1975) argued that this can be modeled by the following goal-recursive logic:

> to get the 5-tower to Peg C, get the 4-tower to Peg B, then move
>   the 5-disk to Peg C, then move the 4-tower to Peg C
> to get the 4-tower to Peg B, get the 3-tower to Peg C, then move
>   the 4-disk to Peg B, then move the 3-tower to Peg B
> to get the 3-tower to Peg C, get the 2-tower to Peg B, then move
>   the 3-disk to Peg C, then move the 2-tower to Peg C
> to get the 2-tower to Peg B, move the 1-disk to Peg C, then
>   move the 2-disk to Peg B, then move the 1-disk to Peg A.

To implement this strategy, one needs to be able to stack a good number of goals. Simon discussed a number of other ways of solving the problem, some of which do not involve goal stacking. With appropriate instructions, however, one can more or less guarantee that subjects will use goal structures to solve the Tower of Hanoi problem. A number of other researchers (e.g., Egan & Greeno, 1974; Karat, 1982) have found evidence for spontaneous use of hierarchical goal structures in the Tower of Hanoi task.

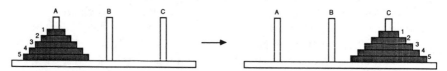

FIG. 6.1. The Tower of Hanoi problem. There are three pegs—A, B, and C—and five disks of different sizes—1, 2, 3, 4, and 5—with holes in their centers so that they can be stacked on the pegs. Initially, the disks are all on Peg A, stacked in a pyramid. The goal is to move all the disks to Peg C. Only the top disk on a peg can be moved, and no disk can ever be placed on top of a smaller disk.

6.2 THE EXPERIMENTAL TASK

Twenty-eight subjects were recruited from the Carnegie-Mellon undergraduate population to participate in the experiment. Figure 6.2 illustrates the configurations presented to subjects in the experiment. There were 8 five-disk problems and 8 four-disk problems. All the four-disk problems required a minimum of $2^4 - 1 = 15$ moves, and all of the five-disk problems involved $2^5 - 1 = 31$ moves. Problems began with either towers or rather flat configurations of disks. There were also two possible types of goal states. Crossing start state with goal state yielded four possible combinations. Two instances were created of each combination for four-disk and five-disk problems. Each subject saw one of the instances of each combination in each difficulty set. Half of the 28 subjects saw four of each set, and the other half saw the other four. The problems were presented in random order. These subjects, then, saw a much richer range of problems than most subjects in Tower of Hanoi experiments, and so would not be expected to have the opportunity to evolve special-case strategies.

6.2.1 Production Rules

It is not possible to reason about all of these problems just in terms of towers, as in Simon's (1975) analysis, but there is a slight generalization of this strategy that can be applied to all of these tasks. It is described by the following three productions:

SUBGOAL-DISKS
    IF   the goal is to achieve a particular configuration of disks
              and disk D1 is on peg P1 but should go to peg P2 in the
                configuration
              and D1 is the largest disk out of place
              and one cannot directly move D1 to P2
              and disk D2 is one smaller than D1
              and peg P3 is different than P1 or P2
    THEN set a subgoal to move the D2 tower to P3 and D1 to P2.

MOVE-DISK
    IF   the goal is to achieve a particular configuration of disks
              and disk D1 is on peg P1 but should go to peg P2
              and D1 is the largest disk out of place
              and one can directly move D1 to P2
    THEN move D1 to P2.

SATISFIED
    IF   the goal is to achieve a particular configuration of disks
              and it is achieved
    THEN pop the goal.

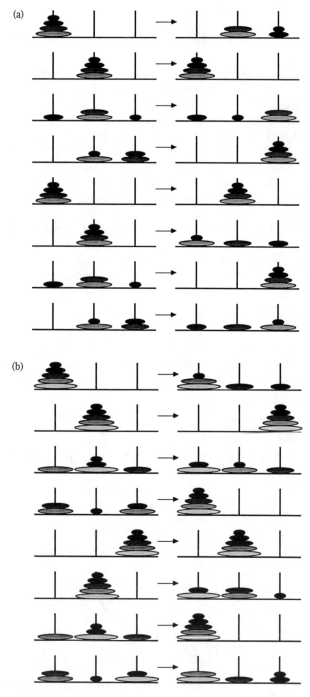

FIG. 6.2. (a) Four-disk Tower of Hanoi problems; (b) five-disk Tower of Hanoi problems.

The basic strategy is embodied in the first production rule. This strategy is to identify the biggest disk out of place, and if it cannot be directly moved, to set a subgoal of getting all of the smaller disks on another peg so that they will be out of the way so that the larger disk can be moved. Moving the other disks out of the way creates a subtower of disks on the extra peg. The strategy replaces the goal of getting an arbitrary configuration with the goal of achieving a tower configuration of the smaller disks and getting the largest disk in place.

In all of the problems, the disks were placed so that they were maximally distant from the goal configuration. This meant that to solve a four-disk problem, the subject would have to go through the following sequence of goal settings and moves illustrated in Table 6.1.

TABLE 6.1
Goals, Subgoals, and Moves in Solving the Tower of Hanoi Problem

Action	Production Fired
Goal main configuration	
subgoal 3-tower and 4-disk	SUBGOAL-DISKS
subgoal 2-tower and 3-disk	SUBGOAL-DISKS
subgoal 1-tower and 2-disk	SUBGOAL-DISKS
move 1-disk	MOVE-DISK
move 2-disk	MOVE-DISK
pop subgoal	SATISFIED
move 1-disk	MOVE-DISK
move 3-disk	MOVE-DISK
pop subgoal	SATISFIED
subgoal 1-tower and 2-disk	SUBGOAL-DISKS
move 1-disk	MOVE-DISK
move 2-disk	MOVE-DISK
pop subgoal	SATISFIED
move 1-disk	MOVE-DISK
move 4-disk	MOVE-DISK
pop subgoal	SATISFIED
subgoal 2-tower and 3-disk	SUBGOAL-DISKS
subgoal 1-tower and 2-disk	SUBGOAL-DISKS
move 1-disk	MOVE-DISK
move 2-disk	MOVE-DISK
pop subgoal	SATISFIED
move 1-disk	MOVE-DISK
move 3-disk	MOVE-DISK
pop subgoal	SATISFIED
subgoal 1-tower and 2-disk	SUBGOAL-DISKS
move 1-disk	MOVE-DISK
move 2-disk	MOVE-DISK
pop subgoal	SATISFIED
move 1-disk	MOVE-DISK
pop main goal	SATISFIED

The critical features of this model are the number of goal-setting firings of SUBGOAL-DISKS and the number of goal-popping firings of SATISFIED. These two productions occur between MOVE-DISK firings and so should determine the latencies with which subjects move the various disks. Of the two, SUBGOAL-DISKS should be more critical because it is the more complex production rule. A number of alternative production-rule formulations make the same predictions about firings of goal-setting productions. For instance, rather than setting a subgoal of moving both a tower and the disk it blocks, it might seem more natural to cast the subgoal as simply moving the tower. It turns out that a model that assumes that just towers are subgoaled makes the same predictions about where subgoals need to be created and how many are necessary.

Alternatively, it might seem more natural to some to have multiple goals pushed such that to achieve a four-disk tower, one (a) subgoals moving the 3-tower out of the way, (b) subgoals moving the 4-disk to the target disk, and (c) subgoals moving the 3-tower to the target disk.

This is basically Simon's original (1975) suggestion. This model involves creating more subgoals, but does not differ in terms of how many subgoaling productions fire and where. It struck us as somewhat implausible because it created a lot of unnecessary subgoals on the stack.

6.2.2 Special Instructions

There is no guarantee that subjects will adopt a goal-recursive strategy, under any of these descriptions, in trying to solve the problem. We were afraid that subjects would only gradually learn to use this strategy as they went through the experiment. To try to assure that subjects would conform to this goal-recursive strategy, we informed them at the outset of the critical piece of information required to execute the strategy: that is, the dependency among disk movements. Specifically, we told them it was important to get the largest disk to its destination first. The instructions used were:

> It is up to you to figure out how to solve the problems but the following hint may be helpful: As you work with the problems you will quickly realize that it is important to get the larger disks to their goal pegs first, since the ability to move a disk becomes more restricted as it becomes larger. It is a good idea to try to create a situation in which you can move the larger disks, and concentrate on the smaller disks only after this has been done.

Half of the subjects were also instructed in subgoaling and given a computer facility to remember their subgoals. These subjects, however, almost never used that facility, and their performance was in no way different from that of subjects who were not so instructed and had no access to such a device. Thus, if subjects do subgoal in this experiment, they can apparently do it without any very specific instruction or external assistance.

We want to make clear the motivation in instructing the subjects this way. There are many ways to solve the Tower of Hanoi problem, and we did not want to be in the business of analyzing the statistical stew that results from a mixture of strategies. There is already ample evidence that subjects can spontaneously adopt or discover the means–ends strategy (e.g., Anzai & Simon, 1979; Kotovsky, Hayes, & Simon, 1985), so there is nothing "unnatural" in the strategy we were asking subjects to adopt. The goal was to study this strategy in a relatively pure form, to see if we could simulate subjects' behavior in ACT-R and find evidence for the critical prediction that processing time would be a function of the number of goal pushes.

The prediction that processing time would be a function of number of pushes is a relatively unique prediction of the ACT-R architecture. Other implementations of goal structures might well relate processing time to the depth of the goal stack or to the number of pops. Depth of goal stack has no effect in the model. Number of pops should have some effect, due to the SATISFIED production, but it is a definite prediction that it will be less than the number of pushes. In the simulation, a MOVE-DISK or SUBGOAL-DISKS production takes about 1 unit of time, whereas the SATISFIED production takes about .05 units of time.

6.3 RESULTS FROM THE TOWER OF HANOI TASK

Subjects solved the problems using a Mac II that enabled them to move the disks by means of a mouse. The computer recorded each move a subject made and the time per move. Table 6.2 presents the average time per problem and the average number of moves per problem. Subjects took somewhat more than the minimum number of steps per problem. They averaged 19.2 moves on the four-disk problems, which is just 4.2 more than the minimum of 15, but they averaged 53.5 moves in the five-disk problems, 22.5 more than the minimum. There is relatively little difference in time per move (3.42 sec for four-disk problems, 3.67 sec for five-disk problems, $t(27) = .96$, *n.s.*). These performance measures are similar to those reported by Karat (1982).[1]

In some of the cases where subjects did not follow the prescription of the optimal goal-recursive strategy, they still made moves suggesting their behavior was controlled by goals. On a few occasions, for example, when the optimal next step called for a move of the smallest disk from Peg A to Peg C, subjects would move Disk 1 from Peg A to Peg B and then to Peg C, inserting an extra move. Subjects would sometimes execute a sequence of 15 moves to get a tower of four disks to Peg C, where the ideal strategy called for its move to Peg B.

---

[1]Note that there is little evidence in this data that tower-to-tower problems are simpler, in contrast to the predictions of some theories, such as Ruiz and Newell (1989).

TABLE 6.2
a. Performance on Tower of Hanoi Four-Disk Problem*

	Number of Moves	Time Per Move
Tower-to-Tower		
(4 3 2 1) ( ) ( ) →		
( ) (4 3 2 1) ( )	21.4	2.96 sec
( ) (4 3 2 1) ( ) →		
(4 3 2 1) ( ) ( )	16.9	3.07 sec
Tower-to-Flat		
( ) (4 3 2 1) ( ) →		
(4 1) (3) (2)	19.3	3.49 sec
(4 3 2 1) ( ) ( ) →		
( ) (4 3) (2 1)	21.1	3.90 sec
Flat-to-Tower		
(2) (4 3) (1) →		
( ) ( ) (4 3 2 1)	21.2	3.22 sec
( ) (4 1) (3 2) →		
( ) ( ) (4 3 2 1)	17.0	3.35 sec
Flat-to-Flat		
( ) (4 1) (3 2) →		
(2) (3) (4 1)	18.5	2.98 sec
(2) (4 3) (1) →		
(2) (1) (4 3)	18.4	4.35 sec

b. Performance on Tower of Hanoi Five-Disk Problem*

	Number of Moves	Time Per Move
Tower-to-Tower		
( ) ( ) (5 4 3 2 1) →		
( ) (5 4 3 2 1) ( )	55.4	3.22 sec
( ) (5 4 3 2 1) ( ) →		
( ) ( ) (5 4 3 2 1)	54.2	3.42 sec
Tower-to-Flat		
( ) (5 4 3 2 1) ( ) →		
(5 2) (4 3) (1)	53.2	3.45 sec
(5 4 3 2 1) ( ) ( ) →		
(5 4 1) (3) (2)	49.0	4.41 sec
Flat-to-Tower		
(4) (5 2 1) (3) →		
(5 4 3 2 1) ( ) ( )	58.2	3.63 sec
(4 3) (1) (5 2) →		
(5 4 3 2 1) ( ) ( )	50.6	3.66 sec
Flat-to-Flat		
(4 3) (1) (5 2) →		
(5 4) (3) (2 1)	58.5	4.06 sec
(4) (5 2 1) (3) →		
(5 2) (4 1) (3)	48.6	3.81 sec

*Each problem is described by which disks are on which pegs in the start state (before arrow) and in the goal state (after arrow). The numbers of the disks are given in a list for each of the three pegs.

128

Although these 15 moves were perfectly executed to move the tower, they were entirely wasted.

Comparing first-half performance to second-half reveals modest evidence for learning. Mean number of moves dropped marginally, from 38.1 to 34.0, $t(27)$ = 1.70, $p < .10$, the time per move dropped significantly, from 3.95 sec to 2.99 sec, $t(27) = 3.15$, $p < .001$. This latter time effect probably reflects subjects' simply learning to use the interface. Therefore, in contrast to some previous experiments (e.g., Anzai & Simon, 1979; Kotovsky et al., 1985), there was only a little learning in terms of improved strategy. Furthermore, informal inspection of the solution records showed no apparent strategic changes. The failure to find any learning trends or differences among problem types justified collapsing across problem types for further analysis.

6.3.1 Evidence for a Goal Stack

Were subjects actually setting subgoals as prescribed by the model? One way to answer this question was to look at that subset of the data involving sequences of moves that seemed clearly in service of a goal. Thus, if subjects subgoaled moving a 3-tower to get a 4-disk in place, the disks should be moved in the order 1-2-1-3-1-2-1-4, and with a particular pattern of placement of the disks on the pegs. The odds of producing such a sequence by chance are quite low.[2] So, if we see such a sequence, we can be quite confident in the inference that subjects had subgoaled moving the 3-tower to get the four disk in place. Table 6.3 shows how many of these occurred. It lists a smaller sequence only if it did not occur as part of a larger sequence. Thus, there were really 261 occasions on which the 4-disk was subgoaled (Part c of Table 6.3), but 32 occurred as part of the 5-disk subgoal (Part d). The data in Table 6.3 represents two thirds of all moves. Thus, subjects engaged in what appears to be a lot of subgoaling. Admittedly, the interpretation of the case where only the second disk is subgoaled (Part a) is a bit shaky, as it only involves a sequence of two disks (a 1 followed by a 2), which might well occur by chance, but in the other cases it is quite probable that the subjects were, in fact, pursuing the ascribed goal. The claim that two thirds of all moves were in service of a goal is actually an underestimate, because it ignores situations in which there were slight deviations from the goal-controlled sequence. By another measure (Table 6.4) at least 79% of moves were in direct service of goals.

Each move shown in Table 6.3 is followed by an indication of the number of subgoals that had to be set in the model before making that move, and the

---

[2]There are three choices at each move except the first, where there are two or three, depending on circumstances. We can view the first move as defining the hypothesis (and so ignore it) and use subsequent moves as confirmation. Thus, the odds of getting this by chance is no more than $(1/3)^7$, which is about 1 in 2,000.

TABLE 6.3
Latency Patterns for Sequences of Moves That Perfectly Fit the Subgoal Model

a. Subgoal Second Disk	Number of Inferred Subgoal Pushes (734)	Latency (sec)
Disk Moved		
1	1	4.56
2	0	2.18

b. Subgoal Third Disk	Number of Inferred Subgoal Pushes (375)	Latency (sec)
Disk Moved		
1	2	5.22
2	0	2.41
1	0	2.81
3	0	2.24

c. Subgoal Fourth Disk	Number of Inferred Subgoal Pushes (229)	Latency (sec)
Disk Moved		
1	3	8.95
2	0	2.46
1	0	2.76
3	0	2.24
1	1	3.00
2	0	1.89
1	0	2.28
4	0	2.13

d. Subgoal Fifth Disk	Number of Inferred Subgoal Pushes (32)	Latency (sec)
Disk Moved		
1	4	14.92
2	0	2.27
1	0	2.68
3	0	2.42
1	1	3.39
2	0	2.03
1	0	2.67
4	0	2.40
1	2	4.92
2	0	2.07
1	0	2.68
3	0	1.83
1	1	2.50
2	0	1.80
1	0	2.14
5	0	1.79

130

time taken to make the move. There is a strong relationship between the number of subgoals set and time. The average time[3] was 2.32 sec with zero subgoals, 4.13 with one, 5.20 with two, 8.95 with three, and 14.92 with four. Thus, it appears that subjects took a couple of seconds or more for each additional subgoal they had to set. Each subgoal setting involved firing a production of similar complexity to the move production, so subjects needed approximately 2 sec per firing of either the SUBGOAL-DISKS or MOVE-DISK production. Egan and Greeno (1974) reported error data that were similarly related to the number of subgoals that needed to be set. This performance data is strong evidence for the existence of subgoals in problem solving.

Note that the data provide evidence not only for the setting of subgoals, but also for their maintenance on a stack. Suppose one took the view that subjects recomputed from scratch what they wanted to do after each move, because they could not remember their subgoals (this would be a variant of Simon's, 1975, perceptual strategy). This would predict, for example, that three subgoals would have to be generated before moving the 2-disk in the second step of Table 6.3d. On the other hand, if the subject saved the goals on a stack, he or she would not have to create any additional goals. The data support the stack notion, which claims that subjects do not have to recompute goals.

Figure 6.3 displays latency data from Ruiz's (1987) dissertation, which provide further support for this analysis.[4] Ruiz had subjects solve five-disk tower-to-tower problems. Unlike our subjects, however, his were not allowed to wander off the minimum 31-move path. Thus, he did not have the problem of splicing out of a longer protocol islands of inferred goal-structured problem solving. Figure 6.3 notes, above each move that involves pushing goals, the number of goals to be pushed. Our analysis basically predicts one or more subgoals must be pushed every fourth move. This captures all the major peaks in the data, although it is superimposed on some generalized improvement across the problem. The speed-up probably reflects learning, as this was the subjects' first pass through the problems.[5] Occasionally, there are peaks at other odd-numbered moves (three of the eight times). These are always points where, in the model, one goal is being popped and a SATISFIED production would then be fired.

The data in Table 6.3 show more reliable peaks at the odd-numbered positions where a 1-disk is being moved and a goal is being popped rather than pushed. On all seven occasions, that time is longer than the two adjacent even times, but much shorter than the odd points where a push would be predicted.

---

[3]The average is weighted by number of observations.

[4]Dirk Ruiz generously provided us with a copy of the figure.

[5]Even our more practiced subjects show some speed-up, in the data of Table 6.3. As we discuss in more detail in the next two chapters, ACT-R actually predicts acceleration across the problem.

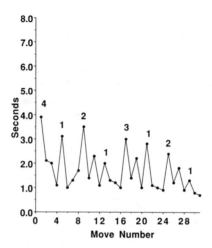

FIG. 6.3.   Goal-recursive median move-initiation times for the first five-disk task
of Ruiz (1987).

The average latency difference between these 1-disk moves and the adjacent moves
is about .4 sec, which is considerably less than the differences involving 1-disk
moves where goals have to be pushed; those differences averaged many seconds.

6.3.2   Fitting the Data to Models

Table 6.3 reports the islands of data that fit the subgoaling model perfectly,
but what fraction of the subjects' moves can be predicted by this subgoal model,
and what fraction cannot be? To address this question, we applied the same
model-tracing methodology to this data that we applied to the navigation experiments in chapter 5. This required having a production-system model that
was capable of generating any move that the subject could generate so that it
could trace the subject's cognitive state. Thus, there must be productions that
will make any move, no matter how peculiar. In addition, subjects sometimes
embarked on the wrong subgoal: for instance, moving a 4-tower to the wrong
disk. There must also, then, be productions capable of generating any subgoal,
no matter how bizarre. Nevertheless, this model should always generate as its
first choice the moves required by the ideal means–ends strategy.

The enhanced model included the production SATISFIED, given earlier, and
the following two productions, one for generating subgoals and one for generating legal moves:[6]

---

[6]A simulation of this is contained in the Tower of Hanoi file in the Examples folder on the accompanying disk. It is discussed further in Section 12.4.1. The Tower of Hanoi problem that comes
coded in working memory with this file is the simpler one illustrated in Fig. 12.1.

SUBGOAL-DISKS′

IF   the goal is to achieve a particular configuration of disks
        and disk D1 is on peg P1
        and one cannot directly move D1 to peg P2
        and disk D2 is one smaller than D1
        and peg P3 is different than P1 or P2.

THEN set a subgoal to move the D2 tower to P3 and D1 to P2.

MOVE-DISK′

IF   the goal is to achieve a particular configuration of disks
        and disk D1 is on top of peg P1
        and one can directly move D1 to P2

THEN move D1 to P2.

These are weakened versions ("primes") of the SUBGOAL-DISKS and
MOVE-DISK productions given earlier. At any point these two productions would
have as their instantiations all legal moves and all possible tower-to-peg subgoals. For conflict resolution, the model preferred any instantiation that moved
or subgoaled a disk to the target peg over an instantiation that moved to a nontarget peg. It ordered the instantiations that moved or subgoaled to the target
peg according to the size of the disk, with the largest disk preferred most. It
also ordered the instantiations that moved or subgoaled to the nontarget peg
according to the size of the disk, but with the smallest disk preferred most.
Thus, if it started out with the goal of moving a 5-tower from Peg A to Peg
C (with B as the other peg), it would generate the instantiations in the following
order of preference:

Subgoal	Disk 5	to	Peg C	and 4-tower to Peg B
Subgoal	Disk 4	to	Peg C	and 3-tower to Peg B
Subgoal	Disk 3	to	Peg C	and 2-tower to Peg B
Subgoal	Disk 2	to	Peg C	and Disk 1 to Peg B
Move	Disk 1	to	Peg C	
Move	Disk 1	to	Peg B	
Subgoal	Disk 2	to	Peg B	and Disk 2 to Peg C
Subgoal	Disk 3	to	Peg B	and 2-tower to Peg C
Subgoal	Disk 4	to	Peg B	and 3-tower to Peg C
Subgoal	Disk 5	to	Peg B	and 4-tower to Peg C

It chose the highest ordered instantiation (Subgoal Disk 5 to Peg C) and
would subgoal the 4-tower to Peg B and Disk 5 to Peg C. In response to that
subgoal, it would generate the following instantiations in the following order of
preference:

Subgoal	Disk 4	to	Peg B	and 3-tower to Peg C
Subgoal	Disk 3	to	Peg B	and 2-tower to Peg C
Subgoal	Disk 2	to	Peg B	and Disk 1 to Peg C
Move	Disk 1	to	Peg B	
Move	Disk 1	to	Peg C	
Subgoal	Disk 2	to	Peg C	and Disk 1 to Peg B
Subgoal	Disk 3	to	Peg C	and 2-tower to Peg B
Subgoal	Disk 4	to	Peg C	and 3-tower to Peg B

And so on. We will not really test this proposal for the complete instantiation ordering. We are only concerned with the top choice, and whether it matched the subject's behavior. The top choice corresponds to the prediction of the original means–end model. The other instantiations allow us to match deviant behavior produced by the subject.

There is a problem with trying to match the behavior of this simulation with subject behavior. All we see from subjects are moves, but the model also predicts the occurrence of subgoals. Table 6.3 displayed strong evidence that subjects do, indeed, set subgoals, but it can be a bit difficult in any particular circumstance to know for sure if a subgoal was set. We could use the criteria used in Table 6.3—of a subsequent move sequence that gives a perfect match to the moves required by that subgoal—but that would be requiring too much from a subject. We have to allow for some random variation on the subject's part. We could just see if the next move was consistent with that subgoal, but this is a rather weak and shortsighted criterion. We felt that more than 75% of the moves had to be the ones predicted by the sequence of moves associated with the subgoal. With this in mind we used the following criteria for ascribing subgoals:

1. For ascribing a subgoal of enabling the second disk to be moved and then moving it the 2 predicted moves had to occur with no deviations.

2. For ascribing a subgoal of enabling the third disk to be moved and then moving it the 4 predicted moves had to occur with no more than 1 extra move.

3. For ascribing a subgoal of enabling the fourth disk to be moved and then moving it the 8 predicted moves had to occur with no more than 2 extra moves.

4. For ascribing a subgoal of enabling the fifth disk to be moved and then moving it the 16 predicted moves had to occur with no more than 4 extra moves.

This process enriches the subjects' behavior with inferred subgoals, but not necessarily with the subgoals predicted by the model.

TABLE 6.4
a. Fit of Means–End Subgoal Model

		Observed		
		Move	*Subgoal*	
Predicted	Move	6,299 match 30 mismatch	1	6,330
	Subgoal	1,646	2,574 match 455 mismatch	4,675
		7,975	3,030	

b. Fit of Hillclimbing Model (Anderson, 1990a)

		Observed		
		Move	*Subgoal*	
Predicted	Move	5,520 match 1,972 mismatch	2,701	10,193
	Subgoal	483	138 match 191 mismatch	812
		7,975	3,030	11,005

6.3.3 Comparative Fit of the Data to Alternative Models

Table 6.4 presents an analysis of the data in terms of whether a subgoal or a move was predicted by our model, and whether a match, a different subgoal, or a different move was observed.[7,8] Seventy-nine percent of the subject moves were predicted by the subgoal model, and 85% of the ascribed goals were predicted. Overall, 81% of the actions were predicted. Individual subjects' data varied from 65% to 100%, in terms of the number of moves that were predicted. The largest number of mismatches were the many occasions (1,646) when the model predicted that a subgoal would be set, but the subject took a move unrelated to any subgoal. These reflect wanderings in the problem space and constituted about 20% of the move data.

As a comparison, Table 6.4 also reports the fit of the model used in Anderson (1990a) to the Tower of Hanoi isomorphs. This model has the same productions but usually prefers moving a disk to its target position over subgoaling

---

[7]This analysis ignores the SATISFIED productions, whose matching is guaranteed given the SUBGOAL-DISKS production matches.

[8]The fit of this model is not sensitive to the setting of the parameters, which played a key role in the previous chapter. Rather, the fit is only sensitive to the assumed subgoal structure.

a disk to its target position. Thus, it can generate goals or moves and, so, be fit to the same protocols, although it prefers hillclimbing to subgoaling. That model only predicted 69% of the moves and only 5% of the subgoals (occasionally, the model lowered its evaluation of the direct moves because they had been repeated to a point where the subgoals could come in). Altogether, 51% of all actions were predicted by this alternative model. As a third comparison, we implemented the model described by Karat (1982). This model only predicts moves, and it fit 67% of the moves. Thus, the goal-recursive model does appear to capture more of the behavior of the subjects than alternative models do.

6.3.4 The Issue of the Architectural Reality of Goal Stacks

One interpretation of these results might be that they indicate nothing about architecture, but much about how we instructed our subjects to solve the problems. The argument would be that we instructed our subjects to simulate a goal stack, and they obediently did. Our results would then tell us how subjects performed such a simulation and not about an architectural primitive of a goal stack.

The first point to emphasize, in response to this argument, is that half the subjects received no instruction on goal stacks, and they were indistinguishable from the half that did. If anything in the instructions affected their behavior, it would have to be the instruction on the dependency relationships, which all subjects received and from which they could all have constructed subgoals. Thus, if our results reflect the result of a "simulated" rather than a "real" goal stack, then subjects added a lot of interpretation to the instructions and did so rather uniformly. Clearly, then, the subjects brought something with them to structure the task, even if it was not a "real" goal stack.

If one is to argue that subjects have the natural wherewithal to simulate goal stacks given just dependency information, then it is unclear what prediction would separate the proposal of simulated goal stacks from real goal stacks. In our opinion it becomes a distinction without a difference, another item to add to the long list of identifiability problems in psychology.

It is worth noting the features that our analyses imply, which would have to be replicated by a simulation proposal, or indeed any different proposal, that involved real stacks:

1. The important variable is number of pushes.
2. There is a weak effect of number of pops.
3. There is no effect of depth of goal stack, which would be expected if the goal stack had to be rehearsed or recomputed.

4. Subjects' behavior is not totally controlled by the goal structure. As in the previous experiment, there is a certain variability in their choice behavior, which is in keeping with ACT-R conflict resolution.

In our opinion it is these claims that are the significant consequences of the ACT-R theory and not the issue of whether goal structures are a "real" architectural primitive.

6.4 ANALYSIS OF TOWER OF HANOI ISOMORPHS

The suspicious reader might wonder to what degree the subgoaling behavior that was observed simply reflected the logical structure of the Tower of Hanoi task. One way to address this question is to look at tasks that have the same logical structure as the Tower of Hanoi task, but where that structure is not so obvious. If subjects behave differently on these problems, then the critical factor is in the subjects' treatment of the problem and not the logical structure of the problem. The Tower of Hanoi isomorphs (Kotovsky et al., 1985; Kotovsky & Fallside, 1988) offer an opportunity to address this question. Table 6.5 gives two isomorphs. Kotovsky et al. (1985) used the three-disk Tower of Hanoi problems that require five moves for their solution. Although these would be trivial problems in the original Tower of Hanoi format, subjects find these to be much more difficult, and can solve these problems, particularly the change problems, only with the greatest of difficulty.

The difficulty with these problems reflects a general defect in applying a means–ends strategy to them. Kotovsky et al. (1985) argued that subjects have difficulty both in perceiving the dependencies that enable means–ends strategy to be evoked and in simultaneously representing all the information that would be required to execute the means–ends strategy. They suggested that subjects solve these problems only after they have overcome these limitations so that they can apply a means–ends strategy. Thus, these isomorphs are excellent choices for testing whether the fit of the model to the Tower of Hanoi data reflects problem structure or psychological structure: The problem structure is isomorphic to the Tower of Hanoi, but the psychological structure is quite different.

6.4.1 Fit to Tower of Hanoi Isomorphs

Kotovsky and Kushmerick (1991)[9] collected some data on the moves in Tower of Hanoi isomorphs. They analyzed this data according to the overall model of Kotovsky et al. (1985), which divides subject solution paths into a final critical

---

[9]A subset of this data had been fit in Anderson (1990a) by the hillclimbing model used in Part b of Table 6.4.

TABLE 6.5
a. A Monster Move Problem

Three five-handed extraterrestrial monsters were holding three crystal globes. Because of the quantum-mechanical peculiarities of their neighborhood, both monsters and globes come in exactly three sizes, with no others permitted: small, medium, and large. The small monster was holding the large globe; the medium-sized monster was holding the small globe; and the large monster was holding the medium-sized globe. Since this situation offended their keenly developed sense of symmetry, they proceeded to transfer globes from one monster to another so that each monster would have a globe proportionate to its own size.

Monster etiquette complicated the solution of the problem since it requires that:

1. Only one globe may be transferred at a time.
2. If a monster is holding two globes, only the larger of the two may be transferred.
3. A globe may not be transferred to a monster who is holding a larger globe.

By what sequence of transfers could the monsters have solved this problem?

b. A Monster Change Problem

Three five-handed extraterrestrial monsters were holding three crystal globes. Because of the quantum-mechanical peculiarities of their neighborhood, both monsters and globes come in exactly three sizes, with no others permitted: small, medium, and large. The small monster was holding the large globe; the medium-sized monster was holding the small globe; and the large monster was holding the medium-sized globe. Since this situation offended their keenly developed sense of symmetry, they proceeded to shrink and expand the globes so that each monster would have a globe proportionate to its own size.

Monster etiquette complicated the solution of the problem since it requires that:

1. Only one globe may be changed at one time.
2. If two globes have the same size, only the globe held by the larger monster may be changed.
3. A globe may not be changed to the same size as the globe of a larger monster.

By what sequence of changes could the monsters have solved this problem?

path and a portion that is just prior to that. The final critical path begins the last time the subject is five states from the goal. Kotovsky et al. claimed that it was only during this final critical path that subjects used means–ends analysis and subgoals.

The criteria described in the previous section were used to infer the setting of goals. Of the 814 actions ascribed to subjects in the precritical path, only 11% involved goal setting, whereas 25% of the 330 critical-path actions involved goal setting. This is a large and highly significant difference, $\chi^2_{(1)} = 31.44$, $p < .001$. It is unclear how many of the 11% ascriptions in the precritical path reflect false alarming of the classification criteria. Table 6.6 reports the fit of three different models to the precritical-path data. These models are the subgoal model we have fit to the Tower of Hanoi data; the model reported in Anderson (1990a), which is a combination of a hillclimbing and a subgoal model; and a pure hillclimbing model, which never sets subgoals. Although the subgoal

TABLE 6.6
a. Fit to Precritical Path

	Moves	Subgoal	Weighted Average
Means–Ends Subgoaling	28%	46%	30%
Anderson (1990a)	36%	25%	35%
Pure Hillclimbing	45%	0%	40%

b. Fit to Critical Path

	Moves	Subgoal	Weighted Average
Means–Ends Subgoaling	79%	98%	83%
Anderson (1990a)	67%	24%	56%
Pure Hillclimbing	68%	0%	51%

model does a reasonable job of accounting for the critical path, the hillclimbing model does the best job of accounting for the data *before* the critical path.

Kotovsky et al. argued that their subjects were initially overwhelmed by the working-memory load of the task and were only capable of subgoaling later. The transition between the non-subgoal phase and the subgoal phase corresponds to the transition between the precritical path and the critical path. On the basis of the analysis in Table 6.6, their theory seems reasonable. The outcome in Table 6.6 also indicates that the good fit of the subgoal model to the original Tower of Hanoi task in Table 6.4 is by no means trivial and is certainly not a response to the logical structure of the Tower of Hanoi task.

6.4.2 Predictive Validity of Hillclimbing

The hillclimbing model fit to the subjects' data is one that preferred moves that got disks to their target pegs[10] and avoided revisiting old states. Recall that production rules in ACT-R are evaluated according to whether they move subjects closer to the goal. Thus, ACT-R predicts hillclimbing in the absence of a means–ends analysis. Moreover, it claims that such hillclimbing leads, on average, to better moves. It is worth investigating to what extent subjects were

---

[10]In isomorphs, the target peg becomes the target monster (move isomorph) or the target globe (change isomorph).

hillclimbing on these problems and whether hillclimbing led to better moves on the Tower of Hanoi.

One can classify moves by whether they take a subject back to previously visited states or not and whether they move a disk to its target location. One can also classify moves by whether they are on the path leading to the goal or not. During the course of problem solving, potential moves arise that realize all eight possible combinations of these three binary features. Table 6.7 provides an analysis of the data from our experiment, the precritical-path data of Kotovsky, and the critical-path data of Kotovsky, according to these three dimensions. The table gives the number of possible moves of each kind that arose and the proportion chosen by the subjects. Chance performance would be about 33%, because in all but three states there are three possible moves.

Subjects were somewhat alike on the Tower of Hanoi task and the critical path of the isomorphs. They showed a strong tendency to select moves on the solution path. The Tower of Hanoi subjects showed some aversion to backtracking, and the isomorph subjects showed some tendency to move to the target

TABLE 6.7
Proportion of Moves Chosen
(Number of Possible Moves in Parentheses)

	Solution Path		Non-solution Path	
	Backtracking	No Backtracking	Backtracking	No Backtracking
a. Tower of Hanoi				
To Target Peg	26% (253)	76% (3,028)	7% (2,355)	26% (2,706)
Not to Target Peg	28% (490)	69% (4,204)	6% (5,693)	26% (5,077)
b. Tower of Hanoi Isomorphs—Precritical Path				
To Target Peg	23% (101)	58% (216)	35% (245)	52% (130)
Not to Target Peg	24% (198)	26% (206)	32% (477)	30% (556)
c. Tower of Hanoi Isomorphs—Critical Path				
To Target Peg	100% (27)	98% (130)	12% (81)	15% (13)
Not to Target Peg	82% (11)	43% (80)	3% (245)	20% (152)

peg. In the precritical path, however, the isomorph subjects exhibited no tendency to select solution moves, but did show a strong influence of the target peg and backtracking. They clearly favored moves that simultaneously approach the goal state and avoid backtracking to a previous state.

Another question of interest is how well tuned the subjects used the antibacktracking and hillclimbing heuristics. Table 6.8 (which is derivable from Table 6.7) provides the proportion of potential moves of each kind that were on solution paths. Chance, again, would be 33%. As can be seen, both hillclimbing and backtracking are quite reasonable heuristics, and a much larger proportion of moves were on the solution path if the moves avoided past states and approached the target peg. This is one piece of evidence for the general value of reducing differences from the goal state, which, as described in chapter 3, is an important basis for evaluating productions.

6.5 CONCLUSIONS

This chapter provides evidence that subject behavior can be under the control of hierarchical goal structures, as predicted by the ACT-R theory. The timing data confirmed specific predictions of the way goals are managed in the ACT-R

TABLE 6.8
Proportion of Moves on Solution Path
(Number of Possible Moves in Parentheses)

	Backtracking	*No Backtracking*
a. Tower of Hanoi		
Hillclimbing	10% (2,608)	53% (5,734)
No Hillclimbing	8% (6,183)	45% (9,281)
b. Tower of Hanoi Isomorphs—Precritical Path		
Hillclimbing	29% (346)	62% (346)
No Hillclimbing	24% (675)	27% (762)
c. Tower of Hanoi Isomorphs—Critical Path		
Hillclimbing	25% (106)	91% (143)
No Hillclimbing	4% (256)	34% (232)

architecture. These predictions would not be satisfied for many architectural realizations of subgoaling. The model also accounted for a majority of the subject moves. This is not at all a trivial outcome, given how different subject behavior is in the Tower of Hanoi isomorphs. In the precritical path of the solutions to these isomorphs, subjects appeared to be free from any subgoaling: They were wandering to some degree and hillclimbing to some degree.

7

The LISP Tutor and Skill Acquisition

John R. Anderson, Frederick G. Conrad, and
Albert T. Corbett
Carnegie Mellon University

7.1 SKILL ACQUISITION

The preceding two chapters gave some evidence for the view that skills are organized and executed in line with the implications of the ACT-R theory. The next four chapters provide empirical evidence for the heart of this book, which is the theory of skill acquisition. That theory is actually quite simple. In essence, all the theory says is that:

1. The knowledge underlying a skill begins in an initial declarative form (an elaborated example), which must be interpreted (problem solving by analogy) to produce performance.
2. As a function of its interpretive execution, this skill becomes compiled into a production-rule form.
3. With practice, individual production rules acquire strength and become more attuned to the circumstances in which they apply.
4. Learning complex skills can be decomposed into the learning functions associated with individual production rules.

The simplicity of the ACT-R theory of skill acquisition is an important part of its theoretical claim. It certainly is a counter-intuitive claim about the nature of complex skill acquisition, which appears to be anything but simple. The comparison between Figs. 2.2 and 2.3 in chapter 2 showed how skill acquisition that appears chaotic on the surface can become very orderly when it is analyzed into production rules. This is perhaps the strongest evidence for the psychological reality of the production rule.

Given the importance of the claim that skill acquisition under a production-rule analysis is simple, it becomes important to provide empirical evidence for this simplicity. This is done by performing analyses that look for the effects of plausibly complicating factors and failing to find them. One of these plausible factors involves individual differences. One might believe that different students would learn in different ways: For example, some students would learn concrete material more quickly, whereas other students might learn abstract material more quickly. Although the ACT-R theory allows for different overall rates of acquisition (as reflected in different parameter values for different students), it does not allow for different types of learning. Another way things could become complicated is that skill acquisition might take different forms in different environments. Again, the ACT-R theory does not allow for such a complication.

7.2 THE LISP TUTOR

This chapter begins the empirical analyses of skill acquisition with a review of data from the LISP tutor. Chapter 2, in motivating the production-rule construct, has already presented some of this data. The LISP tutor has been important in the development of the theory, not so much because of the success of the tutor, but because of the careful series of empirical studies that have followed it. Although we have built a number of other tutors in our lab, some with equal or even better success as educational instruments, none of them has been subjected to anything like the thorough empirical scrutiny that the LISP tutor has received.

This chapter extends the generality of the results with the LISP tutor that were originally reported in Anderson et al. (1989), including a study of what happens when different tutoring modes are used in the LISP tutor. Later chapters are concerned with the course of skill acquisition in other programming languages and in geometry. None of these other topics has had the same thorough analysis behind them, but they do help to establish the generality of the picture created in the initial work on the LISP tutor.

The discussion of skill acquisition, therefore, is mainly devoted to reporting work collected with computer-based tutors. There are basically two advantages to be gained from studying skill acquisition with our tutors. First, the tutors are involved in complex skill acquisition. Our conclusions about the simple nature of skill acquisition have much greater force if they can be shown to hold in the face of complexity. Second, the tutors use a model-tracing methodology, which places the performance of the students in correspondence with production rules from a model of the skill. The previous two chapters have already displayed the advantages of such model-tracing methodology in the analyses of the navigation task and the Tower of Hanoi task. To summarize, then, tutors provide the analytic power of the model-tracing methodology in complex domains where conclusions about skill acquisition will have substantial force.

The analytic power of the model-tracing methodology is only as good as the underlying cognitive model being used. Another advantage of the LISP tutor is that its production rules have probably the highest overlap of any of our tutors with what is actually in the student's head. Again this is because of the great deal of work that has gone into the study of LISP programming skills by a number of developers.

We have been engaged in the study of programming in LISP since 1980. Around 1983, it seemed that we had a good enough understanding of programming in LISP (reported in Anderson, Farrell, & Sauers, 1984) that we might actually use it as a basis for instruction. Chapter 11 expands on our approach to tutoring, but the basic idea was to organize instruction around the individual production rules that we felt the student should acquire. This set of production rules defines the ideal student model. The tutor tries to match up, in real time, the student's problem solving with some path of performance in the production-system model of the skill. In the version of tutoring we describe first, called *immediate-feedback tutoring*, whenever the student makes a problem-solving move that fails to match some allowed move in the student model, the tutor corrects the student and forces him or her to make a move that does match the student model. Section 7.5 describes what happens with less restrictive modes of tutoring.

The model-tracing approach used in an immediate feedback tutor is different than that used in the performance studies of the previous two chapters. In those studies, whenever the student and the model disagreed as what to do next, the model was set to match the student. In the present investigations, if the student's choice reflected a possibly correct solution path, our tutor would match it. If, however, it represented an error, the tutor tried to reset the student to match the tutor by correcting the student. There are two motivations for this change: The first is so as to have positive instructional impact; the second is that it is difficult to interpret behavior in error states when the skills get complex.

7.2.1 A Sample Interaction With the LISP Tutor

The first thing we need to do is illustrate what it is like to interact with the tutor. We have constructed a number of different LISP tutors. This section describes an interaction with the original tutor we created.[1] Figure 7.1 depicts the computer screen at the beginning of an exercise. The screen is divided into two "windows." The problem description appears in the tutor window at the

---

[1]Called, affectionately, "LISP Tutor classic" in our laboratory.

Define a function called "create-list" that accepts one argument, which must be a positive integer. This function returns a list of all the integers between 1 and the value of the argument, in ascending order. For example,

(create-list 8) returns (1 2 3 4 5 6 7 8).

You should count down in this function, so that you can just insert each new number into the front of the result variable.

CODE for create-list

```
(defun create-list <parameters>
    <process>)
```

FIG. 7.1.   The appearance of the tutor screen at the beginning of a coding problem.

top of the screen; as the student types, the code appears in the code window at the bottom of the screen. This exercise is drawn from Lesson 6, in which iteration is being introduced. Students are familiar with the structure of function definitions by this point, so the tutor has put up the template for a definition, filling in defun and the function name for the student. The symbols in angle brackets represent code components remaining for the student to supply. The tutor places the cursor over the first symbol the student needs to expand, < parameters >.

As the student works on an exercise, the tutor monitors the student's input, essentially on a symbol-by-symbol basis. As long as the student is on some reasonable solution path, the tutor remains in the background, and the interface behaves much like a structured editor. It expands templates for function calls, provides balancing right-parentheses, and advances the cursor over the remaining symbols that must be expanded. If the student makes a mistake, however, the tutor immediately provides feedback and gives him or her another opportunity to type a correct symbol. When the student types another response, the feedback is replaced either by the problem description (if the response is correct) or another feedback message (if the student makes another error). If the student requests an explanation or appears to be foundering,[2] the tutor provides a correct next step in the solution, along with an explanation.

---

[2]Students are judged to be foundering when they repeat the same type of error three times or make two mistakes that the tutor does not recognize.

Table 7.1 contains a record of a hypothetical student completing the code for this exercise.[3] This table does not attempt to show the terminal screen as it actually appears at each step in the exercise. Instead, it shows an abbreviated "teletype" version of the interaction. As described earlier, while the student is working, the problem description generally remains in the tutor window, and the code window is updated on a symbol-by-symbol basis. Instead of portraying each update to the code window in the interaction, the table portrays nine key "cycles," in which the tutor interrupts to communicate with the student. At each of these cycles, the complete contents of the code window are shown, along with the tutor's response. The tutor's response is shown below the code to capture the temporal sequence of events; on the terminal screen, the tutor's communications would appear in the tutor window above the code. In each cycle, all the code that the student has typed since the preceding key cycle is shown in boldface in Table 7.1. In each case, however, the tutor is responding specifically to the last symbol the student typed.

In the first of the cycles displayed, the student has typed in the parameter list and has called loop in order to iterate. The tutor reminds the student that it is necessary to create some local variables before entering the loop.

In the second cycle, the student has called let and is about to create a local variable. The template for numeric iteration calls for two local variables in this function, so the tutor puts up a menu to clarify which variable the student is going to declare first. This illustrates the tutor's need to know at all times what the student's intentions are, so that it can follow along. If there is an ambiguity, it will query the student by the means of such menus.

In the third cycle, the student has coded an initial value that would be correct if the function were counting up. This exercise is intended to give the student practice in counting down, however, so the tutor offers redirection.

In the fourth cycle, the student has made a typing error, which the tutor recognizes.

In the fifth cycle, the student is attempting to return the correct value from the loop, but has forgotten to call return. The tutor also reminds the student here that a special function call is required to exit a loop.

In the sixth cycle, the cursor is on the symbol <LOOP-ACTIONS2>, and the student has asked the tutor for an explanation of what to do next. The tutor explains what the current goal is and what symbol to type next in order to accomplish the goal. In addition, the tutor puts the symbol setq into the code for the student.

In the seventh cycle, the tutor recognizes that the student is computing the

---

[3]Undoubtedly, the use of LISP creates a barrier to communication with that fraction of the readership that is not familiar with LISP. However, the semantics of LISP are not really necessary to understanding how the tutor interacts or how these interactions depend on the underlying production-rule models.

TABLE 7.1
A Teletype Depiction of a Hypothetical Student Completing the Code
for the Function Create-List with the Tutor

The Problem Description

Define a function called "create-list" that accepts one argument, which must be a positive integer. This function returns a list of all the integers between 1 and the value of the argument, in ascending order. For example,

(create-list 8) returns (1 2 3 4 5 6 7 8).

You should count down in this function, so that you can just insert each new number into the front of the result variable.

Cycles in Which the Tutor Communicates With the Student

---

1. (defun create-list (num)
   (loop)
   You will need local variables in this function. So before you code anything else, there is a particular LISP operator you need to code.
2. (defun create-list (num)
   (let (( )
   <BODY>))
   Which of the following do you want to do?
   PRESS: IF YOU WANT TO
   1 Initialize a variable to hold the list of digits between
       1 and the value of the parameter.
   2 Initialize a counter variable to keep track of how
       many times we go around the loop.
   3 Have the tutor choose.
   Menu choice: 2
3. (defun create-list (num)
       (let ((count 1)
       <OTHER-INITIALIZATIONS>)
       <BODY>))
   In this problem we won't want to start counting at the same value each time we call the function, so we can't initialize the counter to a constant like 1. How is the starting value being communicated to the function?
4. (defun create-list (num)
       (let ((count num)
       (numlist (list num)))
       (lop))
   Did you mean loop (y or n)? y
5. (defun create-list (num)
       (let ((count num)
           (numlist (list num)))
       (loop
           (cond ((equal count 1) numlist))
       <LOOP-ACTIONS2>)))
   You do want to return the variable "numlist" here, but just typing it into the code won't accomplish that. What LISP operator will allow you to return something from a LOOP?

(Continued)

TABLE 7.1
(Continued)

6. (defun create-list (num)
     (let ((count num)
           (numlist (list num)))
       (loop
         (cond ((equal count 1) (return numlist)))
         <LOOP-ACTIONS2>)))

In numeric iteration the first thing you should do after the exit test is update the counter variable. You can use the function SETQ to do this.

7. (defun create-list (num)
     (let ((count)
        (numlist (list num)))
       (loop
         (cond ((equal count 1) (return numlist)))
         (setq count (1- count))
         (cons)))

You've got the right idea, since you'll need to use the function "cons," but remember you are trying to insert the new value of the counter into the list. What LISP function allows you to assign the results of this function call to a local variable?

8. (defun create-list (num)
     (let ((count num)
        (numlist (list num)))
       (loop
         (cond ((equal count 1) (return numlist)))
         (setq count (1- count))
         (setq numlist (list))))

If you LIST together arguments like 7 and (8) you get (7 (8)). What you want is (7 8). Try another function that combines things together.

9. (defun create-list (num)
     (let ((count num)
        (numlist (list num)))
       (loop
         (cond ((equal count 1) (return numlist)))
         (setq count (1- count))
         (setq numlist (cons count numlist)))))

-----YOU ARE DONE. TYPE NEXT TO GO ON AFTER-----
-----TESTING THE FUNCTION YOU HAVE DEFINED-----

THE LISP WINDOW

= > (create-list 10)

(1 2 3 4 5 6 7 8 9 10)

= > next

149

new value for the result variable, but has forgotten that the new value must be assigned to the variable with setq.

In the eighth cycle, the student has gotten mixed up on the appropriate combiner function to use in updating the result variable. The tutor tries to show, by means of an example, why list does not perform quite the right operation, and why another combiner is needed.

Finally, in the ninth cycle, the student has completed the code.

In the interest of illustration, this interaction shows the student making more errors than our students usually make. Typically, the error rate is about 15%, whereas it is approximately 30% in this dialogue.

After each exercise, the student enters a standard LISP environment called the *LISP window*. Students can experiment in the LISP window as they choose; the only constraint is that they successfully call the function they have just defined (which the tutor has loaded into the environment for them).

7.2.2 Simulation of Learning With the LISP Tutor

The remainder of the chapter is concerned with comparing the data collected from the LISP tutor with the predictions of ACT-R. The predictions of ACT-R are relatively straightforward. To illustrate how ACT-R applies to the acquisition of such a skill, the disk contains a simulation of learning in Lesson 1 of the LISP tutor. This simulation goes through the required exercises of Lesson 1, compiles productions from examples to deal with new situations, and strengthens these production rules with practice. The simulation is to be found in the file called "Learning Ch. 1 LISP" in the Examples folder. It can be observed to generate latencies for each production-rule application. These latencies display the learning trends that we discuss in this chapter. These observed learning trends reflect the processes of production-rule compilation and production-rule strengthening.

7.3 GROUP DATA ANALYSES

7.3.1 Analysis of Computer Records

The interactions in Table 7.1 are segmented into units, and each unit is associated with a production rule. The data from the LISP tutor comes in as a stream of keystrokes and responses by the tutor. This data can be partitioned into cycles in which (a) the tutor sets a coding goal (i.e., places a cursor over the goal symbol on the screen), (b) the student types a unit of code corresponding to a production firing (generally a single atom or "word" of code), and (c) the tutor categorizes the input as correct or incorrect (or as a request for help) and responds accordingly. If the response is correct, the tutor sets a new goal in the next cycle. If it is incorrect, the tutor provides feedback and resets the same goal in the next cycle. If the student asks for an explanation or appears to be lost, the tutor provides the correct answer and sets a new goal in the next cycle.

Suppose the student is coding a function called insert-second and has just typed cons as the beginning of the body of the function. At this point the screen would look like this:

```
(defun insert-second (lis1 lis2)
   (cons <elem1> <elem2>))
```

In the following cycle, the tutor would place the cursor over the goal symbol <elem1>, the student would type code, for example, (*car*. When the student has typed the final space after car, the tutor would evaluate the input and respond. This segment of code would be placed in correspondence with a production rule in the ideal model, which recognizes that it is appropriate to use car as the first step toward extracting the second element from a list. Typically, two measures of the production's firings are collected: time and accuracy. Time is measured only when the student's first response is correct. The measure of time is from when the tutor is ready to accept input (cursor over <elem1> in this example) to when the student has completed the code for that element. Two measures of accuracy have been extracted: (a) the probability that the student's first attempt at a goal is correct, and (b) the number of extra attempts (cycles) required to achieve a correct answer at a goal (the maximum is three). The second measure is used more frequently because it proves to be more sensitive: Often, initial errors are just slips, whereas repeated errors are signs of real difficulty. As a rule of thumb, the number of extra attempts is about one and a half times the number of errors.

What is happening during the period of time attributed to a production? It is not just a single correct production rule firing. There must be an encoding of the screen, the setting of subgoals to type the individual characters, and the actual typing of those characters. Moreover, students can delete characters in order to correct typing errors, or even change their minds about the correct code unit to type. The tutor also intervenes to block syntactically illegal characters. Thus, the time for these segments involves much more than simply the time for the target production to fire. The target production just sets the top level organization for the episode. It is the rule of interest, however, because it represents the new thing that the student must learn. Also, because typing and interacting with the tutor presumably represent skills at relatively high, asymptotic levels of proficiency, learning the coding rules accounts for much of the variation in performance across segments.

7.3.2 Learning Curves

Chapter 2 already described some of the data from the LISP tutor. This chapter presents a more exhaustive and systematic analysis of data collected from the LISP tutor, in the fall of 1985 and the spring of 1986. This data comes from a full semester course that was taught in the fall and spring semesters to Carnegie Mellon undergraduates.

Of the approximately 60 students who took part in these studies, only 43 had complete data sets, and it is these that were used for this analysis. There were 12 lessons in the tutor at that time. Regression analyses were performed in which an attempt was made to find best predicator equations for both log coding times and errors for productions new to the particular lesson separately and for productions introduced in an earlier lesson. Among the predictor variables were lesson number, amount of practice of the production rule within the lesson, depth of the code that was being written, number of pending goals (or unexpanded symbols to the right), left-to-right position in the pretty-printing of the code, familiarity of the concept behind the production (as rated by a panel of four judges), number of keystrokes in typing the symbol, and number of symbols that had been written.

There were approximately 100,000 observations but these were too many for our regression program, so we collapsed into a single number all observations in which a student applied the same production (according to the tutor's analysis) in the same serial position on the same LISP function in a particular lesson. This resulted in approximately a 10-to-1 compression of the data, yielding 6,409 observations of coding old productions and 3,350 observations of coding new productions.

The following regression equations were determined as the best fitting functions for new productions:

$$\log(\text{time}) = 1.35 - .03(\text{lesson number})$$
$$- .31 \log(\text{within lesson opportunity})$$
$$- .15 \log(\text{absolute position in code}) \qquad (7.1)$$

$$\text{mean errors} = .23 - .11 \log(\text{within lesson opportunity})$$
$$- .03 \log(\text{absolute position in code}) \qquad (7.2)$$

where *lesson number* is just the number 1 through 12, *within lesson opportunity* is the number of times the production had been used in the lesson before and including the current opportunity, and *absolute position in code* is the serial position of the code in the function definition. The best fitting equations obtained for the old productions were rather similar:

$$\log(\text{time}) = 1.31 - .01(\text{lesson number})$$
$$- .25 \log(\text{within lesson opportunity})$$
$$- .26 \log(\text{absolute position in code}) \qquad (7.3)$$

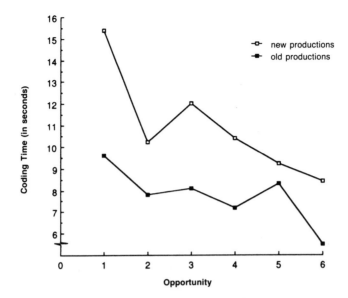

FIG. 7.2. Mean coding time for old and new productions as a function of coding opportunity.

$$\begin{aligned} \text{mean errors} = .16 &- .09 \ \text{log(within lesson opportunity)} \\ &- .02 \ \text{log(absolute position in code)} \end{aligned} \quad (7.4)$$

Each of these predictor variables was statistically significant.[4] Their appearance in these equations is particularly interesting considering the predictor variables that did not prove significant when placed in competition with these variables. Also, note that the logarithm of lesson opportunity and the logarithm of absolute position were better predictors than are untransformed scores.

The effect of lesson number was only significant for latencies. This may just reflect an increased familiarity with the tutor interface. The fact that the same variable showed up for both old productions and new suggests that at least part of the phenomenon was a matter of general interface learning. Also, lesson number was not significantly related to error rate. This is further evidence that the effect may be an interface effect and may not reflect any real proficiency in coding.

---

[4]The regression equations account for 18% of the variance in times for new productions and 17% of the variance in times for old productions. This might not seem like large fractions of the variance, but keep in mind the inherent noise in observations at this fine grain. In typical reaction time experiments, it is rare to get main effects to account for this much variance in individual times. Reliable data is only gotten by extensive aggregating. Aggregation in our case (Figs. 7.2 and 7.3) show large main effects with on the order of 2-to-1 differences.

The within-lesson opportunity effect reflects the amount of learning that was occurring within lessons. It is illustrated in Fig. 7.2, which displays data averaged over the entire course. The difference between the intercepts for the old and new productions reflects the advantages students had when using the same productions during a second or later session. It is interesting to compare the shapes of the graphs of the old and new productions in Fig. 7.2. The new productions show much larger speed-up from first to second use, but after that they show similar rates of improvement.

In the past (Anderson et al., 1989), we had attributed the special advantage from first to second opportunity for new productions to knowledge compilation. The idea was that the production rule was formed on its first use and strengthened on later uses. In retrospect, this seems like making too much out of an apparent discontinuity. As discussed in chapter 4, it seems more likely that it would require many trials to compile an efficient procedure, which is what a production really is. Moreover, not all of our data displays this apparent first-trial discontinuity. Section 7.5 presents some data that do not exhibit this discontinuity. Moreover, recent carefully controlled laboratory experiments (Anderson & Fincham, 1992) have also failed to find any evidence for first-trial discontinuity.

7.3.3 Interaction Between Production Practice and Problem Practice

The effect of absolute serial position in the code is interesting because it has been established that the effect is logarithmic, not linear, and that it is not a result of potentially confounded variables, such as depth of embedding, number of pending goals, or left-to-right position in a pretty-printing. Furthermore, log absolute serial position is a better predictor than either relative serial position or total length of the function. Figure 7.3 illustrates the average serial position effect over the first 33 positions. The initial long pause is due, at least in part, to reading the problem specifications and planning. The subsequent speed-up is thought to be attributable to students using, and hence practicing, their problem understanding as they go through the problem. This would strengthen their declarative representation of the problem and so speed their access to it. Chapter 3 noted that, according to the ACT-R theory, there should be effects of both production strength (influenced by procedural practice) and activation (influenced by declarative practice), and the overall performance improvement should be the product of the two power practice functions (Equation 3.4). Thus, the effects of procedural practice and declarative practice should be superadditive.

A more direct test of this proposed superadditivity was attempted. Productions were broken into two categories, those above and those below the median frequency of use for all productions. Serial positions were similarly broken

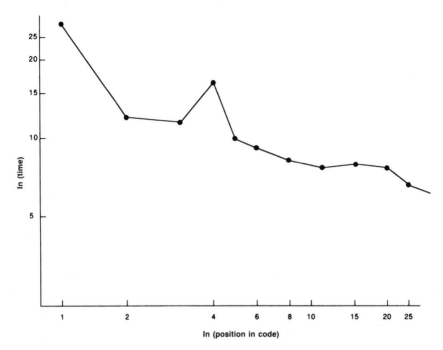

FIG. 7.3. The effect of serial position in code on production time in Lessons 2 and 3.

into those above and below the median position of all symbols in the code. Data was then classified into a 2 × 2 matrix, according to whether the production involved was above or below the median frequency and whether the serial position was above or below the median position. This analysis was done separately for each student. An analysis of variance (ANOVA) was then performed, in which the factors were student (43 values), production frequency (2 values), and serial position (2 values). Separate ANOVAs were performed for old and new productions on mean coding time. These data, as well as mean frequency and mean serial position, are reported in Table 7.2. There are main effects for both production frequency and serial position, but what is critical here is the interaction between them, $F(1, 42) = 9.09$, $p < .01$ for new; $F(1, 42) = 21.75$, $p < .001$ for old. In both cases, as predicted, the effect of production frequency is greater at lower values of serial position.

7.3.4 Summary

As anyone who has taught can appreciate, a class of students learning material is not a carefully controlled experiment, even when it is structured by one of our tutors. Thus, it is all the more remarkable that we have obtained such clear

TABLE 7.2
Results of Superadditivity Analysis

Reported in Each Cell Are Mean Time, Mean Frequency, and Mean Serial Position

New Productions

| | | Serial Position | |
		Low	High
	Low	17.3 sec 1.0 6.2	10.1 sec 2.1 16.1
Opportunity			
	High	13.8 sec 7.9 6.3	8.5 sec 8.9 20.4

Old Productions

| | | Serial Position | |
		Low	High
	Low	13.5 sec 2.0 6.8	8.9 sec 2.1 18.2
Opportunity			
	High	9.6 sec 10.1 7.8	6.1 sec 13.3 20.6

effects of practice on the production rules and on the problems. These are the two critical factors in the ACT-R analysis, one reflecting the new procedural information and the other the new declarative information. As ACT-R predicted, both of these learning effects approximate power functions. Moreover, as ACT-R predicted, they combine multiplicatively. These are nontrivial confirmations of the theory in a truly complex situation.

7.4 INDIVIDUAL DIFFERENCES IN LEARNING

There are substantial differences among students in their performance with the LISP tutor. The question is whether there is anything more involved than some raw, undifferentiated factor of ability. In one attempt to answer this, we looked to see if certain groups of students found certain sets of productions difficult. A factor analysis was performed on the data from Spring 1985; a second factor analysis was then performed on the combined data from Fall 1985 and Spring

1986. Two separate analyses were performed because the Spring 1985 students worked with a somewhat different version of the tutor. In these factor analyses, we were interested in seeing what patterns of individual differences might appear. Specifically, we wanted to learn whether a subset of students would have difficulty with a subset of productions. The details of the factor analysis of the Spring 1985 data and the details of the methodology are reported in Anderson (1990b). Student performance (as measured by mean number of errors) on each production for each lesson was examined for systematic patterns. In the Spring 1985 data, and more clearly in the combined Fall 1985 data and Spring 1986 data, factors emerged that loaded on thematically related productions. For instance, in Lesson 1 a factor emerged that loaded on arithmetic operations, and in Lesson 3 a factor emerged that loaded on logical operations. This meant, for instance, that in Lesson 1, one group of students tended to do relatively poorly on all arithmetic productions, whereas another group of students tended to do well, but that performance on arithmetic productions was relatively unrelated to performance on nonarithmetic productions.

The initially frustrating feature of these within-lesson factors was that they did not show any across-lesson consistency. Thus, productions that loaded on one factor in one lesson would split up and load on different factors in a later lesson. To help organize these within-lesson factors, a metafactor analysis was done. That is, a factor analysis was performed on students' factor scores from particular lessons. Two metafactors emerged fairly strongly in the Spring 1985 data and in the combined 1985–1986 data. When the Spring 1985 data was examined, we noticed that most of the productions that loaded on the first metafactor were new to that lesson (22 out of 34), whereas most of the productions that loaded on the second metafactor were old (20 out of 23).[5] This led to a labeling of the first metafactor as an acquisition factor and the second metafactor as a retention factor. A similar analysis was done in the 1985–1986 data. Most of the productions associated with one metafactor were new to that lesson (18 out of 23), whereas most of the productions associated with the other metafactors were old (23 out of 31).

Thus, what seemed to be stable across lessons were only the very general learning attributes of acquisition and retention.[6] We think we understand why thematic clusters of new productions appeared in individual lessons but disappeared thereafter. These thematically related productions were discussed in the text in close proximity. If a student's attention waxes and wanes while reading the text, this will produce a local correlation among thematically related productions. Another factor that would produce this thematic clustering is that many of the new productions in a lesson are thematically related. For instance, a large

---

[5]That is, productions that loaded on a within-lesson factor that loaded on the metafactor.

[6]There is a temptation to relate them to strength and decay parameters in the ACT-R model for production strengthening, but there are many alternative possible explanations, as well.

fraction of the productions in Lesson 3, on conditionals, are concerned with logical operations of some sort or another. Thus, to the extent that there is an acquisition factor, within a lesson it produces a thematic clustering of productions.

There was also some external validation of these two metafactors. Although both were defined on behavior internal to the LISP tutor, both were strong predictors of performance on paper-and-pencil midterm and final exams. These factors were also associated with scores on the Math SAT but not on the Verbal SAT. The correlation of the retention factor with Math SAT was .62 for Spring 1985 data and .38 for 1985–1986. The correlation of the acquisition factor with Math SAT was .03 for the Spring 1985 data and .60 for the 1985–1986 data. Except for the 1985 correlation coefficient for the acquisition factor, all coefficients were significant.

These factors and the Math SAT were equally good predictors of performance on the final paper-and-pencil test at the end of the course. The failure to find any consistent thematic individual differences in the LISP learning is further evidence for the view that learning is, essentially, simple. The only stable individual differences are very general acquisition and retention factors. This means that the acquisition of a production rule is not sensitive to its content.

The implication of the data analyses to this point are quite startling in their simplicity: If we want to predict a student's performance on a particular problem, we should:

1. Decompose each problem into a sequence of productions.
2. Apply to each new production Equations 7.1 and 7.2, plus a measure to reflect that student's standing on the acquisition factor.
3. Apply to each old production Equation 7.3 and 7.4, plus a measure to reflect that student's standing on the retention factor.
4. Sum the numbers in 2 and 3.

7.5 LEARNING UNDER DIFFERENT TUTORING MODALITIES

So far, the data presented has come from the immediate-feedback version of the tutor. The suggestion has been made a number of times that the simplicity of the learning results reflect the peculiarities of that tutor and are not representative of learning in general. Over the past few years, we have begun to look at other ways of providing feedback to the student and allocating control between the student and the tutor. In addition to the immediate-feedback tutor, we have looked at learning in the following instructional regimens:

No Tutor.   Students receive no guidance at all and must solve the problems on their own. All they are told is whether their final solutions are correct. They can use the LISP environment to try out their solutions, which provides a feedback of a sort. Essentially, these students are in the same kind of environment of students who learn without a tutor, but they enter their code into the same structured editor as do the tutor students. This enables comparable analyses of their data.

Demand Feedback.   Students are not interrupted by the tutor with feedback but can request feedback on their solution at any time. The tutor tells them if their solution so far is correct and, if not, where the first error is. It provides the same feedback about this error as the immediate-feedback tutor would. As much as 80% of the time, students wait until they have finished their solution before they request feedback. So, by their own choice they tend to turn this into a delayed-feedback condition.

Flag Tutor.   Whenever the student makes an error, the part of the code where the error lies is highlighted by the tutor. The student can, however, ignore this and continue to code. Indeed, if the student can come up with code that works despite this error message (i.e., the tutor made an incorrect judgment), he or she is given credit for solving the problem. Students can request the tutor's error message on any piece of code. About 10% of the time, students ignore the error signal at least initially and continue coding, about 15% of the time they request the tutor's explanation of the error signal, and the other 75% of the time they try to correct their code without any information from the tutor as to the nature of their error or what the correct code would be. Thus, students tend to turn this into an immediate-correction tutor, but one in which they receive only minimal feedback.

7.5.1 Effects of Tutoring Modalities

More information about these various tutors can be found in Corbett and Anderson (1989, 1990). Figure 7.4 shows the results from one comparison of the tutoring modalities in terms of time to complete coding of a problem. Students took longest to get through a fixed set of problems in the no-tutor condition, next longest with the demand-feedback tutor, and next longest with the flag tutor; they were fastest with the immediate-feedback tutor. The effects, comparing the extremes, can be as large as a 3-to-1 difference. Thus, it seems the more rope we give students, the more they hang themselves. There tends to be no difference among tutors in final achievement, measured by paper-and-pencil posttests. In some evaluations, when students did not solve all the problems successfully in the no-tutor condition, they gave inferior posttest results. The lack of posttest effects when all problems are successfully solved

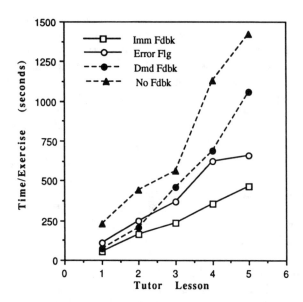

FIG. 7.4. Mean exercise completion time for five tutor lessons.

is important to an understanding of the learning process. Students go through very different trajectories (and take very different amounts of time) to reach essentially the same final solutions. It seems that learning is a function of the solutions that they achieve and not the process by which they achieve them. Students achieve at higher levels if they solve more problems, whatever the regimen.

Although we do not have empirical evidence on this point, it seems only logical that there should be one qualification on this generalization. The problems' solutions must be understood. Our general instructional environment tries to guarantee this for all conditions. The written instructions and problems are constructed to yield a gentle, incremental progression through the material.

This pattern of results is in accord with the expectations of the ACT-R theory. Recall that initial production formation takes place by analogy to an example. Thus, the essential ingredient for learning is a product, the solved example, from which the analogy can take place. Once the production is in place, further learning is in response to a process: Further use of the production leads to further strengthening of it. Because learning is both in response to a product (the initial compilation) and in response to a process (subsequent strengthening), it might not be obvious why ACT-R predicts that the number of problems should be the critical variable. This requires going into more detail as to what happens according to the ACT-R theory in particular situations.

When solving their first problems in a lesson, students are in a state where they have adequately studied the instructional examples so that they can perform about 50% of the new production rules without error. This 50% will be learned and compiled into production rules in all conditions without a hitch, and the compilation will occur in the same way in all conditions. The remaining 50% will be learned when the student comes to an understanding of one of the problems that involves that production and uses memory of that problem as the example for a later problem. This latter 50% of the learning will therefore be based on the products of later problem-solving episodes. In all conditions students come to essentially the same solutions and understanding of these solutions, so there should be no difference in the learning involved in this 50% either.[7] Once the productions are learned, they are strengthened on each subsequent trial to which they apply. Because the tutoring conditions only differ in their response to errors, strength will accumulate across conditions in the same way.

The differences among conditions can have large consequences when the student makes an error and has to correct it. In conditions that provide little guidance, the student may have to spend a lot more time finding out how to correct errors. According to ACT-R, however, students do not learn from errors or from error correction.[8] The only thing they learn from, when an error is made, is the final correct code. Thus, the differences among the conditions are not relevant to learning as long as students come to the same understanding of the same correct code at the end of the correction episodes. Students do not always come to the same code, and there can be other subtle differences among conditions, but the learning consequences of the various conditions are substantially the same, and so one would not expect to see substantial differences in learning outcome.

In summary, then, ACT-R predicts that learning should be a function of the *product* of the problem-solving process and not of the process itself. That is, different processes that produce the same products (solutions) will have the same learning outcome. This is because ACT-R compiles rules from sample solutions. In this, ACT-R is in sharp contrast with Soar, which creates new rules from a trace of the problem-solving process, and predicts that different processes should result in different rules.

7.5.2 Learning Curves

It is also of interest to consider what the learning curves are like in the various tutoring modalities. A difficulty in collecting such learning curves is that only in the immediate-feedback condition are students guaranteed to stay on an in-

---

[7]It is conceivable that the different conditions might impact differently on the degree of understanding. Subjects in immediate-feedback conditions might learn the solutions by rote and subjects in on-your-own conditions might come up with highly patched code that they do not understand. The instructions in our experiment, however, tend to preclude such degeneracies. This is because our material was carefully shaped over many classes to yield effective learning.

[8]That is, with respect to writing correct code. They may learn how to debug their code.

terpretable path of behavior, which can be model-traced. Our response to this problem has been to analyze only that fragment of the data that is on an interpretable path. As soon as the student makes an error in a function that is not immediately corrected, we stop trying to analyze any subsequent data for that function. With the flag tutor, 87% of the interactions were, thus, analyzed, with the demand-feedback tutor 70% were analyzed, and in the no-tutor condition 67% were analyzed. In addition, the data have only been analyzed for Lessons 2, 3, and 4 from the LISP tutor curriculum in Fig. 7.4, and only for 10 students per lesson. Therefore, we have a much smaller data base for these analyses than for the analyses in Section 7.3.

Figure 7.5 presents the change in error rate as a function of production opportunity, and Fig. 7.6 presents the change in coding time as a function of production opportunity. The learning functions are comparable across all tutoring modalities. In the case of error rates, there appears to be no difference as a function of tutoring modality. With respect to times, the two conditions with more delay in feedback (no tutor, demand) were initially faster than the two conditions with more immediate feedback (flag, immediate). This may reflect a selection artifact, in that we only looked at data on a correct path, and students may have been, so to speak, on a roll, in the delayed conditions. Another possibility is that students might be more cautious in the two immediate-feedback conditions. Also, because no feedback was given to students, they do not have

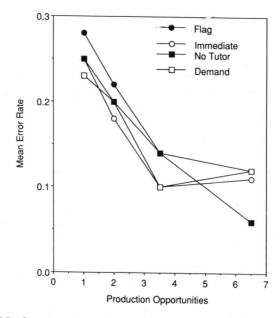

FIG. 7.5. Learning in the various tutor modalities as a function of amount of production practice: mean number of errors per coding attempt.

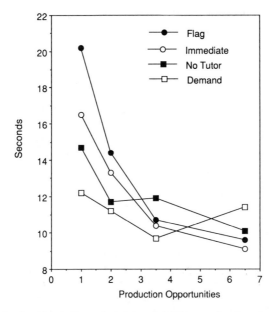

FIG. 7.6. Learning in the various tutor modalities as a function of amount of production practice: mean time per correct coding attempt.

the implicit positive feedback to process. It is interesting in this regard that students were slowest in the flag-tutor condition, where they had to identify the type case of the feedback in order to discriminate correct responses from errors, which were printed in bold.

Unlike the curves in Fig. 7.2, these learning curves do not show a first-trial discontinuity. Rather, if there is a discontinuity, it appears after Trial 2, when learning slows down. We have no clear explanation for this apparent difference in the shape of the learning functions, but there were numerous differences between the conditions that generated Fig. 7.2 and the current conditions, including student population, curriculum covered, tutor interface, and conditions of learning (classroom versus experimental).

The basic similarity of the learning functions across tutoring conditions within this experiment offers further support for the ACT-R conception of the learning process. As discussed earlier, learning should be a function of the number of solutions the student has passed through and not of how the student passes through those solutions.

7.6 CONCLUSIONS

Most of this chapter has been concerned with the effects we have found with our research on the LISP tutor. Perhaps more interesting are the effects we did *not* find. There were no interesting effects of different problem content, of individual differences, or of instructional style. The picture of learning a complex skill was every bit as simple as advertised at the beginning of the chapter. Learning individual production rules underlying a complex skill does not appear much different from learning simple paired associates. The resulting skill is complex because of the interrelations among the units, but the learning of the units is quite straightforward.

This picture of skill learning has important implications for instruction, which will be expanded on in chapter 11. Specifically, it becomes important to do a complete cognitive task analysis to identify a skill's underlying production rules. Having identified them, it becomes critical to arrange for a learning situation that efficiently practices those rules with understanding. Subsequent chapters provide more evidence for this prescription of cognitive task analysis followed by drill and practice that focuses on the production rules revealed by the task analysis.

As a final comment, this chapter reflects a transition point in the book. Much of this chapter was concerned with the global predictions that follow from an ACT-like production-rule analysis of skill, although some points (e.g., Table 7.2) addressed specific predictions of the ACT-R theory. The remainder of the data chapters (8 through 10) focus largely on what follows from a general ACT-like production-rule analysis although not specifically the ACT-R system.

The Geometry Tutor
and Skill Acquisition

John R. Anderson, Francis S. Bellezza, and
C. Franklin Boyle
Carnegie Mellon University

8.1 GEOMETRY PROBLEM SOLVING

As noted in the previous chapter, in this chapter we move from a focus on providing evidence specifically for ACT-R to a focus on providing evidence for the general utility of production rules for understanding skill acquisition. Although this chapter and the next two have a few connections with the specifics of ACT-R, most of the results would be relevant to most production-system theories. In this chapter we report on our research with the geometry tutor (Anderson et al., 1990; Anderson, Boyle, & Yost, 1985). This research was completed before ACT-R (or rational analysis, for that matter) was even conceived.

The geometry tutor focused on instruction of traditional Euclidean proof skills. It is probably the most successful of all the tutoring projects we have undertaken, in terms of its positive educational effect. Like the LISP tutor, it had as its foundation a long history of study of the acquisition of geometry problem-solving skills by students (e.g., Anderson, Greeno, Kline, & Neves, 1981). This chapter looks at the data the geometry tutor has provided about the nature of the acquisition of problem-solving skill. The results reinforce some of the conclusions made in the previous chapter, based on data from the LISP tutor, but call into question the generality of others.

Part of the reason for the perception of success of the geometry project is the very poor character of the traditional geometry classroom. Geometry is considered by high school students to be their least favorite subject (Hoffer, 1981). Classrooms are characterized by low achievement, low motivation, and significant management problems. Against this low base, the tutor has been able to significantly enhance classroom achievement and dramatically enhance classroom motivation (Schofield & Evans-Rhodes, 1989; Wertheimer, 1990). It is our be-lief that the dramatic gains reported in student morale occurred because the tutor made geometry what it is supposed to be: a challenging task, but one at which students can achieve a degree of mastery. Their positive response was due to their mastering a difficult academic topic.

Our conception of geometry expertise is one of managing a difficult search task by means of heuristics. This is what the tutor tried to convey to students. By the time students reach the end of the geometry course, they have learned on the order of 100 rules of inference that enable them to prove various geome-try problems. At any point in a geometry problem, a large number of these rules are potentially applicable. Koedinger and Anderson (1990) estimated there are hundreds of thousands of legal sequences of inferences that could apply at a particular point in a problem; the student's task is to find the rare sequence that will allow the conjecture to be proven. Because most of these paths of in-ference are implausible, students need to learn how to identify the paths that are plausible.

Figure 8.1 presents a typical high school geometry problem that most stu-dents would find difficult. It turns out to be very useful to make the inference that the segment CK is congruent to (≅) itself but it proves to be totally useless to prove that the segment GH is congruent to itself. How is a student to know what is useful and what is not?

Rather than reasoning from the givens of a geometry problem to what has to be proven, one can reason in a backward direction, from what is to be proven to what needs to be proven. So, given the goal in Fig. 8.1 to prove CD perpen-dicular to AB, one might choose to prove ∠ADC congruent to ∠BDC, and then use a theorem called *congruent adjacent angles*. This proves to be a good idea.

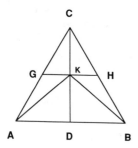

Given: $\overline{AC} \cong \overline{BC}$

$\overline{AK} \cong \overline{BK}$

Prove: $\overline{CD} \perp \overline{AB}$

FIG. 8.1. A geometry problem that students find difficult.

It would not, however, have been a good idea to show that $\angle$CAD plus $\angle$DCA sum to 90° and use the fact that the sum of the angles in a triangle is 180°. Again, how is a student to know this?

8.1.1 The Expert Model

The geometry tutor has an expert model that knows when to apply various rules of inference. It uses various contextually bound rules that recognize the circumstances in which a particular geometry inference is likely to be useful. So, for instance, although it generally makes little sense to infer a segment congruent to itself, it does make sense when the goal is to try to prove two triangles congruent to each other, and they happen to share that side. Thus, corresponding to this insight is the following rule:

IF   the goal is to prove $\triangle$XYZ congruent to $\triangle$WYZ
THEN conclude that $\overline{YZ}$ is congruent to $\overline{YZ}$ by the reflexive rule.

There are also contextually bound, backward-inference rules that recognize when it is reasonable to set particular subgoals.

So that the tutor could follow any moves that students make, there are also low-rated versions of legal rules of inference. Thus, corresponding to the highly rated production rule just stated is the low-rated production rule:

IF   there is a segment YZ
THEN prove YZ is congruent to YZ by the reflexive rule.

These rules are much weaker, however, and so are not preferred by the production system if any higher rated rules apply. Some of the inferences in geometry do not have to be contextually bound. They prove to be good ideas whenever they were applicable. Almost every time there is side–side–side configuration, it is a good idea to prove the triangles congruent. Therefore, the side-side-side inference was encoded in just one production rule:

IF   there are $\triangle$ABC and $\triangle$DEF
         and $\overline{AB}$ is congruent to $\overline{DE}$
         and $\overline{BC}$ is congruent to $\overline{EF}$
         and $\overline{AC}$ is congruent to $\overline{DF}$
THEN conclude $\triangle$ABC is congruent to $\triangle$DEF.

In this tutor, production rules have a single, unidimensional quantity associated with them, which we call their *rating*. As discussed in chapter 3 on conflict resolution, however, ACT-R makes a distinction between how likely a production is to fire, which is measured by production strength, and how successful the production will be if it fires, which is reflected in various measures of cost and probability of success. The rating measure in the geometry tutor is better conceived of as some amalgam of cost and probability of success, rather than as strength. The geometry tutor predated this distinction between these aspects of conflict resolution, and at the time we wrote and thought of the rating measures, quite frankly, in a somewhat blurry manner.

The expert system embodied by these rules is able to find proofs quite efficiently. It also represents the kind of expertise we saw building up in successful students as a function of their experience with different problems. Since we built this expert module, Koedinger and Anderson (1990) have speculated that there may be an even better model of expertise based on reasoning about geometric patterns. They found it in the pattern of reasoning exemplified in some teachers and graduate students in mathematics. To some degree, it may also be the model used by high school students, particularly the better ones. We are currently engaged in research to see if it cannot serve as the basis for a more powerful tutor.

The production rules used by the tutor probably only partially correlate with the actual rules students were using. Nonetheless, these are the rules we tried to communicate to students, and they provided the only useful basis for organizing the data that we obtained from the students.

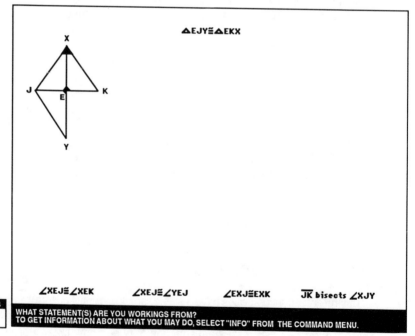

FIG. 8.2. An initial screen configuration with the geometry tutor.

8.1.2 Interacting With the Geometry Tutor

Figure 8.2 illustrates how a problem is initially presented to a student on the computer screen. At the top of the screen is the statement the student is trying to prove. At the bottom are the givens of the problem. In the upper left corner is the problem diagram. The system prompts the student to select a set of statements using a mouse. It then prompts the student to enter a rule of geometric inference that takes these statements as premises. When the student has done so, the system prompts the student to type in the conclusion that follows from the rule. The screen is updated with each step to indicate where the student is. The sequence of premises, rule of inference, and conclusion complete a single step of inference. Figure 8.3 illustrates the screen at the point at which the student has selected the definition of *bisector* to apply to the premise, JK bisects ∠XJY, but has not yet entered the conclusion. A menu has been brought up at the left of the screen to enable the conclusion to be entered. It contains the relations and the symbols of geometry. By pointing to symbols on the menu and to points on the diagram, the student can form the new statement ∠XJK ≅ ∠KJY. The student has to actually point to the diagram to confirm he or she really knows the references of the abstract statements.

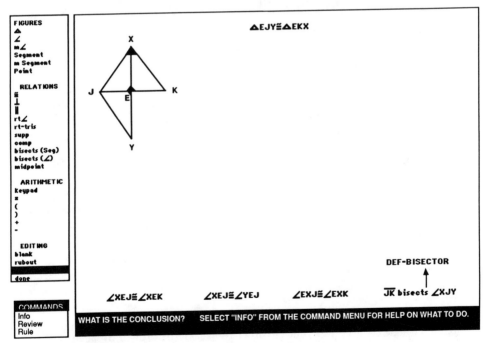

FIG. 8.3. The screen configuration after the student has selected the premises and the rule, and is about to enter the conclusion.

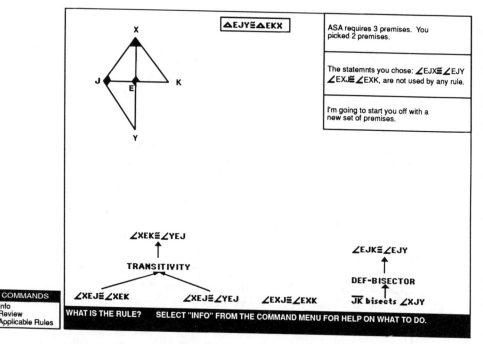

FIG. 8.4. The student has just tried to apply angle–side–angle to the two premises, ∠EJX ≅ ∠EJY and ∠EXJ ≅ ∠EXK.

Figure 8.4 shows the problem at a still later point. The student has completed the bisector inference and added a plausible transitivity inference, but one that proves not to be part of the final proof. At this point, the student begins to flail: He or she has tried a series of illegal applications of rules, the most recent being application of angle–side–angle (ASA) to the premises ∠EJX ≅ ∠EJY and ∠EXJ ≅ ∠EXK. The tutor points out that ASA requires three premises, so it is inappropriate when applied to only two premises. Because the student is having so much difficulty, the tutor points the student to the key step in solving this problem: To prove △EJY ≅ △EKX, he or she will have to prove △EJY ≅ △EJX and △EJX ≅ △EKX, and then apply transitivity to these conclusions. The tutor indicates this key step by boxing the conclusion. Thus, the student is asked to use backward inference to enter a rule and a set of premises from which the conclusion logically follows. If necessary, the tutor can step the student through how transitivity of the two triangle congruences enables the conclusion to be proven. The student would then have the task of proving the two triangle congruences.

Figure 8.5 brings us to a still later point, where the student has proven one of the triangle congruences, but the other remains to be proven. It nicely illustrates how students can mix reasoning forward from the givens and reasoning backward from the conclusions.

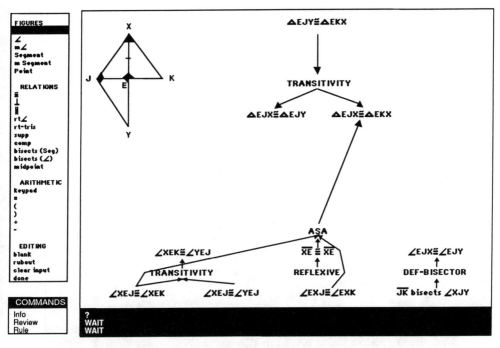

FIG. 8.5. The student has succeeded in proving one of the two requisite triangle congruences.

Figure 8.6 shows the completed proof, in which there is a graph structure connecting the givens to the to-be-proven statement. Students find such representations of proof solutions enlightening in two ways. First, they are able to appreciate how inferences combine to yield a proof, something they tend not to get from the traditional two-column formalism. Second, the search inherent in proof generation is explicitly represented. So, for instance, students can easily identify those inferences, such as the angle transitivity inference, that are off the main path.

The example in Figs. 8.2 through 8.6 illustrates what Brown (1983, 1985b; Collins & Brown, 1987) has referred to as reification. The proof graph makes concrete two abstract features of problem solving in geometry: the logical relationships among the premises and conclusions, and the search process by which one hunts for a correct proof. Normally, students have a great deal of difficulty with both of these constructs. By creating an external referent, the proof graph facilitates instruction on these abstract concepts. Students report that they prefer this proof graph structure to the more traditional two-column proof form. They typically justify their preferences with the assertion that it is "easier to do a proof" with this formalism. Scheines and Sieg (in press), who used such a

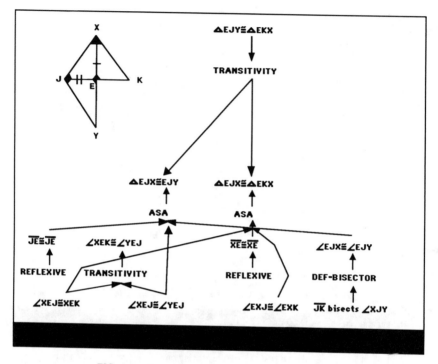

FIG. 8.6.   The proof of the problem is now complete.

representation for proofs in formal logic, found evidence that such a graphical
representation helps problem solving even without a tutor.

8.1.3   Backward Reasoning

This interaction illustrates use of the backward reasoning facility in the geometry tutor. In the first evaluation of the geometry tutor in the 1985–1986 academic year, we found that all but the gifted students had great difficulty with
this backward reasoning facility.[1] Interestingly, this contradicts the opinions of
many people in the field of intelligent tutoring, who thought this backward reasoning capacity of the tutor was one of its strong features. It does, however, replicate the results obtained with the Logic Theorist 30 years before: Students would
not match the backward reasoning of that model, either (Newell & Simon, 1972).
Trafton and Reiser (1991) have similarly found that people have more success

---

[1]That evaluation, which preceded the one reported in this chapter, involved four classes: a "gifted" class of students with IQs over 130, a "scholars" class of high-achieving students, and two
classes of regular academic-track students.

in the graphical data-flow programming languages when they develop their programs in the same forward direction as the data flows through the graph.[2]

There were probably many reasons for the difficulty of the backward reasoning mode, but a significant factor was simply the unnaturalness of it. This is what would be expected from ACT-R. Recall that production rules in ACT-R are selected on the basis of their producing some change in the current state that moves one closer to the goal state. For instance, in the exploratory phase of the research on navigation (chapter 5) it was found that no subject planned backward, from the destination to the start location. This does not mean that it is impossible for ACT-R to reverse its planning. We (and ACT-R) can plan from the goal by treating it as the start state and re-representing operators as producing transformations in the reverse direction, but it takes considerable effort and talent to re-represent the problem space this way.

Many students displayed confusion that reflected the difficulty they had in turning this around. For instance, many students would try to set as a subgoal to prove something the goal implied rather than something that implied the goal. For this reason, in the 1986–1987 academic year we deleted the backward reasoning feature from the tutor. It is the data from this year that were subject to analysis and that are reported here.

8.2 LEARNING WITH THE GEOMETRY TUTOR

In the 1986–1987 academic year, the tutor taught a curriculum that covered over half of the topics in geometry, including congruence, angles, parallel lines, triangles, and quadrilaterals. Only a fraction of that data was subject to analysis, however: that from congruences, angles, and parallel lines. A large fraction of the data was lost due to the demise of the Psychology Department computer at CMU. We only have access to printouts of analyses, not raw data, and so cannot do some further analyses that we would like to do. Nonetheless, what we have does serve nicely to help define the scope of the generalizations that can be made from the LISP tutor.

The time involved in each rule of inference was analyzed into three components: *premise time*, measured from when the tutor was ready until premises have been chosen; *rule time*, the interval between choosing the premise and typing in the rule; and *conclusion time*, the interval between typing in the rule and choosing the conclusion. In terms of the production-system model, the premise time is the most significant, because it corresponds to recognizing the applicability of the rule, which is what the underlying productions do. The re-

---

[2]Scheines and Sieg (in press) did not find similar difficulties in a graphical tutor designed to teach proof skills in formal logic to CMU undergraduates. This may be a replication, in effect, of our result with gifted high school students. Sufficiently capable students, apparently, can adapt to a backward-reasoning system.

maining time may be viewed as simply executing the selected rule within the tutor's interface.

We found it necessary to make a distinction between two types of steps of inference: the last inference a student makes to complete a proof and all the others. The last inference is distinguished by the fact that the conclusion of this rule of inference is posted as the main goal. There are special production rules that recognize that the conclusion can be directly proven from some combination of the statements posted on the screen. It is also easy to enter the conclusion, because the student can simply point to it rather than creating it.

The premise times and conclusion times were significantly shorter for last rules. The reason for the effect on premise time is that the productions that recognize last rules are very highly rated and so should apply quickly. This advantage for conclusion times reflects the considerably greater ease of simply pointing to the conclusion over trying to enter the conclusion through the tutor's interface. There was no significant difference between last and nonlast rules with respect to rule time.

8.2.1 Regression Analysis

Separate regression analyses were performed for premise times, rule times, and conclusion times; all analyses were performed on log times. The dependent variables were:

V_1: Practice. Measured as log number of uses of this inference. This would pick up a learning effect.

V_2: Position. The log position of this inference in the sequence of inferences in the proof. Recall that there was such a serial position effect in the LISP tutor.

V_3: The number of givens in the problem. We thought it might be a measure of problem complexity.

V_4: The number of known solutions to the problem. We thought it might be another measure of problem complexity.

V_5: Whether the inference was last or not.

V_6: Length of the proof, in number of steps. Again we thought this might be a measure of problem complexity.

The first two variables, practice and position, had significant effects on all three times. The third, fourth, and sixth had no significant effects anywhere. The variable of last versus nonlast had significant effects for premise time and conclusion time. The following equations can be extracted from these regression analyses:

$$\text{Log premise time} = 3.91 - .13\ V_1 - .17\ V_2 - .48\ V_5$$
$$\text{Log rule time} = 2.89 - .19\ V_1 - .04\ V_2$$
$$\text{Log conclusion time} = 5.23 - .13\ V_1 - .13\ V_2 - 1.23\ V_5$$

This basically replicates the results from the LISP tutor, that subjects show improvement with practice of the rules and with increasing familiarity with a specific problem. Only the premise time effect do we interpret as implicating production rules in the student model, but learning is apparently also going on in the skills of entering rules and entering conclusions.

The practice effect in these equations reflects the number of times a particular geometric rule of inference occurs. In many cases, multiple production rules correspond to a single rule of inference. Thus, the effect of practice that we see only correlates with the underlying theoretical variable of production-rule practice. The rules of inference can be divided into rules like the side-side–side rule, which have essentially a single production rule in the expert model prescribing their application, and rules like the reflexive rule, which have multiple production rules for different contexts. The following are the inference rules, within the restricted curriculum, that have single production rules in the expert model:[3] congruence-from-equality-last, transitivity-of-congruence-last, transitivity-of-congruence-prelast, definition-of-bisector-prelast, definition-of-right-angle-prelast, definition-of-perpendicular-prelast. The following are inference rules that have many production rules associated with them: reflexive-prelast, definition-of-betweenness-prelast, substitution-prelast, angle-addition-prelast, adjacent-supplementary-angles-prelast. There were many other inference rules that had two or three productions associated with them and so did not land clearly in either camp. With the single rules, every repetition of the rule of inference is a repetition of a production rule. With the multiple rules, almost every repetition of an inference rule occurs in a new context where the old production rules do not apply. Thus, the student has to learn yet another production rule.[4]

Figure 8.7 compares the learning curves for these two kinds of inference rules with respect to premise time. The differences are quite marked. There is very little learning for the same-inference, different-production rule situation, whereas there is substantial learning when the same inference, and same production rule are invoked. Thus, it is the production rule and not the inference rule that is the appropriate unit of analysis for geometry.

One might infer from Fig. 8.7 that individual production rules took about a minute to fire, which is at least an order of magnitude greater than the time

---

[3]We considered geometric rules for last and nonlast position separately.

[4]What this means is that students cannot really come to mastery of the individual rules. The assumption of the curriculum designers is that students come to master more general skills that enable them to make such novel first-time inferences. The evidence for such optimistic expectations is weak, at best.

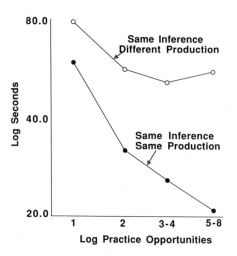

FIG. 8.7. Comparison of improvement on inference rules that correspond to a single production with those that correspond to multiple productions. Times plotted are premise times.

scale envisioned in ACT-R. It seems unlikely that a single production rule is behind the behavior involved in premise selection. Moreover, an error in a production rule can lead to the need for corrections and repeated entries. So, the times in Fig. 8.7 should not be taken as measures of the times for production rules to fire, but rather as measures of their success in application.

8.2.2 Learning to Learn

The previous section provided evidence that students were getting better with practice on specific rules. We also thought we were seeing evidence that students were in some sense "catching on" to geometry and finding it easier to learn new rules. To see if this was the case, we examined performance on the first use of a rule (a logical rule in the geometry sense, not a production rule) over the first three chapters of the geometry course. The following dependent variables were used:

W_1: Number of premises involved in the rule.

W_2: Length of the proof.

W_3: Log position of the rule in the curriculum sequence of rules.

W_4: Type of rule (last versus nonlast).

The regression equation for premise time was particularly simple, and accounted for 51% of the variance:

$$\text{Log time} = 4.80 - .68W_3$$

The regression equation for time to enter the rule accounts for 27% of the variance:

$$\text{Log time} = 2.51 - .23W_3$$

The regression equation for time to enter the conclusion accounts for 87% of the variance:

$$\text{Log time} = 3.64 - .46W_3 - 1.38W_4$$

A similar but very weak improvement in the LISP tutor was found over lessons, but it was restricted to time and did not affect errors. The improvement with the geometry tutor was found on both measures. Comparing the first 10 rules with the last 10 rules, total time for first application decreased from 177 sec to 83 sec, and mean number of errors decreased from .64 to .24.

The improvement in the very first use of a rule suggests a problem with our production rules. We were modeling as in a single production rule what should probably have been modeled as multiple rules. Some of these production rules may be shared among multiple logical rules. For instance, with respect to the critical variable of pre-premise time, students might be learning to focus on unused premises, to relate the premises to the diagram, and to check the number of premises against the intended rule.[5] All of these would increase the accuracy and, hence, the speed of their rule application.

Our own inclination is to believe that these smaller grain steps can be successfully modeled as production rules, and we can account for learning in terms of these smaller grain rules. The times associated with production rules (over a minute) are far too long to correspond to a single production rule in the ACT-R analysis. Unfortunately, because of the shift in computer technology, the geometry tutor and its data are no longer available for further analysis to determine the significance of the discrepancies and whether better production rules would eliminate them. They are reported here as they are.

8.3 INDIVIDUAL DIFFERENCES
WITH THE GEOMETRY TUTOR

There was wide variation in how well the students did at the sample geometry problem. To come to some understanding of these individual differences, the 6 worst students in the sample were contrasted with the 9 best (ignoring about 30 intermediate students). The 6 worst all got Ds and Es as final letter grades,

---

[5]In our new tutor development system (Anderson & Pelletier, 1991), we work with such smaller grain rules.

had a mean IQ of 103, averaged 44 out of 80 on a posttest of proof skills, and had gotten Cs and Ds in their prior algebra course. The 9 best students got As and Bs as the final letter grade in their course, had an average IQ of 130, averaged 75 out of 80 in the proof posttest, and had letter grades from As to Cs in their prior algebra course. Thus, they are quite separate populations by almost any measure.

Table 8.1 provides an attempt to understand the learning differences that separate these two populations. It looks at premise time, rule time, and result time, as well as mean numbers of errors per inference (students could make more than one error while making an inference). Table 8.1 also shows the changes in these with practice. It presents the first time an inference rule was used, the average of the second and third, and the average of the fourth through seventh. Finally, it provides a measure of percentage improvement from the first trial to the average of fourth through seventh trials.

The better students appear to do better everywhere, but there is an interesting pattern in the data. Although the differences between the students on the first trial is relatively small, it increases with practice. This effect is visible if one looks at absolute difference between good and poor students, but is more apparent if one uses percentage measures, which are probably more appropriate: On the first use of an inference rule, the good students were 25% faster and made 18% fewer errors. By the last block of use, the good students were 38% faster and made 50% fewer errors. This replicates earlier results from

TABLE 8.1
Changes in Performance Measures With Practice

	Poor Students Opportunities			
Measure	1	2 & 3	4–7	% change
Premise Time	60 sec	49 sec	37 sec	38%
Rule Time	31 sec	26 sec	26 sec	16%
Result Time	62 sec	73 sec	53 sec	14%
Total Time	153 sec	148 sec	116 sec	24%
Errors	.68	.68	.60	12%
	Good Students Opportunities			
Measure	1	2 & 3	4–7	% change
Premise Time	50 sec	40 sec	25 sec	50%
Rule Time	28 sec	22 sec	16 sec	43%
Result Time	36 sec	39 sec	31 sec	14%
Total Time	114 sec	81 sec	72 sec	37%
Errors	.56	.37	.30	46%

the LISP tutor, which showed that students differed not only in their initial ability but also in their learning rate.

There is also a special pattern that involves premise times. First, premise times showed the largest speed-up, consistent with the view that they reflect the critical underlying productions. Second, the good students began by spending a larger portion of their time studying the premises. This is suggestive evidence that the good students behave more in accordance with the model, which predicts that the large investment of time would be in the selection of premises (where the critical production rule should apply), and that this would also be the block of time to show the greatest compression with learning.

From informal observation of the poor students, we suggest their problem-solving model was something like this:

1. Pick some premises that look like they might be related. "Look like they might be related" means things like that the premises appear in similar location on the screen, that they involve common points, that they are all congruence statements, and so on.
2. Try to find some rule of inference that takes these premises as input. Thus, if a poor student had picked two angle statements and a side statement, he or she would use an angle–side–angle premise even if the angle and side pairs did not all come from the same corresponding triangles.
3. Figure out what conclusion derives from the application of this rule to the statements.

Frequently, the tutor would cut them off because what they were doing was not well formed, but they, nonetheless, stumbled through the problems, sometimes guessing right. In contrast to the model, these students did not select premises with an idea of what rule would apply to it or what conclusion would follow. Their procedure could be modeled by a production-rule system, but it would be a very different one than the kind we intended.

As with the LISP tutor, a factor analysis was undertaken on performance on the different inference rules. This time the dependent measure used was premise time per rule.[6] There were a great many holes in the data, with many measures for the students missing for many of the inference rules. Nonetheless, we were able to examine the performance of 20 of the students on 20 of the inference rules. Two factors accounted for 65% of the variance. These are displayed in Table 8.2 along with their weighting on specific geometry rules. The first factor is mainly concerned with the algebraic aspects of doing proofs in geometry; the second factor is concerned with angles and may reflect a spatial ability factor. This is consonant with psychometric wisdom that there is a

---

[6]We report the factor analysis on times because it shows the larger effects. The factor analysis on errors produced similar results.

TABLE 8.2
Results of Factor Analysis

Factor 1	Factor 2
(.90) Definition of Congruence	(.94) Complementary Angles
(.87) Transitive Property of Equality	(.88) Supplementary Angles
(.86) Definition of Bisector	(.85) Alternate Exterior Angles
(.81) Definition of Vertical Angles	(.84) Corresponding Angles
(.76) Addition Property of Equality	(.72) Transitive Property of Congruence
(.70) Definition of Betweenness	(.66) Definition of Right Angles
(.69) Substitution Property of Equality	(.65) Alternate Interior Angles
(.67) Subtraction Property of Equality	(.61) Congruent Adjacent Angles
(.58) Reflexive Rule	(.47) Angle Addition

spatial ability factor that can be separated from a general reasoning factor (Horn & Stankov, 1982). In the domain of LISP, such a difference would not have shown up because there was no real spatial component to the LISP skills.

How might a difference such as that between spatial and symbolic ability be represented in a production system? Perhaps it reflects differences in the pattern matching that underlies the process of identifying the production rules. Some pattern tests in a production condition are tests of spatial information, and some are tests of symbolic information. Presumably, differential success in performing these tests would result in the production rules' being executed with differential success. Another, slightly different, possibility is that chunks representing spatial information could have different levels of activation, resulting in differential success in pattern matching.

8.4   CONCLUSIONS

In broad outline, the analysis of the data from the geometry tutor is consistent with the data from the LISP tutor and has given support to the ACT-R theory. There were three unexpected results, however: One was the evidence for learning to learn. Our response to this potentially discordant result has been to ascribe it to the incompleteness of our production-rule analysis. There are, undoubtedly, substantial flaws in the production rules, but this is hardly evidence that the flaws are the source of the discrepancies. The second unexpected result was the thematic clustering of rules. This points to the failure of ACT-R to have a theory of different abilities. The third surprise was the apparent difference in the approaches of good and poor students (Table 8.1). This is evidence that not all students use the same rules.

On the other hand, a number of the results from the LISP tutor were replicated. One was that the cognitive production rule does a better job of organizing learning than does the domain inference rule (Fig. 8.7). Another was the role of problem practice in performance. The third was that the effects of both rule practice and problem practice appear additive in log scale, implying that time is the product of power functions of these two variables. All of these are predictions of the ACT-R theory.

As noted in the introduction to this chapter, our view is that the data from the geometry tutor have less to say about the specifics of ACT-R, and more to say about the nature of geometry proof skill and about a production-rule analysis of this skill more generally. On this score, we see that geometry can be successfully taught with a tutor built on a production-rule analysis, and that production rules can be used to organize the data. From the current perspective, we would view the production rules in the geometry tutor as rather too large-grained to provide the best models. Future research will attempt to provide more fine-grained student models for tutoring geometry.

9

The Identical Elements Theory
of Transfer

John R. Anderson and Mark K. Singley
Carnegie Mellon University

9.1 INTRODUCTION

Perhaps the most central question in education is *transfer*: how knowledge from one experience—say, an arithmetic class—is utilized in another situation—a science class or shopping in a grocery store. As Singley and Anderson (1989) reviewed, the transfer that actually occurs often compares poorly to naive expectations about how much should occur. The issue of transfer has been one of increasing interest in cognitive science as researchers try to come to grips with the nature of knowledge and skill. One might view the recent surge of interest in situated learning (Collins et al., 1989; Lave & Wenger, 1990) as based on the premises that skills cannot transfer across contexts and that one needs to learn them in the context of application. ACT-R does not take quite as depressing a view on the possibilities for transfer, but it does expect a fair degree of specificity in transfer.

With the ACT-R theory, the most obvious way to get transfer between two tasks is through overlap in the chunks and productions involved in performing them. If two tasks involve the same chunks and productions, then acquiring and strengthening these chunks and productions in one task will facilitate performance of the other task, but there are other possible paths by which one experience can influence another. The most significant involves the processes of analogy and knowledge compilation. *Analogy* extends knowledge from one situation to another situation that is only similar. *Knowledge compilation* crosses the bridge from declarative to procedural knowledge.[1]

---

[1]Another form of transfer, which is very significant (but not analyzed much here because of our focus on skill acquisition), is how past experiences in a domain enable us to understand new declarative information in that domain.

The function of this chapter is to review the highlights of the theory of transfer and the data from Singley and Anderson (1989); that book may be consulted for a more thorough discussion of many of the issues and the data. Much of this research can be viewed as supporting what might be called a *modified identical elements theory of transfer*. The identical elements theory of transfer was first proposed by Thorndike (1906; Thorndike & Woodworth, 1901). His view, simply put, was that one skill would transfer to another skill to the extent that they shared stimulus–response (S–R) bonds.[2] One could cast the identical elements proposal more generally, however, as the claim that there will be transfer to the extent that one skill shares knowledge elements with another. One can then use Thorndike's identical elements proposal as a process assumption that enables the testing of a theory of representation. What will transfer from one situation to the next will be a function of how one represents knowledge. In ACT-R the units of knowledge are chunks and productions, not Thorndike's S–R bonds. Thus, ACT-R predicts that transfer from one skill to another should be a function of the chunks and productions they share. If transfer can be explained in terms of ACT-R knowledge units, this will be evidence for ACT-R's knowledge representation.

Much of the analysis of transfer in Singley and Anderson (1989) focused on trying to account for transfer in terms of the productions one skill shares with another. For this reason we have sometimes called it the *identical-productions theory of transfer*. However, as this chapter shows, there are also times when it becomes important to consider other avenues of transfer.

Section 9.2 reviews some of the work we have done on transfer in the domain of text editing. This provides some of the clearest evidence for the identical-productions theory of transfer. The declarative component in this domain is minor, reflecting the rather insubstantial intellectual content of text editing. Section 9.3 reviews some of the research in Singley (1986) on the topic of transfer in calculus, where there is evidence for both declarative and procedural transfer. The next chapter provides evidence for further avenues of transfer in the ACT-R theory.

This chapter, like the previous one, does not rest on the specifics of the ACT-R theory. This research was originally done as a test of the ACT* theory and would be consistent with numerous (but not all) other production-system theories; the predictions tested do not apply to all theories or, indeed, to all production-rule theories. In particular, the predictions conflict with much common wisdom in their claims (a) that productions are the units in which to predict

---

[2]Thorndike contrasted his view with the *doctrine of formal discipline* (Angell, 1908; Pillsbury, 1908; Woodrow, 1927), which claimed that studying other-worldly subjects, such as Latin and geometry, was of significant value because it served to discipline the mind. This contrast, between general and specific transfer, is still with us: See Singley and Anderson (1989) for a review.

not only will the unit nodes in these traces
accrue strength with days of practice, but also

the element nodes will accrue strength. As will

be seen, this power function prediction

corresponds to the data about practice. A set of

experiments was conducted to test the prediction

about a power-law increase in *the* strength with

extensive practice. In one experiment subjects

studied subject-verb-object sentences of the form

(The lawyer hated the doctor). After studying
these sentences they were transferred to a
~~furthermore, the thought prevents the study~~

sentence recognition paradigm in which they had to

discriminate these sentences from foil ~~by the mind~~

sentences made of the same words as the *target* ~~illustrates~~

sentence but in new combinations. There were 25 days of

tests and hence practice. Each day subjects were tested

on each sentence 12 times (in one group) or 24

times in the other group. There was no difference

FIG. 9.1. Sample page of corrections.

transfer, and (b) that the declarative origins of these skills can, frequently, be ignored.[3]

9.2 TEXT EDITING: EVIDENCE FOR IDENTICAL PRODUCTIONS

9.2.1 Task Analysis

Figure 9.1 illustrates the kind of material that served as the basis for our work on text editing. It is a page from a draft of Anderson, 1983a, on which handwritten corrections have been made. The task was to use a text editor (or word processor) to make these corrections to a computer file holding the text. This

---

[3]The HS production-system architecture of Ohlsson and Rees (1991) is one embodiment of the common wisdom. In contrast to ACT-R, it holds that production rules are under the continuous influence of declarative knowledge.

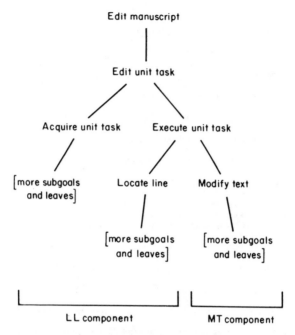

FIG. 9.2.   The top-level goal structure of text editing.

is a task which tens of thousands of people do every day. Text editing is a behavior that has received a fair amount of study in cognitive science. One very important development in this area was the proposal of the GOMS (Goals, Operators, Methods, and Selection) model of text editing by Card, Moran, and Newell (1983). It identified text editing as a fairly routine cognitive skill that is organized into unit tasks, where one unit task is associated with each of the edits to be performed. A goal structure is organized around the unit tasks, and each unit task is decomposed into subgoals and these into subgoals until a level is reached for which direct actions exist.

Figure 9.2 illustrates the top structure of a unit task. It divided into the subgoals of acquiring the unit task (i.e., encoding it from the paper) and executing it. To execute a unit task one must locate where the edits are to be made and then modify the text. Below these goals are more specific subgoals concerned with each particular edit. Card et al. did not cast their GOMS model as a set of production rules, but we and others (e.g., Polson & Kieras, 1985) have done so. The GOMS model provides a useful reference for guiding production-rule models for studying transfer in text editing. Without it there would be a danger of fashioning our production rules to match the results on transfer. Since the GOMS model predates these transfer analyses, we are safe.[4]

---

[4]The GOMS model itself does not identify the units in which to analyze transfer. This is why a production-system translation is necessary.

We looked at the learning and transfer among three text editors that were current at the time we did the study. Two are line editors, called Ed and Edt, and the other is a screen-based editor, called Emacs. Emacs continues to enjoy some popularity, but line editors have passed on; we will see why. Subjects were taught a subset of locative commands for achieving the location goals and mutative commands for achieving the modification goals. They are displayed in Table 9.1.

Although Ed and Edt have different command names, their underlying logics are quite similar; the logic underlying Emacs, however, is quite different. This means that, in terms of a production-rule analysis, there are many similar productions underlying Ed and Edt, but there are few in common with Emacs. Thus, we would expect a great deal more transfer between Ed and Edt than from either of these to Emacs.

We developed a set of 107 production rules capable of simulating editing in these three editors (for details, see Singley & Anderson, 1989). The following is an example of a production rule that spans all text editors:

IF   the goal is to execute-unit-task
THEN set as subgoals to
        1. locate line
        2. modify text

The following is an example of a production rule that applies to both line editors:

IF   the goal is to specify the second argument to the substitution command and the modification is the insertion of a word or string of words
THEN pad the insertion with a space on the end

Our general expectation was that there would be transfer among the text editors to the degree that they shared productions. The first experiment was an attempt to show this. The second experiment was concerned with a curious prediction of this approach: that there are strong limits on the kind of negative transfer that can occur among skills.

9.2.2 Experiment 1: Positive Transfer

Subjects were recruited from a local secretarial school. They were divided into six groups; the conditions are defined in Table 9.2. The subjects had no prior experience with text editing or computers. The groups were balanced on measures of typing speed and spatial reasoning, both of which have been shown to predict text-editing performance (Gomez, Egan, & Bowers, 1986). One group practiced Emacs for 6 days; it is referred to as the one-editor group. A second

TABLE 9.1
Command Summary for the Three Editors

Command Type	Editor	Command	Action
Locative	Ed	1.$p	prints all lines of the file
		3p	prints the third line
		p	prints the current line
		.=	prints the line number of the current line
		RETURN	prints the line following the current line
	Edt	t whole	prints all lines of the file
		t 'dog'	prints the first line following the current line that contains dog
		t - 'dog'	prints the first line before the current line that contains dog
		t	prints the current line
		DELETE	prints the line following the current line
	Emacs	$\uparrow f^a$	moves cursor forward one character
		$]f^b$	moves cursor forward one word
		$\uparrow b$	moves cursor backward one character
		$]b$	moves cursor backward one word
		$\uparrow a$	moves cursor to beginning of line
		$\uparrow e$	moves cursor to end of line
		$\uparrow p$	moves cursor to previous line
		$\uparrow n$	moves cursor to next line
Mutative	Ed	.a	inserts lines after the current line (type '.' to exit the insert mode)
		.d	deletes the current line
		.c	replaces the current line (type '.' to exit the insert mode)
		s/a/b/p	substitutes the first occurrence of 'a' with 'b' on the current line
	Edt	i	inserts lines after the current line (type $\uparrow z$ to exit the insert mode)
		d	deletes the current line
		r	replaces the current line (type $\uparrow z$ to exit the insert mode)
		s/a/b	substitutes the first occurrence of 'a' with 'b' on the current line
	Emacs	$\uparrow d$	deletes the character marked by the cursor
		$]d$	deletes the word marked by the cursor
		DELETE	deletes the character to the left of the cursor
		$\uparrow k$	deletes from the current cursor position to the end of the line
		a	inserts the character 'a' at the current cursor position (Emacs is in insert mode by default)

[a] $\uparrow$ denotes a Control (Ctrl) character.
[b]] denotes an Escape (Esc) character.

TABLE 9.2
Conditions in the Two Experiments on Text Editing

	Days 1 & 2	Days 3 & 4	Days 5 & 6
Experiment 1			
One editor	Emacs	Emacs	Emacs
Two editors	Ed	Ed	Emacs
	Edt	Edt	Emacs
Three editors	Ed	Edt	Emacs
	Edt	Ed	Emacs
Typing Control	Type	Type	Emacs
Experiment 2			
Negative Transfer	Emacs	Perverse Emacs	Emacs

group practiced Ed for 4 days and then learned and practiced Emacs for the last 2 days. A third group practiced Edt for the first 4 days and then transferred to Emacs for the last 2 days. Groups 2 and 3 are referred to as the two-editor groups. A fourth group practiced Ed for 2 days, Edt for 2 more, and Emacs for the last 2. A fifth group practiced Edt for 2 days, Ed for 2 more, and Emacs for the last 2. These groups are called the three-editor groups. Finally, a typing control group practiced retyping the edited pages for 4 days, and then worked in Emacs for the last 2 days. Note that all groups worked in Emacs for the last 2 days of the experiment.

Subjects worked 3 hours a day for each of 6 successive days, starting on a Monday and ending on a Saturday. At the beginning of each odd day (when a new editor might be introduced), they were given a short introduction to a minimum set of commands for each editor. The rest of the time they practiced editing a series of 18-line pages, each of which contained six edits to be performed. The major dependent variable was a modified time-per-edit, which combined both speed and errors. Letting T be the time to perform the six edits on a page, and E be the number incorrectly performed, the derived measure T' was:

$$T' = \frac{T}{6}\left(1 + \frac{E}{6}\right) \tag{9.1}$$

The results were basically the same whether number of errors was corrected or not, but they proved to be more stable (as determined by the ratio of the variance of an effect to error variance) when measured by the corrected formula, T'.

The results are presented in Fig. 9.3 in terms of corrected time to perform an edit. The first, theoretically uninteresting, thing to note is that Emacs was

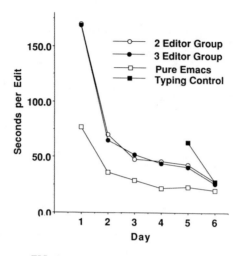

FIG. 9.3.   Transfer among text editors.

much more efficient than the line editors; that is, on Day 1, those in the one-editor group were much faster (using Emacs) than those in the other groups, who were using line editors. The second, and more significant, observation is that there was virtually no difference between the two- and three-editor groups. In particular, on Day 3, when the three-editor subjects were transferring to a new editor, they were almost as fast as the two-editor subjects, who were using that same editor for the third day. Thus, the results indicate almost total positive transfer, as predicted.

In contrast, when the line-editor groups transferred to Emacs on Day 5, they were at a considerable disadvantage compared to the subjects who had been practicing Emacs all along. Still, they were faster than the one-editor (i.e., pure Emacs) subjects were on Day 1. Although Emacs had little in common with the other editors, subjects in all groups were learning to decipher and perform the indicated edits, which was one basis for transfer. Consistent with this interpretation, the control group, which spent 4 days simply retyping an edited text, demonstrated a fair amount of transfer to Emacs. Presumably, this group was also learning how to interpret edits marked on the page.

By looking at the timing of the sequence of keystrokes, one can identify long pauses, during which subjects were presumably planning, and bursts of typing, during which subjects were presumably executing a plan. We, therefore, did an analysis of the data in which we classified any inter-keystroke interval greater than 2 sec as planning. Most of the learning and transfer was due to a decrease in the planning times. *Execution time* was defined as the time left over after the planning times were subtracted out. The actual time per keystroke in the execution phase did not decrease over the experiment, although there was some reduction in the number of keystrokes per edit, reflecting the acquisition of more efficient procedures. This is exactly the pattern we expected. What was being learned were the higher level operations that organize the text editing. The actual execution of the text-editing skill reflected existing typing procedures, which were already well learned in this population.

Thus, a production-system analysis does predict the pattern of transfer in this experiment. Quite independently, Kieras and Bovair (1986) and Polson and Kieras (1985) achieved similar success using a production-system analysis to predict transfer among text editors and other sets of skills. In Section 9.2.4 we consider how well the exact amounts of transfer can be predicted by counting overlapping productions. First, however, we describe Experiment 2.

9.2.3 Experiment 2: Negative Transfer?

It would seem that the ACT-R theory implies that it is impossible to have negative transfer between two skills. The worst possible relationship between two cognitive skills would seem to be their having no productions in common, so that learning of the second would proceed as if the first had not been learned.

Under closer inspection, there *is* room in the ACT-R theory for negative transfer. One possibility is that productions optimal for one skill might transfer to another skill where they are no longer optimal. One might argue that the Einstellung effect (Luchins, 1942) is an instance of this. The *Einstellung effect* refers to a situation in which a subject continues to use a strategy when it is no longer appropriate. An everyday example is one where someone is entering products into a calculator like 436 × 326 and then enters 2 × 200, which can be more quickly done in one's head. What is happening here is not a lack of full transfer of productions from one task to another. Rather, it is perfect transfer. It is simply the case that the knowledge being transferred is not optimal. A more extreme version of this is when the knowledge being transferred is not just non-optimal but is, in fact, wrong, as when Americans find themselves driving on the wrong side of the road in England.

Another way to get negative transfer is to have competition among productions in pattern matching. The assumption in chapter 3 was that productions competed for retrieval of chunks from working memory (although the details of this competition were not developed): A strong production that is partially matched may temporarily gain precedence over a weaker production and, so, slow down its matching. Eventually the weaker production will be matched and recognized as more appropriate, but this will have been delayed. Thus, rather than the inappropriate behavior taking over, there can be a decrement in the performance of the appropriate behavior, typically manifested as a slowing in response time. This is typically what happens to Americans driving in England.

We thought it would be interesting to create a situation in which the two skills studied for transfer were highly similar in logical structure and so would be expected to display high positive transfer on an identical-productions view-point, but which would involve some competing productions, leading to some slowing of production firing. We created what would be a classic interference design in the verbal-learning domain. We created an editor called Perverse Emacs, which was just like Emacs except that the assignment of keys to function was permuted. For instance, in Emacs Ctrl-D erases a letter, Esc-D erases a word, and Ctrl-N goes down a line; in Perverse Emacs Ctrl-D goes down a line, and Esc-R erases a letter. If the functionalities are considered to be the stimuli and the keys are the responses, this is an A–B, A–Br interference paradigm, which produces maximal interference in paired-associate learning (Postman, 1971).

Two groups of subjects were compared. They were recruited from the same population as Experiment 1. One spent 6 days with Emacs; the other spent their first 2 days with Emacs, the next 2 days with Perverse Emacs, and the final 2 days with Emacs again. The results of this experiment are shown in Fig. 9.4. Throughout the experiment, even on the first 2 days, during which both groups of subjects were learning Emacs, the Perverse Emacs subjects performed worse. However, the only day their performance was significantly worse was the third, when they transferred to Perverse Emacs. That difference largely disappeared by the fourth day, when they were still working with Perverse Emacs. Compared with their performance on Day 1 on Emacs, there was large

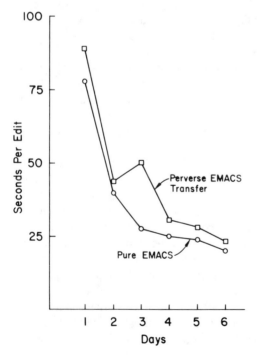

FIG. 9.4.   Transfer between Emacs and Perverse Emacs.

positive transfer on Day 3 to Perverse Emacs, reflecting the production overlap. The difference between the two groups on Day 3 reflects the cost of learning the specific rules of Perverse Emacs. When the transfer subjects went back
to Emacs on Day 5, they picked up at the same point on the learning curve
as if they had stayed with Emacs. (Although they were slower than the pure
Emacs subjects on Days 5 and 6, they were no slower than they were on Day
2, when they had last used Emacs.) This is because they had been practicing
in Perverse Emacs largely the same productions that they would use in regular
Emacs.

Our finding of no negative transfer in this experiment strikes many as counter-
intuitive. Fortunately, a more recent study by Polson, Muncher, and Kieras
(1987) provides further support for the conclusion of no negative transfer. As
in our experiment, they looked at transfer between two editors that differed
only in having the functionality of the keys permuted. They found no statistically significant difference between subjects who had to transfer between these
two editors and subjects who continued to use the same editor—an even stronger
result than we obtained. Although data at this level give no evidence for negative transfer, the next section provides a more fine-grained analysis that does
find some evidence for negative transfer in our data.

Experienced Emacs users who piloted the Perverse Emacs felt that they
were suffering substantial negative transfer, but this simply shows how such
self-impressions can be misleading. Compared to their facility in Emacs, they
performed poorly in Perverse Emacs, and occasionally an Emacs keying sequence
intruded. Compared to the novice subjects in the experiment, however, they
performed very well, reflecting the benefit of their many years of Emacs experience. Nevertheless, they did not compare their behavior in Perverse Emacs
to that of a beginner; they could only compare it to their highly experienced
behavior in Emacs.

9.2.4 Production-Rule Analysis

Our underlying assumption was that the amount of transfer between text editors is a function of the amount of overlap among the skills in terms of the number of shared productions. To test this assumption more precisely, measures
of observed transfer and of amount of production overlap were needed. The
following provides a measure of percent transfer occurring between two skills
relative to the maximum amount of transfer that could occur:

$$\text{Percent transfer} = \frac{OT - TT}{OT - LT} \times 100 \qquad (9.2)$$

where OT is the original time it took subjects to perform the skill, TT is the
time it took to perform the skill after transfer, and LT is the time it took subjects who did not transfer but continued to learn in the same condition. To

apply it to Fig. 9.3, subjects originally took about 80 sec per edit in Emacs; when they transferred to Emacs after 4 days of using a line editor, they took 45 sec. Thus, $OT - TT = 80 - 45 = 35$. In contrast, after 4 days of doing Emacs, they took 30 sec on the fifth day. Thus, $OT - LT = 80 - 30 = 50$ and the percent transfer is $35/50 \times 100 = 70\%$.

To provide more refined data on transfer, the time associated with a unit task was broken into two components: the time until the locate-line goal had been achieved (this included acquire-unit-task and locate-line goals in Fig. 9.2), and the time from then until the unit task had been completed (this included modify-text in Fig. 9.2). The first time was called LL and the second MT.

To get a measure of predicted transfer, we tabulated the number of production rules that the various editors had in common and those that were unique. These results are summarized in Table 9.3 for the LL and MT components separately (see Singley & Anderson, 1989, for further details). There are productions shared by all editors (general), productions shared by the two line editors, Ed and Edt (line, in Table 9.3), productions shared by the two screen editors, Emacs and Perverse Emacs (screen, in Table 9.3), and productions unique to each of four editors. Rather than just tabulate the number of productions, we calculated the average frequency of their firings during two pages of edits, which is reported in Table 9.3. To predict the transfer from any editor designated as Editor 1 to another designated Editor 2, we calculated the proportion of firings in Editor 2 shared by Editor 1 to the total firings. So, for instance, consider transfer from Ed to Edt in LL. There were 8.0 production firings, on average, common to all editors during the LL segment of an edit, 4.6 common to line editors, and 6.2 unique to Edt. Thus, the predicted transfer was:

TABLE 9.3
Categories of Rules and Their Frequency in Two Pages of Edits

Component	Category	Frequency
LL	General	8.0
	Line	4.6
	Screen	7.5
	Ed	4.1
	Edt	6.2
	Emacs	5.2
	Perverse Emacs	5.2
MT	General	2.7
	Line	8.8
	Screen	5.8
	Ed	1.9
	Edt	1.2
	Emacs	1.5
	Perverse Emacs	1.5

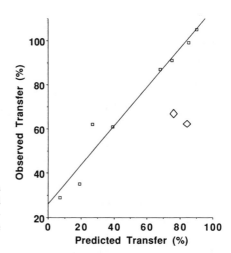

FIG. 9.5. Relationship between predicted transfer and observed transfer. The squares are from Experiment 1; the two diamonds are from Experiment 2.

$$Transfer = \frac{8.0 + 4.6}{8.0 + 4.6 + 6.2} \times 100 = 68\% \qquad (9.3)$$

For Experiment 1, there were production overlap measures for LL time and MT time for four transfer conditions: Ed to Edt, Edt to Ed, line (Ed plus Edt) to Emacs, and typing to Emacs.[5] Corresponding to these eight production overlap measures were eight observed proportion transfers, calculated by Equation 9.2. Figure 9.5 plots the eight observed proportions against the eight production overlap measures. The correlation is .98. The equation relating transfer to overlap is:

$$Transfer = .26 + .88 \; Overlap \qquad (9.4)$$

The linear relationship between the overlap measure and the proportion of transfer is quite stunning. Theoretically, the ideal result would be one in which transfer is identical to overlap, that is, $Transfer = Overlap$. Singley and Anderson (1989) suggested we actually underrepresented the common productions involved in reading the edits in the text and interpreting what they mean, thereby overestimating the difference between the editors.

The two diamonds in Fig. 9.5 represent the transfer for LL and MT times from Emacs to Perverse Emacs. Note that these two times are distinctly below the curve relating the measures for Experiment 2. This might reflect the competition in pattern matching among the similar productions for the two editors.

We observed the importation of certain non-optimal procedures (Einstellung-type interference) from Emacs to Perverse Emacs. For instance, in Emacs one

---

[5]There was a small overlap between typing and text editing because of productions responsible for interpreting the edits on a page.

advances a character by depressing the Control mode key and hitting F. This makes it fairly efficient to move many characters by holding the Control key down and rapidly hitting Fs. The other alternative is to use the Esc-F sequence, which is a two-key sequence for advancing one word at a time. Because it requires two keys, this command offers little advantage. Given the rebinding of keys in Perverse Emacs, however, it took a two-key Esc-R to move one character but a mode-key Ctrl-R to move one word. This made it very inefficient to move forward a character at a time. Still, subjects coming from Emacs continued this inefficient behavior.

Despite such quirks, in general there is a lawful relationship between measures of production overlap and amount of transfer observed among the text editors in these studies. Because of the inadequacies in our model in how edits are read and interpreted, it is not possible to judge whether the exact form of this relationship is what would be predicted by the ACT-R theory; however, it does give strong evidence for the relevance of the production rule as the unit in which to analyze transfer. There may be interference among similar productions, which shows up as a small increase in time, but, when we look at aggregate scores, it is overwhelmed by the positive transfer.

9.3 CALCULUS: DECLARATIVE AND PROCEDURAL TRANSFER

The research effort just described focused only on production rules in performing an analysis of transfer. These production rules are derived from declarative knowledge, but the skill is practiced so much that the declarative origins become almost irrelevant. This section on transfer in calculus presents some transfer data that can also be understood solely in terms of productions, but it also considers other transfer data that require appreciating the declarative origins of the knowledge. We discuss two different procedures that have their origins in the same declarative knowledge. Specifically, we look at the separate skills of deciding when to select calculus operators and deciding how to apply them, and show how initial practice of one procedure strengthens and debugs the declarative knowledge to facilitate acquisition of the second procedure.

The data reviewed here are taken from Singley's (1986) dissertation. Section 9.3.1 presents the first experiment, which showed a pattern of transfer and lack of transfer that is entirely interpretable at the production level. Section 9.3.2 then describes the second experiment, which displays transfer through shared declarative knowledge.

9.3.1 Use-Specificity of Procedural Transfer

The Experimental Situation. Figure 9.6 shows the type of calculus problem Singley presented to his subjects in the first experiment. Each contained a problem statement, describing some situation that the students had

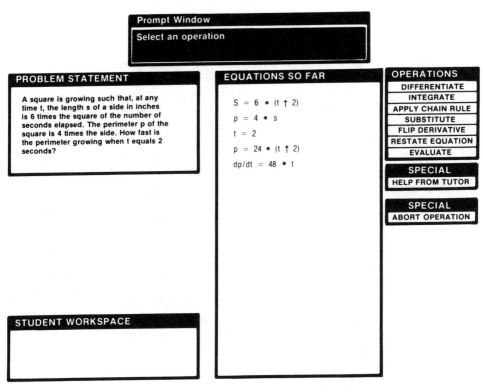

FIG. 9.6. Configuration of the calculus tutor interface.

to convert into a set of equations. These equations would be displayed in the *equations so far* window. The equations that translate the problem in Fig. 9.6 are:

$$s = 6*(t^2)$$
$$p = 4*s$$
$$t = 2$$

Although there were some interesting results involving this equation-writing phase, we ignore them here and look, rather, at the next phase, which involved solving these equations. After translating the problem into equations, subjects had to perform various operations on the equations to transform them into a solution. To do this, the subject selected the operation from the menu on the right and the equations to which to apply this operation. Then the subject had to type the equation that would result from the application of this operator to the equation or equations. In this example, the subject chose to substitute the second equation into the first and got:

$$p = 24*(t^2)$$

After this the subject chose, as a separate operation, to differentiate the equation and typed:

$$dp/dt = 48*t$$

By substituting the third equation into this, the student got the answer, which is that the perimeter is growing at 96 inches per second. Different problems had different starting equations and so had to be solved by different methods.

Thirty-six high school juniors and seniors were selected from a local private girls' school. All of the subjects were taking precalculus, but none had taken calculus nor received any instruction about derivatives.

The experiment was conducted over 3 days, for 2 hours each day. On Day 1, subjects read an introductory text that presented in very direct terms the prerequisite calculus knowledge for solving related-rates problems. The seven operators in Fig. 9.6 were introduced, and the students were required to apply these operators to a series of problems within the tutor interface. Each operator was practiced five times. On Days 2 and 3, subjects were given related-rates problems to solve. There were two experimental conditions, depending on what happened on Day 2. In the selection condition, subjects had to figure out what operators to apply and when to apply them. In the no-selection condition, they were told in a separate window (the prompt window in Fig. 9.6) what operators to select and what equations to apply them to, but they had to figure out themselves what the results of the applications would be. On Day 3, subjects in both groups had to both select the operators and apply them. Thus, on Day 2 the selection subjects had to figure out both when to select the operators and how to apply them, whereas the no-selection subjects just had to figure out the application. If subjects were unable to figure out what to select next or how to apply an operator, the tutor told them.

Results.   Subjects' performance was analyzed with respect to (a) their success at selecting operators and (b) their success at applying the operators. Table 9.4 displays the performance of subjects in terms of mean time to perform operator selection and mean number of unnecessary operators selected per

TABLE 9.4
Operator Selection Results on Both Days
of Problem Solving in the Calculus Experiment:
Time per Selection and Mean Number of Extra Moves

Day	Selection on Day 2	No Selection on Day 2
2	34.9 sec (3.4 moves)	—
3	18.6 sec (2.6 moves)	33.0 sec (3.4 moves)

TABLE 9.5
Time (sec) per Operator Application
on All Three Days of the Calculus Experiment

Day	Selection on Day 2	No Selection on Day 2
1	78.7	83.7
2	43.2	43.8
3	26.3	27.7

problem. Subjects who practiced selection on Day 2 showed considerable improvement on Day 3. Subjects who practiced only application on Day 2, however, were no different when they first tried selection on Day 3 from the other subjects when they first tried selection on Day 2.

Table 9.5 shows mean time to perform an operator application. Both groups of subjects showed steady and substantial improvement over the 3 days. The group that was also practicing operator selection on Day 2 showed no advantage on application on Day 3.

This pattern of behavior is predicted from the assumption of the use specificity of production rules. Even though both selecting a calculus operation and applying it require knowledge of that calculus operation, subjects use that knowledge differently, and so compile different production rules for the two tasks. Singley and Anderson (1989), for instance, considered use of the chain rule in application and selection. The chain rule in calculus says:

$$\text{if } dz/dy = a \text{ and } dy/dx = b \text{ then } dz/dx = ab$$

One of a number of production rules that underlies application of the chain rule in the Singley and Anderson analysis is:

IF   the goal is to apply the chain rule
         and the first equation it is to be applied to is of the form $dy/? = ?$
THEN the result of the chain rule will be $dy/? = ?$

where $?$ indicates that it does not matter what occurs in that position. This rule specifies how to set the ordinate of the derivative in an application of the rule.

The following is one of the production rules that occurs in the Singley and Anderson model of selection:

IF   the goal is to apply the chain rule to derive an equation of the form $dy/? = ?$
THEN set as a subgoal to find an equation of the form $dy/? = ?$
         to be the first input to the chain rule

This rule specifies what kind of input to look for in an application of the chain rule. Both rules embody the knowledge that the ordinate of the derivative of the first equation that is input to the chain rule determines the ordinate of the derivative that is the output of the chain rule. These rules, however, switch which part of the knowledge appears in the condition of the production rule and which part of the knowledge appears in the action of the production rule. One rule is acquired in selection, and the other is acquired in application. Practicing application will not cause the selection rule to be acquired. Therefore, subjects have to start from scratch when they come to doing selection.

It is a striking result that there is no transfer between the rules even though they have similar components. One might well imagine representational systems in which transfer would be a function of degree of similarity, but it appears that if the production rules are not identical there is no transfer.

This replicates a pattern of use specificity of procedural knowledge reported in other chapters. In LISP there was failure to transfer from coding to evaluation or vice versa (Table 2.2), and in geometry (chapter 8) there was failure to transfer uses of the same geometry rule to different contexts (Fig. 8.7). This lack of transfer occurs because multiple production rules are being compiled from a common declarative source, and each rule once compiled is independent of the others. In the next experiment, we attempt to see if we can find some evidence for that common declarative source.

9.3.2 Flexibility of Declarative Transfer

There is a possibility for indirect transfer among different productions that share a common declarative origin. In the example of the previous section, for instance, a student might not really understand that the ordinate of the derivative of the output is the same as the ordinate of the derivative of the first input. This is a fault in the student's declarative knowledge. In learning to apply the chain rule, the student may correct this declarative fault and so be better prepared to learn to select the chain rule. Also, simply using this declarative knowledge in creating one rule will strengthen its representation and so facilitate its retrieval for creation of the other rule.

One might wonder why this transfer was not manifested in the previous experiment. This may have been because both groups of subjects had a first day of familiarization performing applications of the calculus operators. Perhaps this was enough for them to clear up any declarative difficulties and to be able to compile production rules, so that a second day of application training was of no further benefit in accomplishing transfer to selection. The benefit of this indirect declarative transfer should be complete early in the training, while the declarative knowledge is still being accessed (and consequently strengthened and corrected). Once the knowledge passes into correct production form, there should be no further benefit for the declarative representation.

On this analysis, then, the problem with the previous experiment was that it contrasted transfer to selection after 2 days' application practice with transfer after 1 day's practice, and what is needed is to contrast 1 day's application practice with none. This was the primary function of the next experiment. In addition, we wanted to look at transfer both from selection to application and from application to selection.

Method. The experiment used a 2 × 2 between-subjects design. The first factor was whether subjects received operator selection practice; the second factor was whether subjects received operator application practice. The subjects were 32 juniors and seniors from a local private girls' school; they were of similar background to the subjects in the first experiment. There were 8 subjects in each condition. Each one participated in the experiment for 2 days, with approximately 2 hours of work per day.

The experiment used the same interface as before, illustrated in Fig. 9.6. Subjects started with an initial set of equations that they had to solve for rate. Thus, this experiment bypassed the phase of extracting the equations from word problems that was used in the first experiment. In the condition in which subjects practiced both operator selection and operator application, they had to select the operators and the inputs to the operators and type out the result of each application. For those who practiced operator selection only, the result of the application was provided to them by the computer once they had indicated the operator and equation(s) to which it should apply. The result was presented to the students in the prompt window, and they had to type it into the student workspace window (see Fig. 9.6). In the condition in which the subjects only practiced application, the tutor told them which operation to select and what equations to apply it to, but they had to figure out the resulting equation. In the control condition, subjects practiced neither application nor selection: The tutor told them what operation to select, what equations to apply it to, and what equation to enter into the student workspace. Thus, in all conditions the subjects went through all the motions of solving the equations. The conditions differed in terms of what aspects of the problem solving were guided by the computer.

All subjects transferred from whatever condition they were in on Day 1 to the condition of having to do both selection and application on Day 2.

Results. Table 9.6 presents the results from the experiment for each of the 2 days in terms of mean time per selection. Subjects who were told which selections to make on Day 1 were, predictably, faster than those not told. What is a bit surprising is that those who did not have to perform their own applications on Day 1 were faster in selection on that day. It seems that having the application done by the computer made them more reckless, resulting in higher error rates in this condition (Singley, 1986).

The data from Day 2 show that either application or selection practice is beneficial in decreasing time to make a selection. There was no significant difference

TABLE 9.6
Time (in seconds) per Operator Selection on Days 1 and 2

a. Day 1

		Selection		
		yes	*no*	
Application	*yes*	39.1	16.1	27.6
	no	24.4	13.0	18.7
		31.8	14.6	

b. Day 2

		Selection		
		yes	*no*	
Application	*yes*	17.2	21.5	19.4
	no	18.4	41.8	30.1
		17.8	31.7	

Note. The four conditions refer to type of practice on Day 1; on Day 2 all subjects transferred to the yes–yes condition.

among the groups that had only application practice, only selection practice, or both, and all are quite superior to those who had neither sort of practice. Indeed, on Day 2 subjects who had neither selection nor application practice were no different from subjects on Day 1 who had to do both selection and application. Thus, there appears to be no transfer from the manual task of information entry to the problem-solving task of operator selection.

Table 9.7 presents the results for application in terms of mean time to perform an application. Again, on the first day, there are large and not surprising effects of having the computer give instructions on how to perform the application. There is no effect on application of having to perform selection. On Day 2, there is a large and significant effect of having practiced operator application on time to perform the application. The effect of operator selection on application is not as large, but subjects who practiced only operator selection were about 16 sec faster than subjects who practiced neither selection nor application, a statistically significant difference. Subjects who practiced only application were also about 16 sec faster than subjects who practiced only selection, suggesting that application practice transfers more to application than to selection.

According to Table 9.7, subjects with neither application nor selection practice were no different on Day 2 than subjects who had performed both selection

TABLE 9.7
Time (in seconds) per Operator Application on Days 1 and 2

a. Day 1

		Selection		
		yes	no	
Application	yes	74.2	83.3	78.8
	no	24.8	21.8	23.3
		49.5	52.5	

b. Day 2

		Selection		
		yes	no	
Application	yes	41.4	41.3	41.4
	no	57.9	74.1	66.0
		49.7	57.7	

Note. The four conditions refer to type of practice on Day 1; on Day 2 all subjects transferred to the yes–yes condition.

and application on Day 1. Once again, manual entry has no effect on an intellectual task.

The results in this experiment show effects of application practice on selection and selection practice on application. This, in combination with the lack of effect in the previous experiment, indicates that early practice of one use of knowledge transfers to another use of the knowledge, but further practice of one use has no benefit for the other use. This is consistent with the hypothesis that the basis for transfer across different uses of the same knowledge is early access to the declarative knowledge. The current experiment did find evidence for a certain asymmetry, in that application practice has large positive effects on both selection and application, whereas the effects of selection practice on application are somewhat weaker. Singley and Anderson (1989), in a detailed analysis of how the knowledge is used in both selection and application, demonstrated that application makes more thorough use of the declarative knowledge.

9.4 CONCLUSION

The general conclusions of this research are quite supportive for a theory like ACT-R, although as noted, they are hardly unique to ACT-R. Transfer among skills can be predicted by counting up knowledge units, like ACT-R chunks and productions, and understanding the role they play in the target task. In the case of the text editing, this analysis was carried out in great quantitative detail by counting productions. In the calculus research, we were content with general qualitative results, but in many cases we predicted (and obtained) either no transfer or total transfer, which are strong qualitative predictions. Transfer does seem to occur in terms of the units envisioned in the theory.

Computer Programming
and Transfer

John R. Anderson, Fred Conrad, Albert T. Corbett,
Jon M. Fincham, Donn Hoffman, and Quanfeng Wu
Carnegie Mellon University

10.1 INTRODUCTION

The previous chapter described results largely consistent with the identical production theory of transfer. The skills being examined, however, were relatively simple and undemanding. This is certainly true of text editing, and although calculus problem solving can be quite demanding, what was taught in the experiment was only a fraction of what is involved in typical calculus problem solving. The question arises as to what we would find when we look at richer problem-solving skills.

This chapter focuses on computer programming, which is a rich and complex skill. The question of concern here is, What transfers from one programming language to another? We investigate transfer among three programming languages: Pascal, LISP, and Prolog. Sections 10.2 and 10.3 first consider transfer among the languages for subjects who are relative novices and are just learning these languages. Section 10.4 then considers subjects who are relative experts with the languages. This is a report of research in progress, and the conclusions are not final. The chapter serves to highlight the complexity of the transfer question. Section 10.3 shows a surprising lack of transfer by one measure, and Section 10.4 shows a rather substantial transfer by another measure.

Some of the data reported in this chapter come from a tutoring system for various programming languages that we started developing in 1989 (Anderson, Corbett, Fincham, Hoffman, & Pelletier, 1992). This multiple-languages tutoring system was developed on the MAC II, and is somewhat different than the other tutoring architectures described in chapters 7 and 8. Thus, the data constitute yet another test of the generality of the learning results over tutoring

TABLE 10.1
Curriculum

Prolog
  1. Basic Rules and Arithmetic
  2. Conditionality and Problem Decomposition
  3. Recursion
  4. List Processing

Pascal
  1. Programs and Arithmetic
  2. Conditionality and Problem Decomposition
  3. Iteration

LISP
  1. List Processing, Functions, and Arithmetic
  2. Conditionality and Problem Decomposition
  3. Recursion
  4. Iteration

---

architectures. We have implemented in the multiple-languages tutor the material in Table 10.1. We describe that tutoring architecture first and then describe the results on learning in LISP, Pascal, and Prolog.

10.1.1 Sample Interaction With the Pascal Tutor

The way one interacts with the various programming languages tutors is much the same; we illustrate it with respect to the Pascal tutor. Figure 10.1 shows the screen image as it first appears in a problem. In the upper left-hand window is the problem statement. Below it is the code window (both windows are scrollable). At the right top is the skill meter, which displays the student's progress on the various production rules that are being monitored for that lesson. The tutor has an algorithm for determining the student's progress on each rule in terms of a probability that he or she has mastered the rule. The bar graphs represent the individual's progress toward reaching the tutor's threshold for mastery. Below the skill meter is a menu system for entering various coding actions. Finally, at the bottom right, is a window for displaying messages to the student.

In the code window in Fig. 10.1, we see just the root node for the program, as the student is just beginning. The only way to expand that particular node is as a program, and this is the only option in the menu window. When that option is selected, the code is transformed to represent the standard program template. This step corresponds to a production in the ideal student model, but it is a production that has been mastered by the time the student reaches this point in the curriculum.

In Fig. 10.2 the program code is at a state further along, where the student

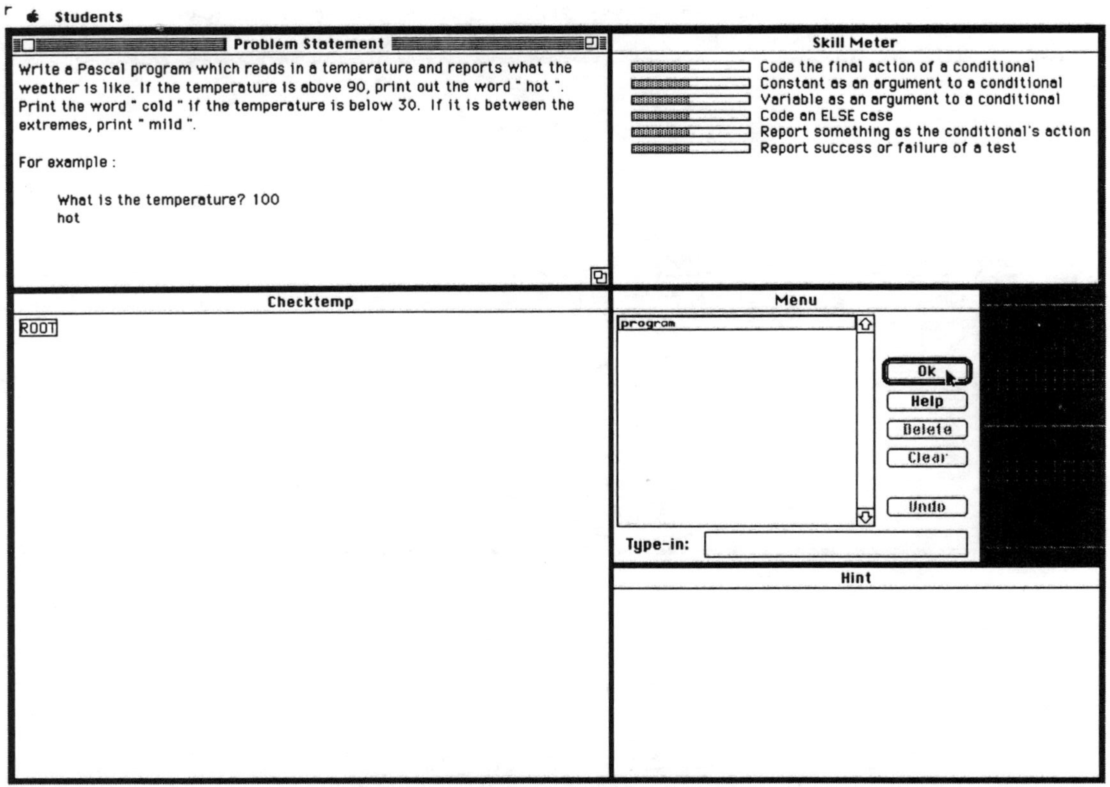

Problem Statement

Write a Pascal program which reads in a temperature and reports what the weather is like. If the temperature is above 90, print out the word " hot ". Print the word " cold " if the temperature is below 30. If it is between the extremes, print " mild ".

For example :

What is the temperature? 100
hot

Skill Meter

▨▨▨▨ Code the final action of a conditional
▨▨▨▨ Constant as an argument to a conditional
▨▨▨▨ Variable as an argument to a conditional
▨▨▨▨ Code an ELSE case
▨▨▨▨ Report something as the conditional's action
▨▨▨▨ Report success or failure of a test

Checktemp

ROOT

Menu

program

Ok
Help
Delete
Clear
Undo

Type-in:

Hint

FIG. 10.1. The screen image at the beginning of a Pascal problem.

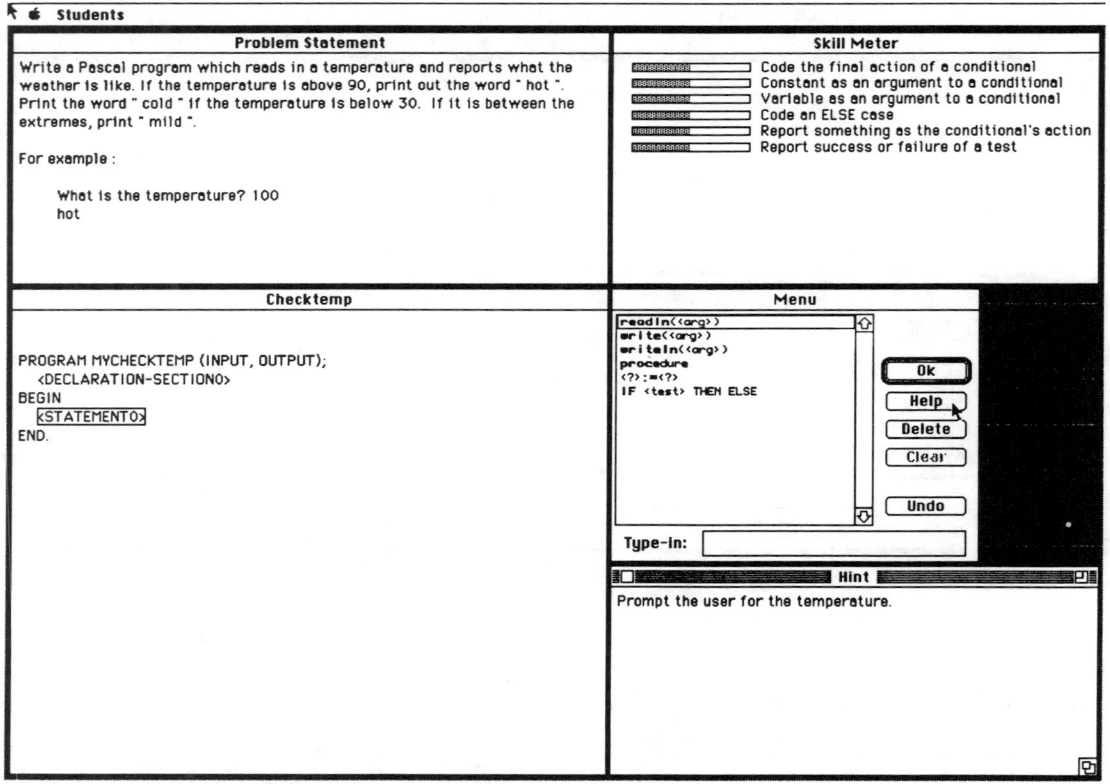

Problem Statement

Write a Pascal program which reads in a temperature and reports what the weather is like. If the temperature is above 90, print out the word " hot ". Print the word " cold " if the temperature is below 30. If it is between the extremes, print " mild ".

For example :

   What is the temperature? 100
   hot

Skill Meter

▭▭ Code the final action of a conditional
▭▭ Constant as an argument to a conditional
▭▭ Variable as an argument to a conditional
▭▭ Code an ELSE case
▭▭ Report something as the conditional's action
▭▭ Report success or failure of a test

Checktemp

```
PROGRAM MYCHECKTEMP (INPUT, OUTPUT);
<DECLARATION-SECTION>
BEGIN
   <STATEMENT0>
END.
```

Menu

```
readln(<arg>)
write(<arg>)
writeln(<arg>)
procedure
<?>:=<?>
IF <test> THEN ELSE
```

Ok Help Delete Clear Undo

Type-In:

Hint

Prompt the user for the temperature.

FIG. 10.2. The screen image near the beginning of a Pascal problem; the student has asked for help.

has entered the name of the program. The node corresponding to the first statement is highlighted in the code window, and in the menu window are all the ways the student can expand that particular node. The student has asked for help, so a message appears in the hint window: "Prompt the user for the temperature."

Figure 10.3 shows the screen at a still later stage. The student has written the code to prompt the user and to read in the temperature. He or she has then decided to expand the next statement as an if–then structure. The tutor has responded with a menu requesting that the student identify which case is to be coded first. This is done so that the tutor can keep track of the student's intentions and follow his or her code. Figure 10.4 shows the final state of the windows when the problem is solved.

The interactions between the student and tutor continue in this way as the student solves other problems by expanding nodes. By default the tutor selects the leftmost node to expand next, but the student can select to expand some other node. At each node the student can enter the code either by means of a menu selection or by actually typing the code (which is required for identifiers, such as TEMP). If the student is stuck, he or she can receive a series of successively stronger hints, up to being told exactly what to enter. (The hint in Fig. 10.2 is the first in that sequence of hints.) If the student's move is ambiguous, the tutor will present a disambiguation menu, as in Fig. 10.3.

The time from the selection of the node (by the tutor or student) to an action by the student (menu selection, type in, or request for help) is taken as the segment of time that corresponds to a production firing. The data that we present is the proportion of those segments for which subjects chose the right response; for those correct responses, we report the mean time taken by that segment.

10.2 THE CLASSROOM EXPERIMENT

We have two sets of data relating to transfer obtained with this tutoring interface. One is from a class that covered most of the curriculum described in Table 10.1, and so involved all three languages. The second involves a set of smaller scale laboratory experiments that looked at transfer between pairs of languages in a more limited way. The more extensively analyzed data set comes from the classroom. Before discussing any of the transfer data, we review in this section some of the basic results related to language learning derived from the classroom experiment. This will help establish that the behavior elicited with the new tutor is similar to that observed with the earlier LISP tutor.

The classroom data were obtained from courses taught in the Fall of 1990 and the Spring of 1991. The Fall course (which yielded nearly complete data from 26 students) involved the first three units of Prolog in Table 10.1, followed by the first two units of Pascal, and then the first three units of LISP. The Spring

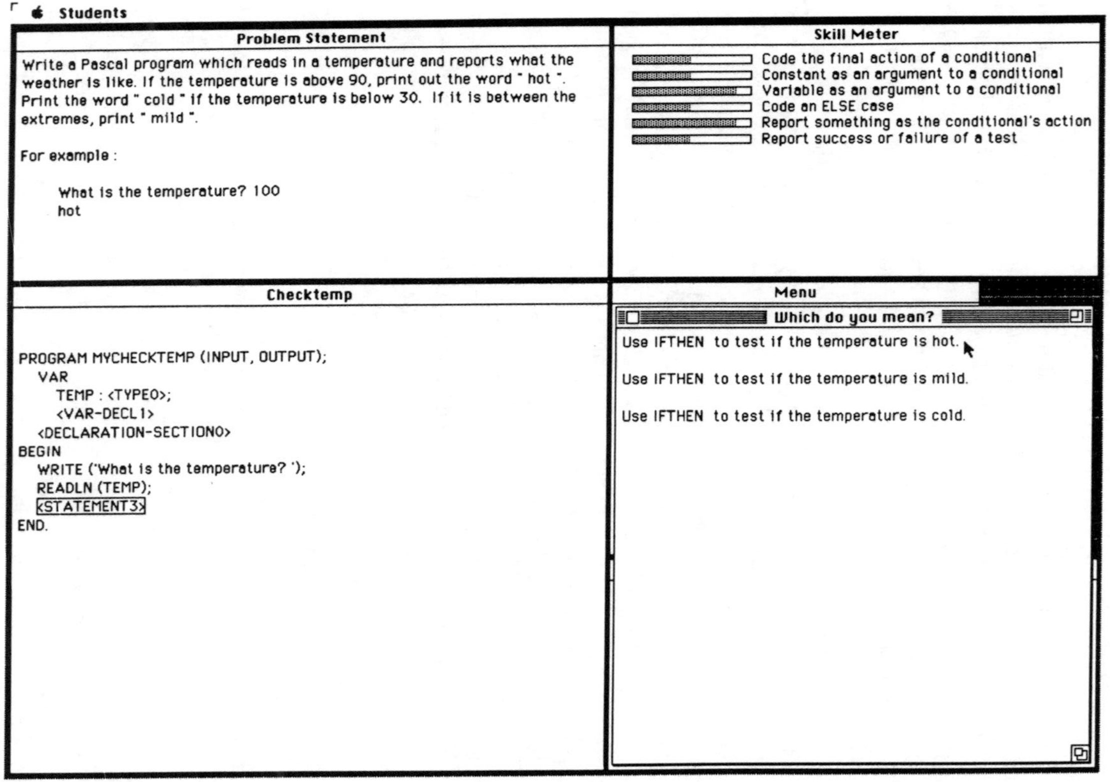

┌ **Students**

Problem Statement

Write a Pascal program which reads in a temperature and reports what the weather is like. If the temperature is above 90, print out the word " hot ". Print the word " cold " if the temperature is below 30. If it is between the extremes, print " mild ".

For example :

What is the temperature? 100
hot

Checktemp

```
PROGRAM MYCHECKTEMP (INPUT, OUTPUT);
  VAR
    TEMP : <TYPE0>;
    <VAR-DECL1>
  <DECLARATION-SECTION0>
BEGIN
  WRITE ("What is the temperature? ");
  READLN (TEMP);
  <STATEMENT3>
END.
```

Skill Meter

▭ Code the final action of a conditional
▭ Constant as an argument to a conditional
▭ Variable as an argument to a conditional
▭ Code an ELSE case
▭ Report something as the conditional's action
▭ Report success or failure of a test

Menu

Which do you mean?

Use IFTHEN to test if the temperature is hot. ⬏

Use IFTHEN to test if the temperature is mild.

Use IFTHEN to test if the temperature is cold.

FIG. 10.3.   The screen image in the middle of a Pascal problem; a disambiguation menu is being presented.

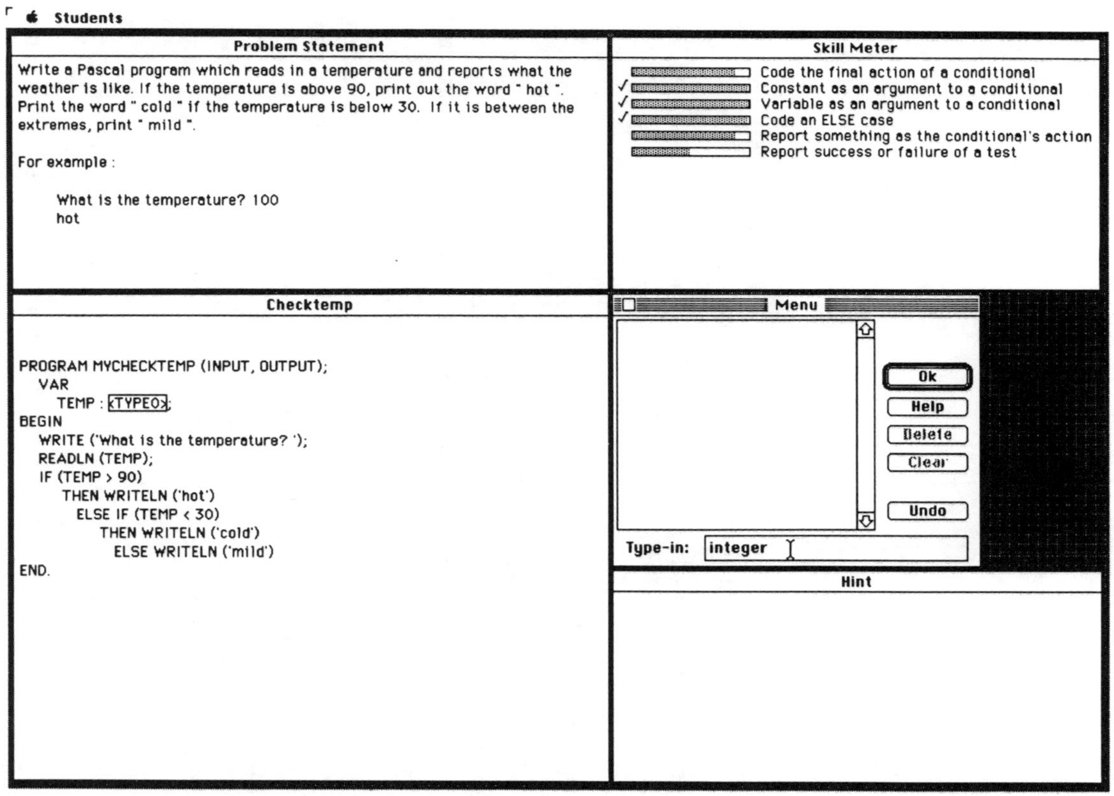

Problem Statement

Write a Pascal program which reads in a temperature and reports what the weather is like. If the temperature is above 90, print out the word " hot ". Print the word " cold " if the temperature is below 30. If it is between the extremes, print " mild ".

For example :

What is the temperature? 100
hot

Checktemp

```
PROGRAM MYCHECKTEMP (INPUT, OUTPUT);
   VAR
      TEMP : TYPED;
BEGIN
   WRITE ('What is the temperature? ');
   READLN (TEMP);
   IF (TEMP > 90)
      THEN WRITELN ('hot')
      ELSE IF (TEMP < 30)
         THEN WRITELN ('cold')
         ELSE WRITELN ('mild')
END.
```

Skill Meter

✓ Code the final action of a conditional
✓ Constant as an argument to a conditional
✓ Variable as an argument to a conditional
  Code an ELSE case
  Report something as the conditional's action
  Report success or failure of a test

Menu

Ok
Help
Delete
Clear
Undo

Type-in: integer

Hint

FIG. 10.4.   The screen image as the student enters the last element of code for the Pascal problem.

211

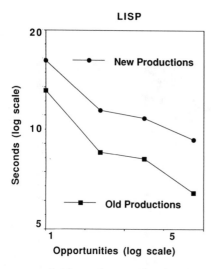

FIG. 10.5.   Time measures for LISP productions as a function of within-lesson practice.

course (with nearly complete data from 23 students) included three units of LISP, followed by two units of Pascal, and three units of Prolog.

10.2.1 Learning Curves

For each language, we calculated learning curves based on accuracy and latency, just as was done for the data from the LISP tutor in chapter 7. A general feature of such a naturalistic curriculum is that all productions do not occur with equal frequency. This means that the number of observations for the nth learning opportunity of a production drops off rapidly as n gets large. Therefore, as in previous graphs, the data presented are aggregated over multiple learning opportunities. Data are plotted for points 1, 2, the average of 3 and 4, and the average of 5 through 8. Only a few productions contributed observations for more than eight learning opportunities.

Figures 10.5 and 10.6 present the data from the LISP tutor, plotted separately for new productions and for productions that had occurred in previous lessons. The results for LISP are similar to those obtained in the examinations of LISP learning in chapter 7.[1] Thus, LISP learning does not depend on the exact nature of the tutor interface or, in this case, the exact curriculum being taught. One result that appears to be discrepant is that, compared to Fig. 7.2, here old productions showed almost the same amount of improvement as a function of within-lesson opportunity as did new productions. The lessons in this cur-

---

[1]The error rates in Fig. 10.6 may seem high even at the end, but it must be kept in mind that this includes performance on the required problems only. Students who were having difficulties were given additional problems, which served to lower their error rates before they went onto the next lesson.

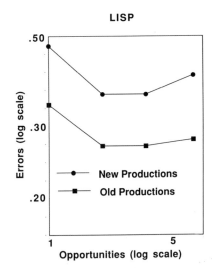

FIG. 10.6.   Error measure for LISP productions as a function of within-lesson practice.

riculum were further apart (almost 2 weeks vs. 1 week, in the earlier study), and the enhancement of productions on repeated use may reflect a beneficial reminding effect.[2]

Figures 10.7 and 10.8 show the learning curves for the Pascal tutor. The results are similar, qualitatively, to what was obtained with the LISP tutor, although the students were a bit faster and more accurate in Pascal. Students did comment that they found the Pascal material the easiest. Finally, Figs. 10.9 and 10.10 present the Prolog material. Again, the same qualitative patterns appear, with Prolog showing roughly comparable times and error rates to Pascal.[3]

Taken together, the results show a remarkable consistency across many variations in tutor discipline and programming languages. Over and over, we find that if we measure learning by the production rule involved we get simple learning curves.[4] As noted in chapter 2, learning of a complex skill is, on the surface, anything but simple.

Figures 10.11 and 10.12 show the data averaged across languages. At this level of aggregation, the data is remarkably straightforward, showing the sharp one-trial drop-off that was noted in learning with the old LISP tutor (chapter

---

[2]The course was taught with slightly different content in 1991–1992. The learning curves for LISP look substantially the same although the later group showed less improvement over trials for old productions than for the new ones.

[3]Pascal was not taught in the 1991–1992 year, but Prolog was. The data from Prolog that year were substantially the same as those we report here for 1990–1991, except that there was greater separation between the curves for old and new productions.

[4]Recently, Corbett and Anderson (1992) looked in detail at the production rules underlying the learning curves, and were able to show that by formulating the rules more carefully, it was possible to improve learning.

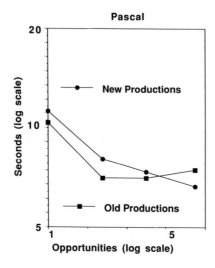

FIG. 10.7. Time measures for Pascal productions as a function of within-lesson practice.

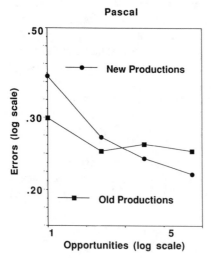

FIG. 10.8. Error measures for Pascal productions as a function of within-lesson practice.

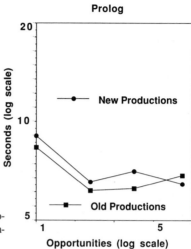

FIG. 10.9. Time measures for Prolog productions as a function of within-lesson practice.

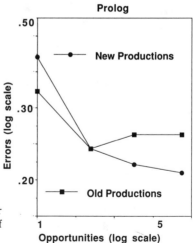

FIG. 10.10. Error measures for Prolog productions as a function of within-lesson practice.

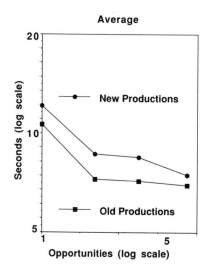

FIG. 10.11. Time measures averaged over LISP, Pascal, and Prolog productions as a function of within-lesson practice.

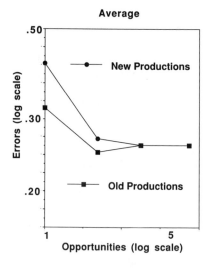

FIG. 10.12. Error measures averaged over LISP, Pascal, and Prolog productions as a function of within-lesson practice.

TABLE 10.2
Categories of Productions for Factor Analysis
(Factor in Parentheses)

LISP	Pascal	Prolog
arithmetic operation (1)	arithmetic operation	arithmetic operation (3)
variable use (1)	variable use	variable use (3)
argument deletion (1)	argument deletion (2)	argument deletion (3)
atoms, numbers, lists (1)	numbers (2)	numbers
function name	identifiers (2)	predicate name (3)
parameter declaration (1)	input–output	goal specification (3)
list extractors (1)	type specification	
list combiners		

7). The amount of aggregation (about 50 students[5] over eight lessons here) is comparable in the two cases.

10.2.2 Individual Differences in Learning

This multiple programming languages tutor provides another opportunity to pursue the issue of individual differences in learning. Are there just general learning abilities, as ACT-R would predict, or do students show specific abilities related either to specific languages or to specific aspects of a language, such as arithmetic?

To get more reliable measures, to enable the use of more productions, and to better satisfy the assumptions of factor analysis, we collapsed the productions into the 21 categories listed in Table 10.2. There were 49 students for whom we had observations of error rates in each of the 21 production categories. A factor analysis—in which we computed the correlation among all pairs of production categories across students—was performed on these data. There were three factors in the orthogonal solution that accounted for 47%, 9%, and 7% of the variance. Table 10.2 lists the association of each production category with a loading over .6. All the productions for the first factor came from LISP, all the productions for the second factor came from Pascal, and all the productions for the third factor came from Prolog. Thus, students could be characterized in terms of three somewhat orthogonal dimensions on how well they performed with each of the three programming languages.

The LISP factor correlates significantly with Math SAT, ($r = .40, p < .01$), replicating the relation found with the LISP tutor (chapter 7). The correlation of Math SAT with the Prolog factor is marginal ($r = .26; p \sim .05$). None of the other correlations among the three factors and Math or Verbal SAT approached significance. The LISP or Prolog subsections of the course were not long enough to allow us to identify separate acquisition and retention factors.

---

[5]The exact number of students varied from lesson to lesson.

We do not know whether to attribute much significance to the language-related factors. Our best guess is that these factors reflect changes in student behavior over the semester. It seemed apparent to us, teaching the course, that one student would, for instance, put a lot of effort into LISP, slack off in Pascal, and perhaps pick up a bit for Prolog. These factors may just be identifying students who had different peaks and troughs in the amount of effort they put into the course. The opportunity existed for productions to correlate across languages according to thematic category, like arithmetic operations or variable use, but they did not so cluster. Such clustering would have been expected if concepts like variables played a critical role in transfer across languages. The lack of thematic clustering is evidence for the independence of production learning.

One could argue that these language factors reflect a significant content dependence: that there are students with the mindset of LISP, and others with Prolog or Pascal mindsets. This strikes us as an implausible conjecture, but it warrants further exploration.

10.3 TRANSFER AMONG PROGRAMMING LANGUAGES

The three languages—Pascal, LISP, and Prolog—can be seen as ordered on a continuum. LISP and Pascal are both procedural in character, in contrast to Prolog. Both LISP and Prolog have primitives to facilitate list processing, and both make extensive use of recursive programming. This leads to the view that Pascal and Prolog define the extremes, with LISP representing a midpoint, but there are similarities between Pascal and Prolog that are not shared by LISP. For instance, both Pascal and Prolog use infix notation for arithmetic and express operations sequentially rather than by functional embedding. Experienced programmers tend to rate these similarities between Pascal and Prolog as rather superficial relative to the similarities that unite the other two pairs of languages. The students in the course, however, voted Prolog and Pascal most similar on the basis of these "superficial" features. This tendency to focus on superficial features has been noted of novices in other domains, as well (e.g., Chi, Feltovich, & Glaser, 1981).

Despite their rather substantial differences, one can approach a core of basic programming problems with relatively equal ease in the three languages. Table 10.3, for example, shows a simple beginning programming problem—classifying a temperature as hot, mild, or cold—written in each of the three languages. For some applications, the differences among the three languages can become quite consequential, but there are basic problems for which such distinctions are not significant. It is worth noting that in Table 10.3, although each of these programs basically solves the same problem, they do so in quite different ways, reflecting the different styles promoted in the pedagogy for these languages.

TABLE 10.3
Equivalent Code in Three Languages

```
Pascal:
    PROGRAM CheckTemp (Input,Output);
    VAR
        Temperature : INTEGER;
    BEGIN
        WRITE ('What does the thermometer say?');
        READLN (Temperature);
        IF (Temperature > 90) THEN
            WRITELN ('Hot')
        ELSE IF (Temperature < 30) THEN
            WRITELN ('Cold')
            ELSE WRITELN ('Medium')
    END.

Prolog:
    checktemp(X,T): –
        X > 90.0,
        T = hot.
    checktemp(X,T): –
        X > = 30.0,
        X = < 90.0,
        T = med.
    checktemp(X,T): –
        X < 30.0,
        T = cold.

LISP:
    (defun checktemp (temp)
        (cond ((> temp 90) 'hot)
            ((< temp 30) 'cold)
            (t 'medium)))
```

The Pascal solution involves explicit IO (Input and Output), as every Pascal program does; the Prolog solution is a set of rules that recognizes the "true" answer; and LISP is a function, which produces the answer as its value. One could have worked to make these three solutions more alike, but this would have distorted how these three languages are typically used.

There are numerous opinions about the effect of learning a first programming language on learning a second. One can find claims that there is considerable negative transfer ("You can never teach a Fortran programmer LISP"), but these are confounded by the same problems that are associated with similar claims about negative transfer in text editing: An experienced Fortran programmer will consider his performance in LISP to be terrible relative to his abilities in Fortran, but he may still be doing much better than someone without Fortran experience given the same amount of training in LISP.

We have observed a large positive relationship in LISP classes we have taught between amount of prior programming experience and class performance in LISP. Such results are hard to interpret, however, because programming experience is confounded with programming aptitude. For instance, there is also a large positive relationship between number of prior programming courses and Math SAT. Anderson et al. (1989) reported an experimental analysis within the LISP tutor of the effect of prior programming experience, partialling out the effects of Math SAT. Although they still found a relationship between prior experience and performance, it was much attenuated after Math SAT was partialled out. There still exist possible confounds with interest and programming-specific abilities that are not adequately measured by the Math SAT. The only way to properly test for transfer is by means of an experiment that randomly assigns subjects either to have or not to have a prior programming language.

There has been a little research on transfer between programming languages. Mandinach and Linn (1987) reported positive transfer from BASIC to a small language called Spider World, and Scholtz and Wiedenbeck (1989) claimed to have found mainly negative transfer from Pascal or C to a new language called ICON, but neither of these took the necessary methodological step of randomly assigning subjects to either learn or not learn a prior language. Studies in which this has been done are generally concerned with whether there is transfer from programming to general problem-solving skills. Here, the evidence for transfer is mixed, at best (e.g., Clements & Gullo, 1984; Dalbey & Linn, 1986; Klahr & Carver, 1988; Kurland, Pea, Clements, & Mawby, 1986; Mandinach & Linn, 1987; Palumbo, 1990; Saloman & Perkins, 1987; Swan, 1989). As Klahr and Carver (1988) pointed out, most of this research has been plagued by the lack of a careful analysis of the skills. Without such analysis it is hard to know how much transfer might be predicted.

10.3.1 Predictions

Does ACT-R predict positive transfer among programming languages? Consider the following production rules that code the arithmetic operation of multiplication for output in Pascal, LISP, and Prolog in the tutors for these languages:

Pascal:
     IF   the goal is to code the output of a writeln statement
            and this is the product of arg1 and arg2
    THEN code arg1 * arg2
LISP:
     IF   the goal is to code the result of a function
            and this is the product of arg1 and arg2
    THEN code (* arg1 arg2)

Prolog:

> IF the goal is to code the assignment of an output variable, var
> and this is the product of arg1 and arg2
>
> THEN code var = arg1 * arg2

These rules are all similar, but they are not identical.[6] The differences reflect the differences in the syntax of the three languages and their separate "style." In fact, in the student models for the Pascal, LISP, and Prolog tutors, there are no identical productions that are responsible for writing code, although there are a few productions in common for reasoning about things like relationships among clauses in a conditional statement. Thus, according to the identical production-rule model of transfer, there should be little transfer from learning one language to learning another, and what transfer there is should not occur in actual coding.

If the programming instruction were extended to the designing of complex algorithms the transfer might become quite substantial. It would then be possible for much of the design of an algorithm to transfer from one language to another. The programming tutors are mainly concerned with coding, however: starting with given or obvious algorithms and converting these to code.

The only proper way to get at the effect of prior experience on programming is by carrying out an experiment that directly manipulates that prior experience and not by using one that trusts to differences among students who present themselves with differing prior experience. Therefore, our experiments involve students learning significant subsets of Pascal, LISP, and Prolog, both as part of the classroom experience described in Section 10.2 and in a series of laboratory experiments.

10.3.2 Transfer in the Classroom Experiment

The data described in Section 10.2 come from two classes. In the class given in the Fall of 1990, students first learned Prolog, then Pascal, and then LISP. In the class given in the Spring of 1991, students learned LISP, then Pascal, and then Prolog. For all students this was their first experience with programming languages. Thus, by comparing performance in two courses we can see the impact of two prior programming languages on learning LISP (in the Fall) and on learning Prolog (in the Spring).

Student performance was analyzed by production rule for each of the first two lessons in each of the three languages. The dependent measures were mean accuracy on production rules and mean coding time when correct. Students were

---

[6]The actual rules in the tutor might be more accurate as cognitive rules if they were generalized across the four basic arithmetic operators.

TABLE 10.4
Mean Percent Correct and Time in Classroom Experiment

	Fall (Prolog–LISP–Pascal)	Spring (LISP–Pascal–Prolog)
Prolog	.73	.80
	7.2 sec	5.2 sec
Pascal	.73	.73
	6.4 sec	6.8 sec
LISP	.72	.71
	7.8 sec	11.2 sec

required to do a fixed set of problems and then additional remedial problems (as required) to reach a mastery level of performance.[7] The data included in Table 10.4 come only from the students' initial performance on the required problems. The final level of performance of students achieving the criteria for mastery was higher. When students learned Prolog as the third language in the Spring, they were more accurate and faster than when it was the first language in the Fall: $t(39) = 4.24$, $p < .001$ for accuracy in the first lesson; $t(47) = 1.52$, $p > .05$ for accuracy in the second lesson; $t(39) = 4.96$, $p < .001$ for latency in the first lesson; $t(43) = 3.01$, $p < .01$ for latency in the second lesson.[8] The reverse relationship held for LISP, although the accuracy effects were not significant: $t(47) = .17$, $p > .20$ for accuracy in the first lesson; $t(45) = .24$, $p > .20$ for accuracy in the second lesson; $t(44) = 5.03$, $p < .001$ for latency in the first lesson; $t(41) = 4.27$, $p < .001$ for latency in the second lesson. Much of the latency effect could reflect a speed-up in using the tutoring interface, which is basically constant across the three languages, so the accuracy results may better reflect the underlying learning. Only one of the four tests for accuracy was statistically significant. The absolute magnitudes of the positive transfer for accuracy were also small.

After each lesson, a quiz was administered. The LISP quizzes involved coding in the regular LISP environment—using a computer, but no tutor; the Prolog quizzes required coding in the regular Prolog environment. Table 10.5 presents the combined scores for the first two quizzes in Prolog and in LISP. The maximum possible score was 20. Here, there is a marginally significant interaction, $t(86) = 1.63$, $p < .10$ (two-tailed) suggesting that students do worse in their last language than their first. This is a bizarre result, and one we attribute to an end-of-semester fatigue. Also, most students were doing relatively well in the course and may have decided to give more attention to other courses. For these reasons, the experimental studies to follow might be more informative

---

[7]Details of the mastery mechanism is described in Corbett and Anderson (1992).

[8]Some students were missing from some lessons, which is why the degrees of freedom vary.

TABLE 10.5
Performance on On-Line Quizzes in Classroom Experiment

	Fall (Prolog–LISP–Pascal)	*Spring* (LISP–Pascal–Prolog)
Prolog	11.4 ± 1.2	8.0 ± 1.2
LISP	7.9 ± 1.2	8.4 ± 1.2

on the transfer issue. The general conclusion one can draw from Tables 10.4 and 10.5 is that students definitely got faster in their interactions with the tutor. The improvement in accuracy, however, was marginal, at best.

10.3.3 Transfer in the Laboratory

LISP and Pascal. Two four-lesson sequences were developed, one for LISP and one for Pascal. The first lesson in each language was an overall introduction to the basic style of programming in each language, the second lesson gave instruction in performing arithmetic computations in that language, the third lesson was concerned with how to write conditional code, and the fourth lesson was concerned with how to write iterative code. One would not expect transfer for the first lessons because they had almost nothing in common. The underlying concepts for the subsequent lessons, however, were basically the same (although the production rules responsible for mapping these concepts into code were not). The analysis was performed on data from these last three lessons.

The experiment involved a 2 × 2 design, with six subjects in each cell. One factor concerned the order in which the languages were learned: either Pascal and then LISP, or LISP and then Pascal. Crossed with this was the factor of sequential versus concurrent learning. In the sequential condition, subjects learned all of one language before learning any of the other language. In the concurrent condition, subjects learned a lesson in one language and then the corresponding lesson in the other language before moving on to the next lesson for both languages. The purpose of the concurrent versus sequential manipulation was to determine how to deploy the tutors in the classroom.

Subjects were taught by an earlier version of the multiple languages programming tutor that ran on a Xerox D-Machine. It is quite similar in character to the tutor illustrated in Figs. 10.1 through 10.4, and is described in Anderson et al. (1992). The instruction also involved a mastery discipline, in which subjects had to achieve mastery on the productions in one unit of a lesson before they were promoted to the next unit. Thus, different subjects would go through differing numbers of remedial problems before they reached criterion. The analyses reported here, however, are drawn only from subjects' performance on their first encounter with a production rule in the lesson in which it is introduced. In focusing on first use of new production rules, we can look for effects of prior language on learning the rule, uncontaminated by any prior learning of that rule. The results are not particularly specific to this restriction, and similar patterns (or lack thereof) would appear if other subsets of data had been examined.

Table 10.6 displays the performance on the Pascal problems and the LISP problems as a function of condition. Reported there are percent correct on the new production rules and mean time for applying the production rules. There was no effect of the order of learning the languages on accuracy, but subjects were more rapid in their interactions with the second language. This replicates the general trend of the classroom results. There is, however, a significant effect of sequential versus concurrent learning on accuracy: Subjects performed better when they got to learn all of one language before having to learn a second language, rather than interspersing the two languages. It is unclear what the basis of this effect is, and it did not replicate in the other analyses reported in this section.

LISP and Prolog. A four-lesson sequence in Prolog, similar to those described earlier, was developed so that we could study the transfer between LISP and Prolog. (The first three lessons for LISP were identical to the first three lessons for the previous experiment.) Thus, the first lesson in both LISP and Prolog was an introduction to the basic programming style of the language, the second lesson involved arithmetic, and the third lesson involved condition-

TABLE 10.6
Transfer Between LISP and Pascal:
Mean Percent Correct and Coding Time
for First Use of New Production Rules

| | Performance on Pascal | | |
	Sequential	Concurrent	Overall
Pascal, then LISP	59.7% 16.3 sec	48.3% 12.8 sec	54% 14.6 sec
LISP, then Pascal	56.8% 10.5 sec	49.6% 12.7 sec	53% 11.6 sec

| | Performance on LISP | | |
	Sequential	Concurrent	Overall
Pascal, then LISP	73.7% 10.0 sec	49.6% 9.0 sec	61% 9.5 sec
LISP, then Pascal	65.8% 11.1 sec	56.0% 9.7 sec	61% 10.4 sec

ality. For this pairing, the fourth lesson for each language involved recursion rather than iteration, because iteration can only be realized in an obscure pseudo-form in Prolog. We used the same 2 × 2 design as before, with the variables being language order and whether the languages were learned sequentially or concurrently. Again, there were six subjects in each cell. The same version of the multiple programming languages tutor was used, and the same analyses were performed on subjects' learning in Lessons 2 through 4.

Table 10.7 reports the transfer results as a function of condition and of which language was being measured. The results are a bit peculiar. It appears that subjects learning Prolog benefited by learning LISP first: Subjects who had previously learned LISP were correct 41% of the time on their first use of a production in Prolog, whereas subjects for whom Prolog was the first language were correct 26% of the time. This is a statistically significant difference ($p < .05$). The conclusion of transfer is not supported in the analysis of the LISP data, however. Here, subjects who learned LISP as their first language did better (33% vs. 26%). There are multiple possible interpretations of this result, but we suspect that, despite our attempt to match subjects by ability, by chance, better subjects were assigned to the LISP-first condition. Because each subject served as his or her own control, there was no significant advantage for accuracy, overall, of learning a language second. In this experiment, those who learned Prolog and then LISP were faster on both languages (but also less accurate). Averaging over groups, there was no latency advantage for the second language.

TABLE 10.7
Transfer Between LISP and Prolog:
Mean Percent Correct and Coding Time
for First Use of New Production Rules

	Performance on Prolog		
	Sequential	*Concurrent*	*Overall*
Prolog, then LISP	27%	25%	26%
	9.4 sec	9.0 sec	9.2 sec
LISP, then Prolog	40%	43%	41%
	9.9 sec	11.7 sec	10.8 sec
	Performance on LISP		
	Sequential	*Concurrent*	*Overall*
Prolog, then LISP	24%	28%	26%
	9.9 sec	9.0 sec	9.5 sec
LISP, then Prolog	33%	32%	33%
	10.8 sec	11.4 sec	11.1 sec

It is worth noting, however, that this partially replicates the effect in Table 10.4, where the only substantial accuracy effect was in Prolog, which was learned better when preceded by LISP and Pascal. It is conceivable that learning, first, a language with a fairly transparent flow of control, like LISP or Pascal, facilitates learning Prolog, which does not have a transparent flow of control. Kessler and Anderson (1986) found that first learning iteration, which has an obvious control flow facilitated learning recursion, which does not.

As a final note, this experiment failed to replicate the significant advantage for sequential learning, which calls into question the conclusion of the previous experiment.

Prolog and Pascal. We had done an earlier experiment on transfer between Prolog and Pascal within the same tutor. At the time, the results had seemed so counter-intuitive that we went on to design the two experiments just reported. The earlier curriculum involved arithmetic, conditionals, and iteration in each language. As already mentioned, iteration is achieved in Prolog in a rather peculiar way, so we thought the results might have been due to that. Table 10.8 reports the results for this experiment. The measures are a little different from those reported for the previous two experiments: Rather than reporting only the first use of a rule, these are measures of average performance on a rule over many uses, as in the analysis of the classroom data in Table 10.4.[9] There were four subjects in each of the four conditions. There is no evidence for an advantage in either accuracy or latency in the second language. With respect to the curious interaction in Table 10.8, there appears to be no advantage of having Prolog second in this experiment.

10.3.4 Overall Conclusions From Transfer Studies

This section has investigated transfer among programming languages using a number of different measures in a variety of situations. The results have been somewhat variable, as would be expected using small numbers of subjects on multiple replications of phenomena that are so variable because of individual differences. Now it is the time to combine the results and try to identify the big picture. Averaging the results of the three experiments, there is no difference in the accuracy displayed in early learning of a programming language between its being the first language or the second language. In both cases, accuracy is 49%. When time per production is measured, the difference is very modest: 11.8 sec per production for the first language versus 11.3 sec for the second language. The results from the classroom experiments show somewhat stronger

---

[9]The decision to focus on first use of a rule or to average use was made arbitrarily by the member of the research team who happened to be responsible for a particular data analysis.

TABLE 10.8
Transfer Between Pascal and Prolog:
Mean Percent Correct and Coding Time
for Production Rules

	Performance on Prolog		
	Sequential	Concurrent	Overall
Prolog, then Pascal	57% 11.7 sec	45% 14.1 sec	51% 12.9 sec
Pascal, then Prolog	39% 12.7 sec	52% 13.8 sec	46% 13.2 sec
	Performance on Pascal		
	Sequential	Concurrent	Overall
Prolog, then Pascal	63% 13.6 sec	67% 12.8 sec	66% 13.2 sec
Pascal, then Prolog	64% 10.9 sec	67% 13.7 sec	66% 12.3 sec

transfer: an overall accuracy difference of 76% versus 72% and a latency difference of 9.2 sec versus 6.5 sec. The classroom experience was more extensive and involved two prior languages rather than one. Our overall conclusion, then, would be that the effects on accuracy are either very weak or nonexistent, but that there can be real effects on latency. As noted earlier, the accuracy effect is the more critical one, because the latency effect can be attributed to familiarity with the interface, which stays constant across languages. Our accuracy results come close to satisfying the prediction of no transfer made by the identical productions theory.

How general is this result of lack of transfer among programming languages? We suspect that more extensive and advanced training in one language would show some transfer, although perhaps only to the corresponding, more advanced concepts in the second language. We would expect this because there are aspects of algorithm design that are common to multiple languages. In addition, we all share the intuition that a massive amount of experience in programming (many courses and many years of experience) has prepared us to be better learners of even the basics of a new language. Whether this intuition is correct is hard to know. It is simply impossible to randomly assign subjects to an experiment that may or may not involve many years of programming experience.

The research described in the next section takes a different approach to assessing the effects of extensive experience. Looking at subjects who already know two languages quite well, we see how well they transfer from coding a problem in one language to coding that same problem in the other language.

10.4 DECLARATIVE TRANSFER OF ALGORITHMS

The previous research failed to find substantial transfer from learning one programming language to learning a second one. Our analysis of that result was that the coding rules used in one language were different from the coding rules used in the other language. At a more advanced level, however, there are features common to programming in different languages. We have referred to this advanced level as the algorithm level. At this level, there is an abstract plan about how to achieve a solution, which is then realized in a specific programming language. Once having worked out this abstract plan in one language, one does not need to work it out for the second language. Table 10.9 shows the recursive code for writing factorial in LISP and Prolog. Although the actual codes are different, they reflect a common understanding of what a recursive solution to factorial is like. Among the components of this understanding are the following:

1. The terminating case occurs when the integer is 1.
2. In the terminating case, the value of factorial should be 1.
3. The value in the recursive case for n is obtained by multiplying the result of factorial of $n - 1$ by n.

According to a theory like ACT-R, subjects should encode the information they have in some declarative representation of the algorithm; this then becomes part of the input to the coding productions. The coding productions considered in the previous section would only take over after a declarative representation encoding these algorithmic facts was deposited in working memory. Having just solved the problem in one language, these declarative algorithm representations would be available for transfer to the second language. Thus, an analysis in a theory like ACT-R predicts large positive transfer from solving a problem in one language to solving it in the second language. Moreover, this benefit should be associated with designing the algorithm and not with coding it.

TABLE 10.9
Code for Factorial

```
In LISP:
  (defun factorial (n)
    (cond((zerop n) 1)
      (t (* n (factorial (1 – n))))))

In Prolog:
  factorial(0,1)
  factorial(N,R): – N1 is N–1,
      factorial(N1,R1),
      R is N * R1.
```

One might have expected some transfer at the level of algorithm design in the experiments of the previous section, but a number of factors worked to block observation of such transfer.

1. There was little cumulative algorithm design skill (as might be embodied by productions) to transfer, because the majority of the problems did not require any significant algorithm design. Those that did were rather idiosyncratic in the design skills that they required and, so, did not involve something that would transfer to other problems.

2. One might have thought that declarative memory for an algorithm for a problem in one language would transfer to solving the same problem in another language, but many of the problems were not the same across the two languages, and those that were the same occurred at intervals of from days to months apart, over which there would be much forgetting of specific algorithms. (See Section 10.4.3.)

3. The dependent measures used in the previous studies were concerned with tapping coding productions and not with any general problem analysis. Thus, even if there were some general algorithm-level transfer taking place, we were not specifically trying to measure it. Wu (1992) provided evidence that the structure of our tutors tends to eliminate any differences in skill at algorithmic design. This is because they provide extensive help at the algorithm level with their hints.

Wu (1992) has been using a somewhat different paradigm to see whether there is transfer in solving the same problem in different languages. He has looked at this issue between Pascal and LISP and between LISP and Prolog.

10.4.1 Transfer Between Pascal and LISP

Eight CMU students, three undergraduates and five graduates, who knew both LISP and Pascal, were recruited for the experiment. Their mean GRE/SAT Math score was 730. All subjects solved five problems that involved coding the Fibonacci function, adding fractions in numerator–denominator form, converting a number from arabic notation into English, calculating the powerset of a set, and searching a database. Except for the Fibonacci series, these problems are more substantial than the problems used in Section 10.3 or, indeed, the factorial problem in Table 10.9. Four subjects solved the first problem in LISP and then in Pascal; the second problem in Pascal, then LISP; and alternated thus with the remaining three problems. The other four subjects did the problems in the same order, but began by using Pascal, then LISP, and continued alternating thereafter. The programs were written on the ANDREW system at CMU using the text editor Emacs. The programs were tested in COMMONLISP and UNIX-PASCAL.

Subjects had to get each of their programs to work. An experimenter was available to help them with the syntax of the programming language and the computer system. The experimenter also determined the final correctness of the programs. Subjects solved one pair of problems (i.e., one problem in each of two languages) on each of 5 consecutive days.

Subjects showed substantial positive transfer, taking an average of 34 min to write their first program and under 23 min to write their second. The overall time was analyzed to determine where that positive transfer was occurring. The total programming time was decomposed into time spent coding and time spent debugging. The coding time was further divided into thinking time and keystroking time. The distinction was made in terms of inter-keystroke times. Any time over 2 seconds was attributed to thinking, any time under 2 seconds was attributed to keystroking. Singley and Anderson (1987) and Katz (1988) have found this to be a useful distinction. The thinking times and keystroking times were then subdivided into time spent on creating the first draft and time spent recoding subsequent drafts after debugging time.

Table 10.10 shows what we think is the most informative aggregation of these units (for more details see Wu and Anderson, 1992). Each aggregate of time is reported as a 2×2 array, where the rows represent different languages and the columns represent whether that language was used first or second. The data in each cell are averaged over subjects and problems.

There are large effects of first versus second language on thinking time for first draft, with subjects taking 66% as long for the second language. On the other hand, there is not much effect in keystroking time for the first draft, with subjects taking 88% as long for the second language. There is a large effect of time spent on additional drafts, with subjects taking 58% as long in the second language, but subjects also made a lot fewer drafts in the second language: 57% as many. With respect to time per draft, subjects took 107% as long for the second language.

Thus, there are basically two transfer effects shown in Table 10.10. When working a problem in the second language, subjects took less time thinking about their first draft and made fewer subsequent drafts. This is quite compatible with the view that the transfer is in terms of the declarative algorithm design, which precedes the coding stage.[10] Subjects needed to spend less time thinking about their first draft because they already had that algorithm design available. Also, it had already been debugged when they wrote the first program, so they needed fewer drafts before they got their program working. Usually, subjects corrected at most one bug per debugging iteration, so number of drafts is a good indication of number of errors in the first draft.

---

[10]Katz (1988), in a similar study of transfer between LISP and Pascal, obtained similar data that are consistent with the view that the transfer occurs in planning the algorithm.

TABLE 10.10
Transfer Between LISP and Pascal

	First Language	Second Language
a. Thinking time for first draft (sec)		
Pascal	520	390
LISP	494	296
b. Keystroking time for first draft (sec)		
Pascal	452	468
LISP	333	225
c. Time spent on additional drafts (coding and debugging—sec)		
Pascal	824	794
LISP	1,484	544
d. Number of additional drafts		
Pascal	5.2	3.8
LISP	4.2	1.6
e. Time per additional draft (sec)		
Pascal	158	209
LISP	353	340

10.4.2 Transfer Between Prolog and LISP

Eight subjects were used in a similar experiment studying transfer between LISP and Prolog, three undergraduates and five graduates. Their mean GRE/SAT score was 760. The five problems from the previous experiment were used, plus a sixth involving writing a little parser. The procedure and analysis in this experiment were identical to those used in the previous one. The results are presented in Table 10.11.

As the table shows, again there is a large positive transfer overall. Subjects took over 22 min to write the program in the first language and less than 14 min in the second language. These overall savings decompose into the same pattern as in the previous experiment. Subjects showed considerable transfer in first-draft thinking time—taking 48% as long on the second program—but little transfer in first-draft keystroking time—taking 89% of the time on the second program. There was considerable evidence for transfer in time spent on subsequent drafts: Subjects required only 59% of the time spent for the first language for the second. All this effect, however, was due to number of additional drafts: There were 52% as many for the second language. Finally, in terms of time per draft, the time required in the second language was 113% of that used for the first.

Thus, the results are quite consistent, with transfer being substantial for the algorithm-design phase, but its being confined to that phase. Our interpretation

TABLE 10.11
Transfer Between Prolog and LISP

	First Language	Second Language
a. First draft thinking time (sec)		
Prolog	288	152
LISP	336	150
b. First draft keystroking time (sec)		
Prolog	283	273
LISP	309	256
c. Time spent on additional drafts (coding and debugging—sec)		
Prolog	592	452
LISP	781	352
d. Number of additional drafts		
Prolog	3.8	2.6
LISP	4.6	1.8
e. Mean time per additional draft (sec)		
Prolog	156	174
LISP	170	196

of these data is that a declarative representation of the algorithm was being transferred from one language to another. The failure to see transfer elsewhere is consistent with the view that there was no transfer of the procedural coding skill from one language to another.

10.4.3 The Effect of Delay

We have followed up this research with a study of the effects of delay on transfer between LISP and Prolog. The delay between solving the problem in one language and solving it in the second was varied from immediate (as in the previous research), to brief (about 20 min, during which subjects solved an intervening problem), to long (a day). With respect to the measure of thinking time for the first draft, subjects took 46% as long on the second problem when it was done immediately (closely replicating the value in Section 10.4.2), 56% as long after a 20-min delay, and 67% as long after a day's delay. This decrease in transfer is statistically significant and is consistent with the notion that subjects access a declarative trace of the algorithm that decays with time. It also explains why there were no benefits for repeated problems in different languages in the experiments of Section 10.3. Those problems were repeated at lags varying from days to weeks. Presumably, much of the memory for the specific algorithms would have been lost during that time.

10.5 DISCUSSION

In sum, the evidence seems quite compelling that there is substantial transfer of algorithms across languages, but not much transfer of coding skill. This is in accord with the analysis in a theory like ACT-R. In going into this research we found this to be a rather counter-intuitive prediction, although our intuitions began to shift once the results came in. The form of each language is unique, but the algorithms are constant. The identical elements theory asserts that it is only the common elements of knowledge that transfer. Algorithmic transfer only showed up in transfer between specific problems because of the great diversity of knowledge involved in algorithm design. Knowing that the factorial of 0 is 1 (part of the algorithm for a recursive solution to factorial) just does not transfer to much else. Thus, there is only transfer from knowledge of one special case to a repetition of that case in another language. Such example-to-example transfer would be declarative in the ACT-R analysis. That is, students would use a declarative representation of the algorithm obtained from solving the problem in one language and would not have to create the algorithm anew for the second language. Wu (1992) has developed an ACT-R model of this transfer, which has independent coding productions for two languages but transfers a common declarative representation of algorithms between the two languages.

This chapter very much reflects an ongoing research project; even as the book was going to press, new results on transfer among programming languages were coming in. Thus, this is by no means the final story but rather an interim report. In our new efforts, we have moved from using this as a domain to test the ACT-R theory to using the ACT-R theory to interpret the data. The theory does a good job of providing the right categories in which to represent the knowledge and understand its acquisition and transfer. What we are learning in our further research is the structure of the knowledge underlying programming; that is, we are articulating the structure of a complex skill. This is perhaps the right note on which to end the experimental section of this book. The theory is being used as a tool to achieve other scientific objectives—in this case, to understand the skill of computer programming. In the next chapter, we discuss the use of the theory to advance the educational goals of our model-tracing tutors.

11

Tutoring of Cognitive Skill

John R. Anderson and Albert T. Corbett
Carnegie Mellon University

11.1 MODEL-TRACING TUTORS

The previous chapter marked the end of what could have been a conventional research monograph. The first four chapters laid out the theory, and the next six laid out the empirical evidence. These next two chapters are concerned with implications and applications of the theory. In this chapter, we discuss the connection between the ACT-R theory and intelligent tutoring. We have always had two perspectives on our work in intelligent tutoring. On one hand, we would like to see cognitive psychology make a real contribution to education. On the other hand, we view the classroom as an ideal situation for testing ACT-R. Certainly, the dominant source of data in the preceding chapters has been model-tracing tutors (chapters 7 through 10) and a simulation technique based on them (chapters 5 and 6).

A major virtue of production rules is that they can be used to model complex phenomena of real significance in everyday life. Given that they have the potential to deal with real-life complexity, it is important to see whether these models actually live up to their potential. This is why the model-tracing methodology is important in our research. It allows us to analyze complex behavior and see whether the behavior is, in fact, generated by rules. Until the use of tutors, there were only two ways psychologists could address complex behavior: One was to look at single subjects in detail; the other was to look at many subjects, but only in terms of gross features. The model-tracing methodology allows us to follow a classroom full of students for a semester in exquisite detail.

Building an intelligent tutor represents an opportunity to create a cognitive model and then do an experiment to collect data to test the model. We call it a *tutor* because we also use our theory to design the experiment so as to optimize skill acquisition. As experimentalists, we typically consider ourselves to have met our ethical obligation if the experiment does the subject no harm. As tutor builders, we do not feel we have fulfilled our ethical obligation unless the tutor does the student substantial good. Thus, our "experiments" are a little out of the ordinary in ways beyond just their length. They are experiments in two senses: The sense that occupied the previous chapters was as a test of whether the microstructure of complex learning fits the ACT-R theory. The other sense is whether instructional manipulations derived from the ACT-R theory do, in fact, enhance learning.

A number of evaluations have been done of the LISP tutor, the geometry tutor, and the algebra tutor in actual classroom situations (for a description of these tutors, see Anderson et al., 1990). Student achievement increased by about one letter grade or one standard deviation in the case of the LISP tutor and the geometry tutor,[1] but there was no improvement associated with the algebra tutor. The positive results are relatively large for educational applications, but they fall short of dramatic. We think the algebra tutor failed to have an effect because control students were already achieving at fairly high levels with respect to the symbol manipulation skills the tutor teaches. Singley, Anderson, Gevins, and Hoffman (1989) have subsequently worked on a word-algebra system, which teaches a part of algebra that students find very difficult. Although these are only laboratory studies, they have produced large positive results.

Traditionally, educational systems are evaluated in terms of achievement gains. The most common measure of achievement is standard deviations of improvement, and one standard deviation is regarded as a very large effect in the educational literature. Such measures are not very meaningful, however. Standard deviations are measured relative to the variance in the population. If the achievement scores in the population were exponentially distributed (not necessarily an invalid assumption), doubling performance would only produce an improvement of one standard deviation. A better measure of accomplishment is the time required to reach a certain level of achievement. On this, we can report that our mature tutors get students to at least the same level of mastery as control students in about one third of the time. This is because the tutors are designed to optimize learning rate. Whether students achieve a higher level of mastery seems to be a function of two factors: (a) whether the tutors employ a more powerful cognitive model than the control environment and (b) whether students are less likely to solve exercises successfully in the control environment. If either of these conditions is satisfied, our tutors will produce

---

[1] In cases in which students are equated for time, the effect comes out as achievement gains. In cases where students are brought to the same performance levels, it is measured by the time to achieve the target level.

higher levels of achievement. Otherwise, they just produce more rapid attainment of the same levels of achievement.

The next section discusses the model-tracing approach to maximizing learning and its basis in the ACT-R theory. Section 11.3 then provides an overview of the field of intelligent tutoring, focusing on contrasts between the modal assumptions of the field and our current approach. Finally, Section 11.4 reviews specific criticisms of the model-tracing approach.

11.2 ACT-R PRINCIPLES OF TUTORING

Our approach to tutoring comes from taking seriously the ACT-R theory of skill acquisition. The goal is to create an environment in which students can practice a skill so that they acquire and strengthen appropriate production rules efficiently. Four principles, which can be derived from ACT-R, shape how we are currently building model-tracing tutors:

1. The skill itself should be modeled as a set of production rules.
2. Instruction should be example based.
3. The major goal of instruction should be to maximize the rate at which students can induce rules from examples.
4. Students should be allowed to correct errors with the minimum possible assistance from the tutor.

The following subsections discuss each of these principles in more detail.

11.2.1 Student Modeling

Our approach to tutoring is different from most others' in that it revolves around a fully specified ideal model of the student; that model is cast as an ACT production system. It is this in-depth analysis of the knowledge to be learned that distinguishes our approach from the behavioristic drill-and-practice approaches, which rest on more superficial analyses of the knowledge. The first step in our approach to tutoring is to come up with a set of production rules that represent the skill we want the student to master. The task of building such a model is not easy, but there are a number of helpful facilities within our systems. Developing the student model is the most labor-intensive aspect of tutor development. The ideal student model is intended to capture the complexity of the domain. In contrast to the complexity of the knowledge representation, the learning and teaching principles we describe further on are quite simple.

There is not necessarily a unique set of production rules that prescribe how students should approach a task. Just as there are multiple possible computer programs for doing a task, there are multiple possible production systems. There is no guarantee that one will come up with the best production system for performing a task. Some of the recent work on geometry tutoring is predicated on the belief that there is a more powerful cognitive model for proof construction (Koedinger & Anderson, 1990) than the expert system that underlay the original geometry tutor (Anderson et al., 1985). The level of achievement that our tutors can produce is a function of the power of their cognitive models. As noted earlier, we can outperform conventional instruction (and also produce more rapid learning) if we can teach students more powerful ways to solve problems.

11.2.2 Example-Based Instruction

The second principle of our approach to tutoring is to use example-based instruction. A fundamental assumption of the ACT theory is that one cannot directly "tell" a production rule to a student. Productions are functional units associating cognitive contexts with cognitive actions, which only form as a by-product of problem-solving efforts. Declarative instruction obviously plays an important role in learning, because it can foster useful declarative encodings of appropriate goals, contexts, and actions. In the case of declarative knowledge, however, there is a second, more pragmatic, sense in which students cannot be "told" rules. Goals, contexts, relations and/or actions are difficult to describe outside a problem-solving context in a way that will allow students to recognize them in practice. As a result, examples are central to instructing in problem-solving skill. They provide contextualized definitions of concepts and—in the case of a generative skill, such as programming—can demonstrate what the student should expect to see as he or she works. Many studies have demonstrated both the importance of grounding instruction in specific examples and the value of students' analogical use of examples in problem solving (Anderson, 1989a; Chi, Bassok, Lewis, Reimann, & Glaser, 1989; Fong, Krantz, & Nisbett, 1986; Reder, Charney, & Morgan, 1986; S. K. Reed, 1987; Ross, 1984, 1987; Van-Lehn, 1986). A number of these studies have also shown the importance of accompanying these examples with appropriate instruction. In our view this instruction serves to indicate the salient aspects of the examples and, so, guide the analogy process.

Consider the geometry problem in Fig. 11.1, which might be used to illustrate the following production rule:

> IF   the goal is to prove $\triangle XYZ \cong \triangle UYV$
> and X, Y, and U are collinear
> and Z, Y, and V are collinear
> THEN conclude $\angle XYZ \cong \angle UYV$ because of vertical angles.

In addition to presenting the example and the inference, one needs to accompany the example with text that communicates the rule. When trying to prove congruent triangles that form a vertical angle configuration, it is a good

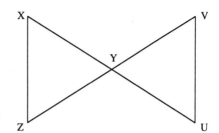

FIG. 11.1. Goal: Prove ΔXYZ ≅
ΔUYZ.

idea to infer that the vertical angles are congruent. When the student next comes across a problem that involves this rule, he or she will be able to solve that problem by analogy to this example. If so, the production rule will be formed by the knowledge compilation process in ACT-R.

The implications of this view of learning for instruction are simple but quite important. These implications are: (a) An example is needed to illustrate each production rule to be taught; (b) enough surrounding instruction must be given to ensure that the students correctly understand the example so that they will generate the right mapping in making the analogy; and (c) problem-solving opportunities should be given for the mapping to occur. These are not very complicated ideas, but they are not often followed. What is complicated is determining, in the first place, the production rules that determine what needs to be represented by the example.

11.2.3 Maximizing Learning Rate

Once the rule set to be learned has been fixed, there is only one thing that can vary and that one can strive to optimize. This is the rate at which these rules are acquired. Because of errors in understanding the examples, it may take multiple opportunities before the correct production rule is formed. Also, it may take multiple trials of practice to compile a rule and strengthen it sufficiently so that it will apply reliably. We have done a number of experiments looking at different modes of tutoring that vary how long it takes subjects to go through a set of problems and the way in which they go through the problems. As noted in chapter 7, what predicts students' final achievement is how much practice they have had on these rules and not how that practice occurred. Section 7.5 compared students who were forced to stay on a path of correct solution with students who were allowed to explore any path of solution they liked, with the only constraint that they finally execute a correct solution. Students in the second condition can take three times as long to get through the problems, but they show the same level of achievement. The basic implication of this principle is that one wants to minimize floundering time in problem solving and select problems that offer practice on those productions on which students most need practice. Much of the overall organization of our tutors is motivated to maximize learning rate.

The model-tracing approach derives its name from this third step in tutoring. To determine where the student's errors are and where further practice is required, the tutor tries to simulate the student's problem solving in real time as it is taking place. As described in previous chapters, the tutor essentially tries to find some path of productions that matches the behavior it observes from the student. Many times, when one of our tutors had serious problems, it was because it could not recognize legitimate problem-solving paths. Basically, there were rules of problem solving that students possessed that we had not given to the tutors. This is more of a problem with nonstudent experts who try out the system, who have had more opportunity to learn methods outside the tutor, but even students working exclusively with our tutors find ways of problem solving we have not represented. Much of the effort in a serious curriculum development should go into identifying the rules that were missed in the "first-pass" design of the system.

Much of the individualization of instruction in our tutoring approach comes from the aspect of our tutors that we call *knowledge tracing*. We maintain a model of what the student knows that takes the form of a series of Bayesian estimates of the probabilities that the student knows specific production rules (for details, see Corbett & Anderson, 1992). We then select new problems that will offer maximal opportunity for the student to learn, and stop presenting new problems when we believe the student has reached a mastery level of performance on all productions in a particular section. In this way we try to get all students to the same high level of mastery in minimal time.

11.2.4 Error Feedback

Whenever the student makes an error, the tutor can retrieve a production rule that would have generated a correct response.[2] The tutor's response to the error is organized around the correct rule that has been identified. There are three possible explanations for the error, presented here in order of increasing severity:

1. The student has the correct rule but it did not fire correctly. This may be because the student misunderstood the problem, or it may reflect some slip in the execution of the rule.

2. The student has no rule. The student may ask for help directly in this state or may make a guess, which appears as an answer.

3. The student has an incorrect rule or misconception.

Each of these situations requires its own remediation pattern:

---

[2]If there is more than one correct production rule (and none of these match the student's), the tutor selects one arbitrarily to organize remediation.

1. The error is pointed out and the student is allowed to self-correct to strengthen the rule. This will put the student back on the correct path.

2. The student needs to learn the correct rule. The assumption in ACT-R is that this is done from an example, and the obvious example from which to learn is the current problem. The student can only learn from the current problem if it is properly elaborated so that it can be used by analogy. Thus, it is important that the student come to a correct solution of the current problem and understand why it is correct.

3. As with the second case, the critical step in dealing with a misconception is to understand the correct rule. In this case, however, the misconception can actively interfere with achieving that understanding. Therefore, it is also necessary to explain to the student why his or her answer is wrong.

Each of these actions is progressively more elaborate, in response to the increasing severity of the problem. Unfortunately, when a student makes an error, the tutor does not necessarily know which of these categories the error comes from. Therefore, we have evolved a system for responding to errors that involves the following components:

1. If an error occurs, the tutor merely signals the error, without any explanation.

2. The student can ask for help, in which case the tutor presents a series of successively stronger messages. The initial message describes the current goal; the final message tells the student what to do. These help messages are intended to help the student understand the correct solution so that it will become an example for future problem solving.

3. The student can also request an explanation of why a response is an error.

It is not clear to us that this reflects an optimal response to error states, but it does achieve a number of goals. In signaling errors right away, the tutor helps optimize learning rate by avoiding entering error states, where a great deal of time can be wasted. By providing a minimal error signal, we allow the student to correct slips without having to process elaborate explanations. Successive hinting also has this effect, in that the first hint is often enough if the student has only a simple misunderstanding of the problem. This policy also allows students to generate their own explanations of the correct response, which in turn should enhance retention of the information (Anderson, 1990c, chapter 7). Furthermore, students only have to process error explanations if they want to.

This policy allows the students to control how much explanation they want to receive. Many students fail to seek enough explanation from the tutor. They often guess at an alternative solution rather than seek explanation. If they seek explanation, they may ignore intermediate messages and only read the last message that tells them what to do. We are currently experimenting with different schemes to motivate them to read and process the messages more deeply.

11.3   REVIEW OF INTELLIGENT TUTORING

Wenger wrote a review of the field of intelligent tutoring systems (ITS) in 1987 that did an excellent job of capturing the state of the field at that time. It is often viewed as reflecting a high-water mark in terms of enthusiasm about artificial intelligence applications to instruction. Since that time there has been a notable disaffection with the approach, with some of the prominent researchers leaving the field, including Wenger himself.

In that book, Wenger introduced a rather favorable review of our work with the following odd sentence:

> John Anderson and his research group at Carnegie-Mellon University entered the
> ITS stage through an interesting side door. (p. 289)

That side door is psychology, which is implicitly contrasted with the front door of artificial intelligence (AI). He suggested, however, that this side door may evolve into the main entrance, as more cognitive scientists enter the field bearing theories of learning and instruction. We agree that this represents the natural development in the field. Early work was driven by the challenge of bringing artificial intelligence techniques to bear on education, but often lacked a coherent, scientific theory of effective education. Interventions were motivated by intuition, as often happens in education, but unlike most educational interventions, there was almost no empirical evaluation. The entry into the field by cognitive scientists of various stripes has brought with it theoretical rationales for instructional manipulations. It has also brought an increased emphasis on getting intelligent tutoring systems out of the laboratory and into the classroom

TABLE 11.1
Intelligent Tutoring Systems Reflecting the Artificial Intelligence Approach

---

Algebraland (Brown, 1983/1985b): A graphical system for teaching algebraic manipulation.

Bridge (Bonar & Cunningham, 1988): A graphical tutor for the plan structure of Pascal programs.

Buggy (Brown & Burton, 1978a; Burton, 1982): A system for identifying bugs in subtraction skills.

Guidon (Clancey, 1982): A system for medical diagnosis based on the MYCIN expert system.

LMS (Sleeman, 1982): A diagnostic model for determining the source of errors in algebra symbol manipulation.

MACSYMA Advisor (Genesereth, 1977): An automated consultant for MACSYMA.

Meno-tutor (Woolf & McDonald, 1984): A domain-independent tutoring system to manage tutorial discourse.

PROUST (W. L. Johnson & Soloway, 1984): A system for diagnosing nonsymbolic student errors in Pascal programs.

SCHOLAR (Carbonell, 1970): A mixed-initiative system for tutoring South American geography.

SOPHIE (Brown, Burton, & DeKleer, 1982): A system for tutoring electronic troubleshooting.

SPADE (M. L. Miller, 1979): A system for tutoring LOGO programming.

Steamer (Hollan, Hutchins, & Weitzman, 1984): A simulation of a steam propulsion plant.

WEST (Burton & Brown, 1982): A couching system for a mathematics game.

WHY (Collins, Warnock, & Passafiume, 1975): A Socratic tutor for rainfall.

WUSOR (Goldstein, 1979): Couches the electronic game WUMPUS.

---

and workplace. Finally, it has led to more empirical evaluation, although, on the whole, the record of the field in this regard is still not very strong.

In this section we reflect on the AI roots of the field. Contrasting our approach with the traditional AI approach serves to highlight what is unique about our approach. Although the AI efforts were not without merit and did set the foundation for some of our applications, they reflect the fundamental flaws in pursuing educational endeavors cut off from concern with a scientific account of human cognition. Of course, it is another question whether ACT-R is the right account of human cognition on which to build an educational application. The last section of this chapter reviews criticisms of our efforts.

Table 11.1 lists some of the principal early systems that were built and what they attempted to teach. We then review some of the features that typify these systems and the approaches they reflect, although it is certainly not the case that all the systems reflect all of these features.

11.3.1 Emphasis on Exercising Artificial Intelligence

As its name suggests, intelligent tutoring is considered a branch of artificial intelligence. Most of the developers (ourselves included[3]) have considered themselves to be artificial intelligence researchers, at least when they were building tutors. From its inception, intelligent tutoring was strongly contrasted with the older and larger field of "conventional" computer-assisted instruction (CAI). Researchers in the new field tended to dismiss conventional CAI as merely "drill and practice" of limited educational value; at best, the field of CAI was viewed as putting the majority of its effort into interface design. AI researchers, in contrast, saw an opportunity to apply AI techniques to bring at least some of the intelligence of the human tutor to the task. The hallmark of this intelligence would be the flexibility of the system, flexibility in the range of behaviors the system would accept from the student and flexibility in response to the student. As we describe further on, these goals involved approaches to "bug diagnosis" (finding bugs in programs), human emulation (by computers), and exploratory systems that stand in contrast with model-tracing tutors. In retrospect, there is a certain irony in this point of view. A decade later, no intelligent tutoring programs have challenged the educational and commercial success of conventional CAI programs. Moreover, interface design has risen to prominence among former and current intelligent tutoring researchers (Bhuiyan, Greer, & McCalla, 1992; du Boulay, Patel, Taylor, 1992; Merrill, Reiser, Beekelaar, & Hamid, 1992).[4]

A number of difficult and important areas of artificial intelligence are naturally engaged when we attempt to bring the intelligence of the instructor on line.

---

[3]Not that we cease to consider ourselves psychologists while we are building tutors.
[4]Larkin and Chabay (1992) attempt to bring the CAI and ITS traditions together.

The one domain of AI that is involved in virtually every tutoring application is natural language, both its generation and its understanding. Many applications have also used AI research in reasoning (e.g., Sophie) and planning (Proust). One might have expected to see research on expert systems used more often because these expert systems can provide the intelligent module for a tutoring system, but, with one notable exception (Clancey's Guidon), existing expert systems have not played a prominent role in the development of intelligent tutoring systems. Clancey (1984) himself concluded that off-the-shelf expert systems are not well suited to tutoring, because they are not cognitive models. They tend to employ computationally tractable algorithms rather than the cognitively viable algorithms that can be communicated to the students.

One of the major goals of AI, which is lacking in most intelligent tutoring applications, is machine learning, although there have been promising attempts (e.g., Langley & Ohlsson, 1984). This might seem surprising, but it is unclear that a detailed computational theory of learning can be involved in the moment-by-moment computations of a tutoring system. Perhaps, theories of learning should only be used to motivate the design of tutoring systems. This is the principal role of the ACT-R theory of learning in our work.

As anticipated, the goal of bringing AI to bear on computer-based tutoring has proven quite challenging. Indeed, many researchers took up intelligent tutoring because it promised to be a challenging domain in which to explore AI issues. There are at least two disadvantages inherent in such a situation. First, relatively few systems have been brought to the point that they actually work (for comments on this, see W. B. Johnson, 1988). Second, there has been little evaluation of the pedagogical effectiveness of the systems. Success is not measured in how well the system instructs, but in how well it handles some of the difficult problems of artificial intelligence.

11.3.2 Emphasis on Bug Diagnosis

A major goal of intelligent tutoring is to tailor the system's responses to the student. Such individualized instruction requires the system to maintain a model of the student's knowledge state. This model can be used in curriculum structuring (as is the student model in model-tracing tutors) and in governing the tutor's direct responses to the student's behavior. For example, a tutor may judge that a particular error is simply a slip and does not require immediate comment. Many of the early systems spent a lot of effort trying to understand the student's misconceptions. This is true, for instance, of the WHY system, which attempted to identify systematic misconceptions about rainfall; of the Buggy system, which was totally devoted to understanding misconceptions in subtraction; and of the PROUST system, which tried to identify misunderstandings in Pascal programs.

As with intelligent tutoring more generally, there are two motivations for this emphasis. The first is the common-sense belief that students have misunderstandings that require correction. This was reinforced by the computer science analogy whereby computer programs make mistakes because they have discrete "bugs." In fact, this approach in intelligent tutoring systems is often called *bug diagnosis*. There was a time when it was felt that educators underestimated the amount of systematic misconception that was at the source of student difficulties. Indeed, this was an area in which intelligent tutors might hope to outperform human tutors in real time, because bug diagnosis can be quite complicated. The very challenge of applying AI methods to this complex task was the second motivation for the endeavor. Aside from the scientific product, it is impressive and satisfying to see a system recognize the misconception underlying an apparently bizarre error and provide a coherent English explanation for it.

The educational justification for this endeavor has fallen on hard times lately on two counts. First, it has been shown, in a number of domains (e.g., Anderson & Jefferies, 1985; Payne & Squibb, 1990), that the majority of student errors do not reflect hardened misconceptions. The majority of errors are often just slips—something expected by ACT-R. Many of the remaining errors simply reflect students' guessing what to do when they come across problems for which they lack adequate knowledge. It is, then, a matter of no knowledge rather than wrong knowledge. Second, there is little evidence that feedback on misconceptions is effective. The most notable research on this issue was carried out by Sleeman, Kelly, Martinak, Ward, and Moore (1989), who found no benefit of explaining errors to students learning algebra; maximal benefit was obtained from simple reinstruction on correct conceptualizations and procedures. AI researchers (e.g., Self, 1988) are reassessing the value of bug diagnosis.

Similarly, there was no lasting benefit of error explanation in the LISP tutor (Anderson et al., 1989). Error explanations had some immediate impact on tutor performance, but they had no impact on long-term acquisition of the skill. McKendree (1990) was able to find a long-term benefit of specially crafted error messages in a study with the geometry tutor. She also provided a theoretical analysis of how error explanations could help the course of skill acquisition. A close reading of her analysis reveals that the conditions for benefit are subtle. What has been lacking in most bug diagnosis work is any coherent analysis of how error diagnosis could facilitate the learning process.

This is not to say that a tutoring system should be silent about errors. Occasionally, students do not believe there really is anything wrong with their solutions. Under those circumstances, students are inclined to ignore what the tutor is telling them. What is needed here is something more on the order of informative error messages, rather than bug diagnosis. Students do not want to know what is wrong with their minds that caused them to make the error. Rather, they want to know why their solution will not work. It is much easier (but by no means trivial) to design informative error messages than to give bug diagnoses.

11.3.3 Emphasis on Human Emulation

The major goal of intelligent tutoring is to introduce flexibility into computer-based instruction. Human tutors are the existing model for such flexible response, and we, among others, have quoted statistics on the effectiveness of private human tutoring (from, e.g., Bloom, 1984). Some research exists on how human tutors structure interactions (Lepper & Chabay, 1988; Merrill, Reiser, Ranney, & Trafton, in press), and a common approach in intelligent tutoring has been to adopt human tutors as models in deploying artificial intelligence approaches to computer tutoring. The goal, in some sense, is to have the tutor behave as if it were a human looking in on the student's computer interactions and commenting on them.

A major component of this is an emphasis on natural language dialogue, so a fair amount of research has gone into how tutoring dialogues are organized (Fox, 1988). Also, more mainstream AI issues of natural language understanding and generation are addressed in tutor design. There has been slow progress on these fronts. Someday there may be a system that does emulate the natural language capabilities of a human tutor, but the field is not there yet.

In our research, we have come to question the wisdom of this emphasis on human emulation for a number of reasons. Although much is known about the behavior of human tutors, and human tutors can undoubtedly be quite effective, very little is known about what, specifically, makes human tutors effective. Certainly, one should only aspire to model those aspects of the human that are effective, rather than aspiring to model them all. Indeed, there is the awful possibility that some features of human tutors are counterproductive, and we would be more than wasting our time in trying to emulate them.

This issue is particularly acute with respect to natural language generation. It is difficult to generate a convincing emulation of human verbal instruction, and the result is often something that is hard to understand. On the other hand, it is not particularly hard to fashion non-human-sounding but comprehensible texts. There are similar difficulties in attempting natural language understanding. The costs of misunderstanding someone's explanation can be considerable. It may be better to generate easy-to-understand menus and have the users select from them to indicate their intention.

As an aside, it is unclear to us from observing human tutors how critical high-performance, natural language processing is. First, as has been observed of human tutors (Lepper & Chabay, 1988), they often do not say a lot—leaving it largely to the student to learn—and many of their comments are linguistic equivalents of yeses and nos. Second, as we have observed informally but have not seen reported, when tutors engage in natural language dialogue, there is often misunderstanding. The student will misunderstand the more complex communications of the tutor, and the tutor will misunderstand the more complex communications of the student. It is unlikely, in such a case, that the human advantage can come from their understanding of natural language. We suspect it more likely comes from their understanding of the problem domain and some basic rules of tutoring, which is the basis on which human tutors are typically selected.

There has been little empirical evaluation of the importance of natural language processing to tutoring, and such evaluation is difficult. One study in the context of the algebra tutor (Lewis, 1989) contrasted natural-sounding feedback with brief, telegraphic feedback. Students did better (although not statistically significantly so) with the telegraphic feedback.

As a more general point, we believe it is a mistake to foster the expectation in the student that a computer tutor is like a human tutor. It is a pretense that is almost certain to fail, and it is one that can give rise to misunderstanding, frustration, and ultimately contempt on the part of the student. It is much better to have students regard computer tutors as what they are: nonhuman tools to help their learning. It is important for the student to have a good model of how the tutor responds; human behavior, by contrast, is notoriously hard to predict or understand.

11.3.4 Emphasis on Exploratory Systems

A rather different trend in intelligent tutoring—by no means reflected in all systems—is the desire to have exploratory systems in which much of the control is in the students' hands. Many of the systems that encourage exploratory learning are constructed around simulations, or *microworlds*, such that intelligence can be built into both the simulation and a pedagogical component. The freedom granted to students varies across systems. Some allow students to interact with a sophisticated simulation with no guidance. The paradigm of this is the steamer system (Hollan et al., 1984), which simulated a power plant. Other systems provide students with a simple simulator, but offer intelligent comments on their behavior. The paradigm of this is Sophie (Brown et al., 1982), which taught students to troubleshoot electronic circuits using a conventional circuit simulator. Finally, some systems simply allow the student to choose the sequence of topics to cover, but provide direct instruction on those topics. The paradigm of this is the WHY system (Collins et al., 1975), which employs dialogue to communicate a database concerning rainfall.

There are at least three motivations behind this exploratory approach. The strongest motivation is probably the intuition that students learn better from discovery than from direct instruction. This is an attitude toward the educational process that can be traced back at least to Rousseau. It has had a poor empirical record when measured in terms of attempts to document the advantage of exploration. More often than not, exploratory learning proves to be highly inefficient because students fail to explore what they need to. Surely, we would have no scientists if we required each child to rediscover all of modern science. More often, *discovery* means guided discovery, but even here the empirical evidence is poor in terms of instructional effectiveness. For discussion and a review of discovery learning that is still relevant today, see Ausubel (1968, chapter 14).

The best evidence we have for discovery learning comes from psychological studies, not from educational studies. These are the many demonstrations that show memory to be better for knowledge that is generated than for knowledge that is received. (See Anderson, 1990c, for a review of the generation effect in memory.) The problem is that, although it is easy to get subjects to generate arbitrary mnemonic devices in an artificial psychology experiment, it is more difficult to get students to generate efficiently the educationally relevant knowledge they need in a true educational situation. When discovery systems work, they manage to guide students to the right discoveries. Less directive learning environments appear to work better for more capable individuals, who, presumably, are better able to organize their own learning (Snow & Lohman, 1984).

A second motivation for discovery systems is that they represent more of a challenge to artificial intelligence. It is much harder to get a computer system to behave intelligently in a situation that it does not control than in one it does. From a purely educational perspective, it would seem odd to seek out difficult instructional situations, but it makes perfect sense from the perspective of AI research.

The third motivation is quite the opposite of the second. If the heart of a system is a simulator the student can explore, one can simply avoid the problem of building an expert system, which would have to be able to solve the problems in order to tell the student how to solve the problem. In many applications it is difficult to build expert systems capable of solving the problems. Therefore, one who wants to make an educational contribution to these domains has to look for a solution that obviates the need to build difficult expert systems, and counts rather on the human ability to figure things out for themselves and learn. The goal of the simulator is to create an environment in which that is easy. Certainly, this is true of simulators of dangerous systems, such as power plants, nuclear plants, and airplanes. It is much better to learn from mistakes that lead only to simulated disasters than from mistakes that lead to real disasters.

11.3.5 Emphasis on Interface Design

One offshoot of this emphasis on simulators has been a growing emphasis on building better interfaces for tutors. This relatively recent trend also occurred in response to increased computer power, enhanced computer graphics, and other interface developments. It has taken two forms.

One starts from the observation that improved interfaces can lead to improved learning and performance. To take a simple example, compare the advantage of screen-based editors over line-based editors (Card et al., 1983; this volume, chapter 9). The belief, which certainly has some justification, is that the need for improved instruction can be eliminated if improved interfaces are created for learning and performing. Note that this trend is really the antithesis of intelligent tutoring, in that it is not trying to automate instruction. Indeed, many of the practitioners of this approach are quite vocal in their opinion that computer-based instruction ought to be eliminated, whether it is intelligent or not.

The less radical trend in this direction is the belief that the effectiveness of tutors can be enhanced by using interface features to communicate hard constructs. The geometry tutor (chapter 8) has often been cited positively for its use of a graph structure to illustrate the goals and structure of a proof. This has also been cited as a virtue of relatively recent systems, such as Algebraland (Brown, 1983/1985b) and the Bridge tutor (Bonar & Cunningham, 1988). A frequently used term, which seems to have originated with Brown (1983/1985b), is *reification*: the idea that one can make abstract but important mental constructs concrete. Once concrete, they can be made explicit objects of instruction. This emphasis has evolved to the point where intelligent tutoring "authoring" systems are being developed whose aim is simply to facilitate the construction of relevant graphical components (e.g., Towne, Munro, Pizzini, & Surmon, 1987).

11.3.6 Lack of Emphasis on Empirical Evaluation

Implied in the foregoing discussion is the observation that there has been relatively little empirical evaluation of the classic intelligent tutoring systems. Until recently, it was a rare paper at a conference that contained any empirical information beyond informal anecdotes of how a particular student or students interacted with the system under discussion. This pattern is beginning to change, although very slowly. At the most recent International Conference on Intelligent Tutoring Systems (Frasson, Gauthier, & McCalla, 1992), approximately 25% of the 72 (non-invited) papers included empirical evaluations. Only 5 of these papers, however, assessed the pedagogical effectiveness of a learning environment by comparing it to some other learning experience and examining student performance. Although many research topics do not call for such pedagogical evaluations, this is a minuscule percentage for the field as a whole.

To the extent that these systems are meant to further AI goals, such evaluations are largely irrelevant. Such empirical evaluations are critical, however, if these systems are to contribute to education or to the understanding of human learning. Perhaps the most discouraging aspect of the field is the wealth of claims about education and human learning that are without any empirical basis at all. Substantial weight is accorded to intuitions about what are, in fact, complex and fundamental issues in human cognition. Empirical results that contradict such intuitions are often taken as casting doubt on the usefulness of empirical research, rather than on those intuitions.

In the world of educational evaluation, there is a distinction drawn between summative and formative evaluations. It is *summative* evaluations that everyone instinctively wants to get: answers to the question, How good is this system? Although such evaluations are necessary, they are relatively uninformative. They have two basic problems. One is that they just tell how well something works; they do not identify what it is in the program that is effective and what is not. Second, they are very expensive to do properly. We also think that positive summative evaluations of a tutor by its authors (including ourselves) should be substantially discounted. There is too much room for even conscientious and honest authors to affect the outcome. The need for second-party evaluation increases their cost.

The real payoff comes in *formative* evaluations, which are attempts to assess various features of a tutor to determine their contributions to educational outcome. Certainly, one of the sobering outcomes of our formative evaluations was how some of the promising features we built into our tutors had no effect, whereas some apparently incidental things turned out to be of substantial consequence. So, for instance, in the LISP tutor, there is little benefit of error feedback (Anderson et al., 1989), but there is some apparent benefit associated with the decision to have students type in answers rather than select them from a menu (Corbett, Anderson, & Fincham, 1991).

11.4 CRITIQUE OF THE MODEL-TRACING APPROACH

11.4.1 Overview of the Criticisms

Before we consider the criticisms of our tutors that others have made, we would like to point out what we think the major problems with our tutors have been and why their achievements have not been greater. The problems are all related to implementing the model-tracing paradigm.

Most fundamentally, the rule sets we have developed have not been as powerful as they could be, in terms of problems they solve, nor as rich, in terms of reflecting different, legitimate problem-solving methods. Consequently, the tutors sometimes teach less than they should and sometimes fail to recognize legitimate solutions. They also have problems in determining which rules the students are using and in deciding which they have mastered. The consequence is that students sometimes receive inappropriate instruction or are promoted at inappropriate points in the curriculum. Developing better models of students and applying them more accurately are major goals in our research on tutoring.

Three classes of criticism have been leveled at the model-tracing approach to tutoring. The first of these concerns the fundamental psychological validity of production-system models. The second involves the pedagogical strategies built into the tutors. The third touches on practical implementation issues. Some of these criticisms have been expressed in print; more have been expressed at conferences and in personal communications; and a few are implicit in competing theoretical formulations.

11.4.2 Criticisms of Production-System Modeling

Production-system models assume that a cognitive skill can be decomposed into a set of independent rules and chunks. Although different levels of analysis have been involved, the notion of decomposability has a long tradition in psychology and education (Gagné & Briggs, 1979; Thorndike, 1922). There is also, however, a strong competing theory in education that directly challenges the decomposability of knowledge (e.g., Shepard, 1991). A related critique of this constructivist camp would argue that a learner constructs an understanding of a skill, rather than acquiring an external specification of the skill. Organizing instruction around a pre-specified student model seems to be at odds with this constructivist approach. Finally, there are theorists who would postulate the decomposability of knowledge, but would contend that production rules and chunks, as conceived in ACT-R, fail to capture a true understanding of a task domain.

Added to this, there is a further unease about our emphasis on the efficiency of learning. Much of the effort in our tutors goes into bookkeeping to maximize rate of learning. As discussed, the tutors typically employ immediate feedback when an error is made in order to maximize the rate of learning. Student modeling in the tutor is directed toward obtaining mastery learning at a maximum pace. Many people believe that this actuarial effort is misplaced, and that education should be focused on *depth* of learning, not *rate* of learning.

In some sense, this whole book is a response to this concern in that it argues that there is nothing to understanding but a rich set of facts and procedures (read *chunks and productions*). It is possible to learn to execute procedures with greater or lesser understanding, as educators have observed. Kieras and Bovair (1984), for example, have demonstrated that people can learn procedures to manipulate a device more readily if they have a model of the device, but the effect of such a device model turns out to just be richer knowledge representations at both the production level and the declarative level. No matter how rich the productions are, however, each has to be mastered individually, and truly skilled performance may simply take years to achieve.

There is a natural inclination to view as important what is learned and not how long it took to learn it. This philosophy leads, in part, to the rather leisurely attitude toward learning that pervades American education and American culture. The longer spent mastering one thing, however, the less time there is to master other things. There is no magical compensation for leisurely learning, such that we suddenly reach the point of critical insight when everything falls into place. Each new unit of knowledge (chunk or production in ACT-R) will not require its own due of effort. All that can be done in education is to try to choose the most important and efficient facts and procedures to teach, and then to avoid spending undue time and effort to master the units that compose these facts and procedures. The normal course of education is notoriously inefficient. It is estimated that 46% of a typical child's class time is actually spent in instruction (Stigler & Perry, 1990). Certainly, the first variable of human learning is time on task. Studies of individual teacher characteristics have tried to determine what kinds of teachers get the most achievement out of their students. Time and again, the answer has been that the successful teacher is the one who manages class time best and increases the relevant learning time (Gagné, 1985, chapter 12; Leinhardt & Greeno, 1986). Furthermore, students also face serious issues of efficiency of learning in their homework exercises. In various studies, we have found that students spend many times as long solving a problem set on their own than they spend with a tutor (chapter 7). Unassisted, they spend long periods of problem-solving time confronting repeated impasses or under enduring misconceptions and still more time trying to track down careless errors that have made their problem solving go astray.[5] Our goal in tutoring is to maximize both the time spent in *productive* problem-solving activities and the rate at which new rules are acquired, by structuring exercise sequences and constraining students' performance.

A key component of our ability to maximize learning rate is that our tutors *individualize* instruction. Classroom instruction is often (but, clearly, not always) very inefficient. When a teacher is meeting the educational needs of some students, he or she is losing others and boring still others. It is interesting that there is little gain associated with reducing class size, whereas there is great improvement associated with one-on-one teaching. Any class size greater than one means that a student's individual learning needs are not being met. Interestingly, the geometry tutor (Anderson et al., 1990) lost almost all of its educational advantage when two students were assigned to work on it together.

11.4.3 Constraints on Student Behavior

Perhaps the most strongly and frequently voiced criticisms of our tutors concern constraints on student behavior (e.g., Bonar & Cunningham, 1988). There are two chief constraints of interest, one structural and one sequential. The

---

[5]One might speculate that bugs are a more serious problem in unsupervised learning than in our controlled studies, because in unsupervised learning, bugs can be reinforced and expanded without correction.

structural constraint is that a student's solution must conform to the underlying production-system model. Ultimately, each step must map onto a rule in the underlying production system. In generating a production-system model, one goal is to be able to recognize any "reasonable" solution to an exercise, not just any possible solution. *Reasonable* is not formally defined, but has to be defined heuristically in each domain. Generally, a solution is considered reasonable if one is not inclined to say, Yes, but there's a better way to do it. If a tutor fails to achieve this goal, it may be because of an intentional, but inappropriate decision, or because of an oversight. As an example of an issue of intention, students must generate code top–down in our programming tutors. This is an intentional curriculum design decision, but it may be an error, in the sense that students may learn to program more efficiently if they can generate code bottom–up. As Reiser has, one could build tutors that tutor bottom–up or in both directions (cf., Reiser, Kimberg, Lovett, & Ranney, 1992). An example of an oversight can be seen when, occasionally, a student figures out a top–down solution that is as good or better than any the tutor can generate. In either case, the deficiency can be repaired by adding appropriate rules.

The stronger, sequential, constraint concerns immediate feedback: Our tutors have most typically used immediate feedback to ensure that the student's behavior conform to the student model, step-by-step. So, not only must the student's eventual solution map onto the student model, but each successive step must map onto the model. There are a variety of criticisms of immediate feedback. First, students are deprived of the opportunity to detect their own errors. Second, in the case of programming, immediate feedback in code generation can preclude practice in debugging. Third, immediate feedback may impede students' monitoring of the learning process and their development of the meta-cognitive skills that characterize skilled performance (Chi et al., 1989; Schoenfeld, 1985). The issue of self-detection of errors is also open to empirical evaluation. In research on feedback control in programming tutors, we have found that allowing students to discover, debug, and correct their own errors slows them down and does not lead to improved learning (Corbett & Anderson, 1990; this volume, Section 7.5). The latter two points, concerning debugging in programming and meta-cognitive skills, are curriculum issues. That is, one can argue that our particular tutors are poorly designed in that they do not provide practice in these skills, but the same model-tracing methodology should be applicable to the specific skills of debugging and meta-cognitive learning.

Our model-tracing approach is not committed to immediate feedback. Chapter 7 discussed two other feedback modes: demand feedback and flag tutoring. The essential requirement of model-tracing tutoring is that the student's solution be eventually put in correspondence with a solution generated by the student model. As these other two modes of feedback demonstrated, this need not be done immediately. As it turned out, these other modes of model tracing were inferior to immediate feedback. We still maintain some hope for flag tutoring, however, and are interested in exploring other options. There is reason to expect some positive results if students are more responsible for generating their solutions and get less guidance from the tutor. The problem is to give them this benefit without requiring a lot of additional learning time.

11.4.4 Criticisms Concerning the Practicalities of Implementation

There are two chief criticisms that have been made of the actual process of implementing model-tracing tutors. One is that this approach will not apply in some domains. All of our tutoring work has focused on teaching relatively formal and quantitative skills, for which expert systems already exist to some degree. There is no reason why the approach could not extend to less formally defined areas, like trouble-shooting, language learning, or social science education. Developing expert student models for such domains appears quite difficult but is not impossible in principle. In the absence of a demonstration, however, our assertions on this matter are rather feeble. A second criticism is that the approach is inherently hard to use. Our own experience is that the time we take to develop instructional modules in our system is no different than the figures typically cited for conventional CAI.[6] It is apparent, though, that the difficulty of using the system outside of our laboratory is a major obstacle. We accept, then, that these implementation-level criticisms have some merit.

11.5 SUMMARY

It is interesting to ask just what can be expected from our model-tracing tutors if the ACT-R theory is correct. Conditional on (a) having an appropriate student model, (b) successfully communicating with the student, and (c) having the students actually try to learn, the expectation is that our tutors should optimize learning rates. This is a powerful prediction, one which could be disconfirmed by simply displaying some instructional regimen that outperformed our tutors for a single student. Unfortunately, the prediction is qualified with some strong conditionals. As noted throughout this chapter, it is quite difficult to come up with the best student model. It is also the case that students do not always correctly interpret the tutor's instruction. More seriously, many students come into real classrooms with no intention of learning, but rather with the view that the classroom is an unpleasant requirement (like cleaning their rooms), to be gotten through with the least amount of effort possible. Instructional manipulations that could change that attitude might well outperform any of our tutors.

---

[6]The traditional figures require between 100 and 1,000 hours of development for one hour of instruction.

Our tutors have been repeatedly observed to accelerate instruction, and when we have made variations on our tutors, we have gotten effects (or lack of effects) consistent with ACT-R. Although these are not results on the order of the quixotical image of our tutors beating all instructional alternatives, they do provide substantial evidence for the ACT-R conception of learning.

12

Creating Production-Rule Models

John R. Anderson
Carnegie Mellon University

12.1 INTRODUCTION

The disk that accompanies this book contains the ACT-R system and the production systems reported throughout the book. Part of the motivation behind making this disk available is to communicate the theory with a precision that would not be possible even if program listings were included in the book. These systems can be run and inspected at any level of detail desired. In doing so, you may well find interesting issues hidden in the code, which may not surface in the book.

Another motivation is to move ACT-R out of our laboratory and allow other people to engage in the modeling. To this end, the disk contains a user's manual written by Chris Lebiere and Nick Kushmerick and a beginner's primer written by Rich Lehrer. Neither of these, however, addresses the more conceptual issues behind cognitive modeling. This is the function of this chapter. It is part of the book, not the disk, on the view that it may be of interest to those who do not have access to the disk or a way to use the disk.

The first question one can ask about production-system models is how one comes up with ideas for these models. The second question is, having decided on a model, how one goes about implementing it in ACT-R. These questions are handled in turn, as we move through the chapter. The detail is built up gradually, as the chapter progresses, so you should feel free to skip to the next chapter when your tolerance for detail is exceeded.[1]

---

[1]As if readers needed author's permission to skip material.

12.2 TASK ANALYSIS AS A SOURCE OF MODELS

One way to create a production-rule model is by task analysis. A production system like ACT-R is a programming language that is quite appropriate for solving many cognitive problems. One can, therefore, set oneself the task of writing a set of production rules to solve a problem. The result of this programming exercise is a putative theory for the task. This is the essence of creating a production-rule model by task analysis. Such task analysis was one source for the production-rule models reported in previous chapters. There is no guarantee that the model created by such task analysis will be a correct theory of how people do the task, but even if it is not quite on target, it is often a good start.

Much of the work in expert system development has just this character, and expert systems are often developed as production rules (e.g., Brownston, Farrell, Kant, & Martin, 1985). The tasks undertaken by expert system developers are often complex, so writing an adequate production-rule system is a considerable accomplishment. Often the developers are not experts at the task themselves and must resort to interviewing domain experts to come up with rules for the task. The resulting system can behave in part like the human expert, but it is a rare expert system that would seriously be considered a simulation of a human.

There are a number of reasons why a model developed by task analysis in ACT-R has more of a chance of being a cognitive model for the task than the typical expert system. One is that a model written in ACT-R has a structure that is plausible as a cognitive system. If one stays within ACT-R (and does not do things like writing LISP function calls to make programming easier), and one avoids writing production rules that have unrealistically complicated conditions (and hence could not be matched under reasonable assumptions about activation), the rules created should reflect things humans are capable of. Furthermore, the tasks being modeled tend not to be nearly as complex as the tasks expert systems solve, and the developer usually has reasonably good intuitions about the steps he or she goes through in solving a particular problem. It is these intuitions that guide the development of a production-rule model.

For certain domains, it seems that the task structure is almost enough to uniquely determine the production-rule model. Bovair, Kieras, and Polson (1990) reported considerable success in this regard for certain routine tasks, such as text editing. They were able to take their production-rule model and a few style rules and essentially derive a single model for each task. The style rules determined both an overall approach to the task (e.g., the style rule "use the GOMS unit task structure") and the way the rules were written (e.g., the style rule "conform to structured programming principles").

Unfortunately, task analysis does not come with this same guarantee of success in all domains. A simple example of the limitations of task analysis would be the Tower of Hanoi task. As noted in chapter 6, there are a number of different models that could be proposed for performing the Tower of Hanoi task. Moreover, many of these models would produce the very same solution to a problem. Another complication is that different subjects could perform according to different models. The solution to this dilemma in chapter 6 was to include in the instructions information that would lead subjects to choose a particular model. In many situations, however, this would defeat the purpose of the research, which is to discover which model subjects adopt on their own.

Thus, for many situations, task analysis will only identify a plausible candidate for the correct model. Determining whether one has a correct model or not then requires the kinds of detailed comparisons between subject behavior and model behavior that occupy the previous chapters. Ultimately, the proof of the production-rule model has to be its ability to account for behavior in detail. As in any scientific enterprise, there is always the possibility for iteration: going back and changing the model until it accounts for the detailed behavior. Obviously, the scientist would want to limit such iterations and have as good a chance as possible of starting out with the right model or, at least, something close to the right model. Thus, it makes sense to seek more information to guide model construction. This is the purpose of verbal protocols, which are the topic of the next section.

12.3 VERBAL PROTOCOLS AS A SOURCE OF MODELS

Task analysis is as effective as it is in guiding cognitive modeling because of the constraint on the resulting model that it be able to perform the target task. Unfortunately, this behavioral constraint is not enough when one gets to non-routine tasks. Many researchers have, therefore, resorted to verbal protocols, in the hope of gaining additional guidance by further constraining the model to correspond to what the subject says. Unfortunately, insisting on exact correspondence to a verbal protocol is too strong a constraint.

There is a strong hint in the field that there is something wrong with constraining cognitive models to correspond exactly to verbal protocols. Since the 1960s, researchers must have collected and transcribed thousands of protocols. During that same time, perhaps as many simulation models were written. Nevertheless, there seem to only be about a dozen cases of a serious correspondence calculated between verbal protocols and simulation models.[2] This is particularly remarkable, because the people who gather protocols tend to be the people who develop simulation models.

---

[2]It is hard to know exactly how to count, but the following seem to be fairly clear and distinct cases of detailed computer modeling of verbal protocols: Baylor (1971), Farley (1974), Feldman (1959), Moran (1973), Neves (1977), cryptoarithmetic by Newell (1991), logic by GPS in Newell and Simon (1972), Ohlsson (1990), Peck and John (in press), and VanLehn (1989).

It should be clear from the outset that the problem with simulating verbal protocols is not a problem with modeling natural language generation. The standard strategy is to abstract away from the verbalizations to some representation that is easier to simulate. The classic methodology here is Newell and Simon's (1972) use of the problem behavior graph. Still, the requirement is that the abstraction preserve all the essential detail of the verbal protocols. The difficulty is in simulating all and only the essential detail in the verbal protocol, not in generating natural language. Undoubtedly, simulating the actual natural language utterances would be much more difficult. There are no cases of anything approaching this except where the subject is restricted to a very small vocabulary of utterances (Feldman, 1959, is an approximation).

The problem with aspiring to simulate verbal protocols can be understood if one examines how the generation of verbal protocols might relate to problem solving in ACT-R. The next two subsections address this goal. Subsection 12.3.3 then discusses how verbal protocols might constrain production-rule modeling in a less rigorous, but more useful, way.

12.3.1 The Status of Verbal Reports

Ericsson and Simon (1984) provided a thorough review of the issues involved in using verbal protocols. The naive notion regarding verbal reports is that you can get subjects to tell you what they are doing, and then you can make your theory conform to just what the subjects say. This idea got into trouble with introspectionism and has a bad name to this day. Current suspicion about the use of verbal protocols reflects, in part, overgeneralization of valid criticisms of the introspectionist program. It also reflects a correct recognition of attempts to import back into psychology the errors of introspectionism.

A modern statement of the criticisms of verbal reports can be found in Nisbett and Wilson (1977). Although these authors did not aim their criticisms at protocol analysis in problem solving, per se, their remarks are often so interpreted. Their basic point was that, in general, people are poor at reporting higher order cognitive processes. A few examples, culled from the wide range of experiments they reviewed, demonstrate this:

1. Nisbett and Schachter (1966) observed the amount of shock subjects would accept under two conditions. In one, they gave the subjects a placebo pill, which the subjects were told would produce heart palpitations, breathing irregularities, hand tremors, and butterflies in the stomach. Subjects in this condition took more shock than subjects who were given no pill. When asked why they took greater shock, however, most of the subjects did not attribute it to the placebo. One subject, for example, explained, "I used to build radios and stuff when I was 13 or 14, and maybe I got used to electric shock" (p. 237).

2. Maier (1931), in one of his insight experiments, gave subjects the task of tying together two cords that were hanging from the ceiling. The cords were sufficiently short and sufficiently far apart that one simply could not bring the cords together. The insight required was that subjects had to make one cord a pendulum and set it swinging in motion, then go to the other cord and bring it toward the swinging cord, and then catch the swinging cord. Maier found that subjects were more likely to come on this insight when the experimenter bumped into the cord apparently by accident and set it swinging. Subjects who solved the problem after this cue, however, never gave credit to the cue. One subject, a psychologist, said, "Having exhausted everything else, the next thing was to swing it. I thought of the situation of swinging across a river. I had imagery of monkeys swinging from trees. This imagery appeared simultaneously with the solution. The idea appeared complete."

3. In an experiment by Nisbett and Wilson (1977), consumers rated four identical pairs of nylon stockings. The majority of the subjects preferred the last pair they examined, replicating a frequently observed serial position effect in evaluations, but none of them acknowledged choosing the fourth pair because of its position.

Thus, subjects' interpretations of their behavior are frequently quite inaccurate. Nisbett and Wilson argued that people do not have access to their cognitive processes, although they did acknowledge that people had access to the products of their cognitive processes. For instance, Maier's subject did not know why he thought of the pendulum solution, although he could, of course, report the solution itself.

Thus, subjects' reports provide glimpses of internal states of working memory. As such they provide useful clues and suggestions that may disambiguate an unclear process. This can be crucial in guiding model framers as they choose among alternative production-system models for a task. However, it is often counterproductive to *require* that a simulation model account for all verbal utterances.

One could defend the program of requiring that a cognitive model account for the utterances of the subject by arguing as follows: These utterances certainly are data, as much as key presses or moves of disks in the Tower of Hanoi are. As long as one treats them in this way, and not as reports of the underlying processes, there is nothing inherently wrong with requiring a cognitive model to account for them. This is certainly the view of Ericsson and Simon (1984), who saw accounting for verbal reports as a particularly important constraint on a cognitive model.

One can imagine administering the Tower of Hanoi task, and gathering data about the actual moves, the subjects' verbalizations, the latency of their moves, and subjects' GSR. There can certainly be different opinions about how to rank these various sources, in terms of how important it is to account for their data.

I would guess that Ericsson and Simon would want to order them: moves, protocols, latency, and GSR. I would order them: moves, latency, protocols, and GSR. There is not a necessarily "correct" ordering, and one could probably justify any of the 24 possible orderings. To do so would require a theory of how the behavioral measures relate to the underlying problem-solving processes. A serious problem with the use of verbal protocols is that such a theory does not really exist.[3] To justify the relatively low priority I have given to verbal protocols, I now show how verbalization of problem solving would be implemented in ACT-R.

12.3.2   Interpretation of Protocols Within a Production System

The first thing to note is that, within a production system, verbal reports would have to be generated by production rules. As a consequence, a production-system theory would predict, in accord with Nisbett and Wilson (1977), that subjects should not have access to an explanation of why they are doing what they are doing. The processes underlying what they are doing are produced by (a) the production rules, which cannot be inspected and reported by other production rules, and (b) conflict resolution among production rules, which is equally inaccessible. The only thing that subjects should be able to report are the contents of their working memory.

Recall that new active elements are written into working memory by the action of productions. To the extent that subjects can focus on new things entering working memory, they should be able to give a report of what the actions of their rules are doing or, in Nisbett and Wilson's terms, the products of their cognitive processes. Such reports would be an aid to theoretical proposals about what the underlying processes are but would still leave a lot for inference.

There are a number of important qualifications about the reporting of the contents of working memory:

1. Reporting the contents of working memory places a premium on *concurrent* reports, in which subjects give reports as they are performing a task, rather than *retrospective* reports, in which they give reports after the task has been completed. Retrospective reports will be defective because of the failure to remember the contents of working memory. Concurrent reports are more likely to have critical sequential information and, therefore, are likely to be more complete.

2. One will get better reporting when the contents of working memory are naturally verbalizable than when they are not. Ericsson and Simon noted that

---

[3]This is a relatively remarkable fact, given that promoters of the use of protocols aspire to precise mechanistic models.

one tends to get interference with the main process if the contents are not easily verbalizable. This is because it becomes necessary to solve the problem of verbalizing what is in working memory while trying to do the primary task. On the other hand, in some cases subjects will want to verbalize as part of the process of rehearsing and keeping active the information in working memory. So, for instance, in mental multiplication special instructions are required to prevent subjects from verbalizing intermediate results.

3. The instructions should emphasize having subjects only say what task-relevant information they are attending to, and instructions should discourage subjects from interpreting what they are doing. Frequently, the former, noninterpretive, process is referred to as *talking aloud*, whereas the latter, interpretive, process is referred to as *thinking aloud*. Not only might subjects' interpretations be wrong, but the process of interpreting could change the primary process that is being studied.

Given that all behavior must be generated by productions, it is of interest to speculate about what sort of productions might be responsible for protocol reports. In the best of cases, verbalization is part of the phenomenon under study. Mental multiplication tends to be such a case. It might involve productions like:

IF subgoal is to find the product of X and Y
    and P is the product of X and Y
THEN say "P is the product of X and Y"

The action calls for verbalization to rehearse the information and make it more active for other productions. In other cases, however, some additional process must intervene to generate the verbal reports. In these situations, subjects are in a dual-task situation, where they must both perform the task of interest and generate verbal reports. This book has not given any real consideration to how dual tasks might be performed in a production-system architecture. One possibility is that the subject maintains multiple goal stacks, one for each task. In the case of verbal reports and problem solving, the subject might maintain one goal stack to do the problem solving and another to perform the verbal reports. Thus, the subject might have productions like the following:

IF the goal is to talk about what I am doing in the task
    and X is an element of the task
    and X is described as expression
THEN say expression
IF the goal is to talk about what I am doing in the task
    and X is an element of the task
THEN set a subgoal to describe X

The first production applies when the contents of working memory are directly verbalizable, and the second applies when they are not. There is no constraint on the element other than that it be task relevant,[4] but conflict resolution will give preference to the more active elements.

These productions might offer some interference to the ongoing primary process, but they would leave it basically unchanged. The second production, setting a subgoal of description, might lead to more demanding processing and hence greater interference. On the other hand, the process of verbalization might rehearse valuable information in working memory and, so, improve performance. In some situations, verbalization has been observed to improve problem-solving performance (Gagné & Smith, 1962).

Thinking aloud instructions might promote a production of the following form:

IF   the goal is to explain what I am doing
        and I do X
THEN set as a subgoal to explain why I did X

This task would take the subject off on a trail of an explanation that might be truly epiphenomenal and could well be so demanding as to substantially interfere with the primary process. Worse yet, the subject might change the primary goal from performing the task to explaining how he or she might do the task. Even worse the subject might have execution productions that would say, in effect, If I say I will do X as part of my explanation then do X. This is when the primary phenomena can be fundamentally changed by the process of reporting.

Because protocols must be generated by production rules, generating verbal protocols is a skill, just like any other we have considered. It might seem strange that subjects appear in laboratories with such a complex skill already largely in place, but if you think about it, it is apparent that we often practice the skill of giving concurrent verbal reports in our daily lives. Whenever we do a task that is demanding of working memory, it can be to our advantage to rehearse task-relevant information verbally to keep it available. Noninterpretive verbal protocols derive from this the skill for concurrent verbal rehearsal. In addition, we often resort to giving interpretive protocols when we need to give instructions. Thus, the typical way I explain to someone how to operate a device is to model how to use it, giving a concurrent explanation of what it is I am doing. Interpretive verbal protocols derive from this skill. Interpretive protocols inherently depend on our making inferences about our processes by observing our behavior and mental products and trying to explain them. As Nisbett and Wilson noted, however, all too often our self-explanations can be considerably off the mark.

---

[4]Just how to formulate a pattern in ACT-R requiring goal relevance is an interesting question.

12.3.3 The Role of Protocols in Model Building

Protocols are almost certainly incomplete, because there is no guarantee that everything of relevance has been reported. If the reports are generated by a concurrent dual process (rather than by a rehearsal process that is part of the primary task), they may also contain things that are not relevant. Because these concurrent processes cannot inspect production rules and can only respond to things that happen to appear in working memory, there is no guarantee that everything they choose to report will be task relevant.[5] In the extreme example of an interpretive process, everything reported could be task irrelevant and truly epiphenomenal with respect to the problem-solving task.

If one were to eschew protocols, one would only have the problem-solving behavior from which to infer the model. Although this behavior is certainly task relevant in a way the protocol may not always be, the visible problem-solving behavior is often a very incomplete record of the processes involved. The job of the theorist is to fill in the gaps between the problem-solving steps. The role of protocols is to provide suggestions for how these gaps are to be filled. For instance, in the Tower of Hanoi task, is the subject setting subgoals or is the subject using the perceptual strategy (Simon, 1975; this volume, chapter 6)? The subjects' report can be quite useful in disambiguating this. Consider, for instance, the protocol in Table 12.1, which was collected by Neves (1977) in response to the Tower of Hanoi situation illustrated in Fig. 12.1. This seems to be pretty conclusive evidence for a certain amount of subgoaling.

The protocol in Table 12.1 is of unusually good quality. Because of the incompleteness of most protocols and the potential irrelevance of portions, they cannot be used as conclusive evidence. Instead one must look for other measures of overall consistency, as discussed in the previous chapters. The role of the protocol should be to provide ideas for how to model the cognitive processes to get a good fit to the primary data (i.e., choices and latencies, in the ACT-R theory). Anything that appears in a protocol could possibly be an intermediate product and provide a clue as to the hidden problem-solving processes.

I think the paucity of instances of detailed simulation models being fit to detailed protocols is due to the incompleteness and irrelevant portions of most protocols. It is just not possible to get a perfect fit, and it is extremely difficult to define a satisfactory fit because the process by which verbal reports are selected is just too hard to specify.

As a final comment, I note that this method of using protocols as a source of good ideas is substantially how they are used in expert system development.

---

[5]This highlights the issue of implementing the task-relevance test, noted in Footnote 4.

TABLE 12.1
Protocol Collected by Neves of a Subject Solving the
Tower of Hanoi Problem in Fig. 12.1

I'm looking at Peg 3, which has 2 at the bottom, which is not the largest. Peg 1 has it, and can't be moved because the smaller one is on top. Go to Peg 2 and try to move the next to the smallest, which is the 3. I cannot move it, because something smaller will be below it. Go back to Peg 3 and try to move the next to the largest, which is already done, which was the 2. Look for the next to the smallest, which is the 1, that is on Peg 2, but can be moved. My move is therefore, 1 to 3.

12.4 DEVELOPING A BASIC PRODUCTION-RULE MODEL

This section describes a set of steps that we and others (e.g., Cooper & Wogrin, 1988) have found useful in developing a production-system model. These basic steps are not unique to developing an ACT-R production system model, but apply to production-rule modeling generally. Indeed, this section describes how to create a production-system model for doing a task in ACT-R without many of the distinctive ACT-R features. We call this a "vanilla" ACT-R production-system model. People often find this level of modeling quite useful. The next section of the chapter then describes how to create some of the distinctive features of ACT-R.

The output of the task analysis and protocol analysis described in the previous sections should be a set of production rules. It is generally thought not wise at this stage of analysis to worry about casting these rules in any production-system formalism. Rather, we try simply to state the rules in English, as, for instance, the rules for addition in Table 1.1 were stated. It is distracting to be concerned with the details of the production-rule formalisms until we have a basic conception of the rule set, although this is not to say that the rule set will not change as the attempt at implementation is begun.

As with any natural language statement, these production rules have vagueness and potential inconsistencies in them. In the process of formalizing them in a production-rule language, these difficulties will be revealed, and part of the

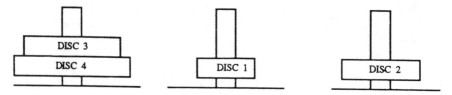

FIG. 12.1. State of the Tower of Hanoi problem when the protocol in Table 12.1 was collected.

correction process could be a reorganization of how we think about the production rules for the task.

Once an English version of the production rules is in place, the next step is not to create the ACT-R production rules but rather to design the ACT-R declarative memory to which these production rules will apply. This reflects the observation, made in chapter 2, that the syntax of the production rules is largely a function of the syntax of declarative memory. This amounts to specifying the working-memory structures, and more specifically in ACT-R, the chunk structures. We need to be able to represent the various problem states, the various types of goals, and the various types of intermediate results. Once having decided this, we are positioned to create both an initial working-memory structure and the actual ACT-R production rules that transform it.

Within ACT-R there are two levels to specifying the knowledge representation. First, we need to specify the various types of chunks; then, we must specify what slots they will take. This can be illustrated with respect to the addition task used in chapters 1 and 2. The overall addition problem was represented as a chunk of the numberarray type, which pointed to the columns. The columns were another type of chunk, with pointers to the top row, bottom row, and answer row. In addition, the production rules involved creating two types of goals: one to represent the goal of getting the overall sum, and the other to represent the goal of processing an individual column. Finally, two other types of chunks were necessary: One was to represent addition facts and the other was to represent numbers. Each of these types must be declared in ACT-R by a command called WMEType:

(WMEType numberarray columns)
(WMEType column toprow bottomrow answerrow note)
(WMEType addition-problem object)
(WMEType write-answer column object)
(WMEType addition-fact addend1 addend2 sum)
(WMEType number value)

Having specified the chunk types, we must specify which actual chunks the system starts out with. Some of these chunks are given in Table 2.1. A complete specification of all the chunks can be found in the Addition example in the Examples folder on the accompanying disk. It turns out that we need quite a few chunks, because we need to specify the complete addition table.

Once we have settled the knowledge representation and the initial declarative memory, we are ready to ask how we can formalize the production rules that will operate on this declarative memory. This is accomplished by trying to translate the clauses in the conditions and actions into the knowledge representation within the computational constraints of the production system. Often, this translation process will reveal holes in the initial English version of the production rules or in the decisions made about the knowledge representation. Table 2.3 displays what these production rules look like in the ACT-R syntax.

Once we have encoded the initial working memory and the production rules, and indicated what the top-level goal is, we can run the production system. It should come as no surprise that first-draft production systems never run. Errors can reflect both careless steps and fundamental misconceptions. ACT-R has a set of facilities for tracking down errors. The disk accompanying this book contains complete documentation of ACT-R and its debugging facilities. It also includes a primer, written by Richard Lehrer, based on his experiences as a novice working with ACT-R.

12.5   ACT-R ELABORATIONS ON THE BASIC PRODUCTION SYSTEM

The preceding section was concerned with creating a very basic production system. ACT-R, as a theory, comes with a lot of additional commitments and we have created facilities that allows these theoretical commitments to be explored. The system that automatically appears has none of these theoretical features turned on. They must be explicitly turned on by the user.

Three features of the ACT-R system might be particularly interesting to experiment with. These are conflict resolution, activation-based computation, and analogy. I leave the details of using each of these features to the manual and primer on the accompanying disk. The following subsections give a brief conceptual introduction to each.

12.5.1   Conflict Resolution

This subsection describes the conflict-resolution principles in the production-system model for the Tower of Hanoi simulation in chapter 6. It illustrates the simple approach to conflict resolution and does not utilize the expected value computations described in chapter 3. Therefore, I also describe a production system that utilizes the expected value computations.

There are only three productions required to implement this model. They were given in English form in chapter 6. They are given in the ACT-R formalism in Table 12.2. One production, SUBGOAL-DISK, subgoals movement of a block disk. Another production, SATISFIED, recognizes when that goal is satisfied. A third one, MOVE-DISK, makes a legal move. The productions SUBGOAL-DISK and MOVE-DISK create all possible subgoals and moves, not just the optimal ones. Thus, it is up to conflict resolution to select the appropriate one.

The conflict resolution is accomplished by associating values with production instantiations through the Parameters statement. The production set in Table 12.2 utilizes one of the simplest schemes imaginable.[6] If the disk is moved or sub-

---

[6]There is a runnable version of this production set in the Tower of Hanoi file in the Examples folder on the disk.

SUBGOAL-DISK
= goal >
  isa disk-configuration
  contents (!choose! (= peg))
  problem = problem
= peg >
  isa goal-peg
  identity = destination
  contents ($1 = disk $2)
= disk >
  isa disk
  size = n
  position = source
  lower = rest
= problem >
  isa tower-of-hanoi
  pegs (!choose! (= newpeg1 = newpeg2))
!eval! (and (not (equal = newpeg1 = source))
  (not (equal = newpeg2 = source)))
- (= source >
  isa peg
  contents (= disk $)
- (= newpeg1 >
  isa peg
  contents (= other $)
= other >
  isa disk
  size = nx
!eval! (> = n = nx)))
== >
= pega >
  isa goal-peg
  contents nil
  identity = source
= pegb >
  isa goal-peg
  contents nil
  identity = newpeg1
= pegc >
  isa goal-peg
  contents = rest
  identity = newpeg2
= newgoal >
  isa disk-configuration
  contents (= pega = pegb = pegc)
  problem = problem
!push! = newgoal

Parameters SUBGOAL-DISK
  :value (if (equal = destination = newpeg1)
    = n
    (- = n))

(Continued)

269

TABLE 12.2
(Continued)

```
SATISFIED
= goal >
  isa disk-configuration
- (contents (!choose! ( = peg))
= peg >
  isa goal-peg
  identity = destination
  contents ($1 = disk $2)
= disk >
  isa disk
  position = source
!eval! (not (equal = source = destination)))
== >
!pop!
```

Parameters SATISFIED
     :value 5000

```
MOVE-DISK
= goal >
  isa disk-configuration
  contents (!choose! ( = peg))
  problem = problem
= peg >
  isa goal-peg
  identity = destination
  contents ($1 = disk $2)
= disk >
  isa disk
  size = n
  position = source
= problem >
  isa tower-of-hanoi
  pegs (!choose! ( = newpeg1))
!eval! (not (equal = newpeg1 = source))
= source >
  isa peg
  contents ( = disk $s)
- ( = newpeg1 >
  isa peg
  contents ( = other $)
= other >
  isa disk
  size = nx
!eval! ( > = n = nx))
= newpeg1 >
  isa peg
  contents ($d)
== >
= source >
  contents ($s)
= newpeg1 >
  contents ( = disk $d)
= disk >
  position = newpeg1
```

(Continued)

TABLE 12.2
(Continued)

Parameters MOVE-DISK
  :value (if (equal = destination = newpeg1)
    = n
    (– = n))

---

goaled to the optimal destination, it is assigned a value corresponding to the size of the disk. If it is moved or subgoaled to the other destination, it is assigned a value corresponding to the negation of the size of the disk. This produces the ordering described in chapter 6, under which preference is given to moving the largest disk to its subgoal position.

The scheme of calculating values of production rules in LISP is quite straightforward and totally general, but it is a stand-in for a more detailed process of conflict resolution according to the ACT-R theory described in chapter 3. One can also have production evaluations ordered according to $PG - C$, which is the ACT-R theory. This requires specifying a global value of G and specifying parameters q, r, a, and b for each production from which P and C can be calculated as described in chapter 3. There is a production set called 8 puzzle in the Examples folder on the disk for doing the eight puzzle, which reflects use of these parameters.[7] The following is one production for moving a tile down a cell. It reflects use of these features.

```
MOVE-DOWN
  = goal >
  isa problem
  current = current
  = current >
  isa puzzle-array
  cells ($ = cell1 $ = cell2 $)
  = cell1 >
  isa cell
  row = row1
  column = column1
  content = value
  = cell2 >
  isa cell
  row = row2
  column = column1
  content blank
  !eval! (equal (1 + = row1) = row2)
```

---

[7]The production sets for the Map experiments of chapter 5, in the Examples folder, also illustrate this, but they have other complications.

```
==>
   =cell1>
      content blank
   =cell2>
      content =value
```

(Parameters move-down
      :q 1.0
      :a 0.1
      :b (EstimateC *TotalEffort* (distanceh =row1 =column1 =row2
            =column1))
      :r (EstimateP *TotalEffort* (distanceh =row1 =column1 =row2
            =column1))

This production sets the parameter q to be 1 to reflect the apparent fact that all moves can be made with certainty in the eight puzzle. The cost of a single move, a, is set to be .1. The parameter b (cost of future moves) and r (probability of future success) are estimated according to the functions EstimateC and EstimateP, which implement the functions in Figs. 3.3a and 3.3b. These functions estimate b and r from the total effort so far and the distance from the goal of the state resulting from the move. This distance is calculated by the LISP function, distanceh.

12.5.2 Activation Computation

The ideas of the ACT theory on activation were developed many years ago from studies of the fan effect (Anderson, 1983c). The general conception has not changed, although the details have been altered to reflect the outcome of a rational analysis (e.g., Anderson & Milson, 1989). Therefore, the fan paradigm is appropriate for illustrating the use of activation computation in the ACT-R theory.

A typical fan experiment has subjects study a list of facts. A two-digit prefix is associated with each fact: the first to indicate the number of facts associated with the person and the second to indicate the number of facts associated with the location, such as:

(1–1) A doctor is in the bank
(1–1) A lawyer is in the park
(1–2) A sailor is in the train
(1–2) A fireman is in the school
(2–1) A teacher is in the church
(2–1) A baker is in the boat
(2–2) A teacher is in the train
(2–2) A baker is in the school

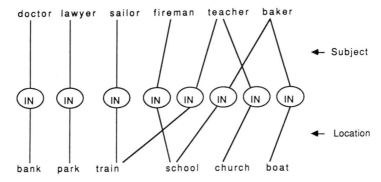

FIG. 12.2. A network representation of the facts in the fan experiment.

Figure 12.2 shows a network representation of these facts. Note that as the number of facts associated with a particular term increases, the fan of elements emanating from it increases. These materials are encoded in the file Fan Exp in the Examples folder on the accompanying disk.

After studying these sentences, the subject is asked to recognize the facts he or she has studied from a list that also includes foils using nonstudied combinations of the same words used in the fact sentences. Thus, the subject might be asked if he or she recognizes the following probes:

(1–1–T: probe1) A doctor is in the bank
(1–2–T: probe4) A sailor is in the train
(2–1–T: probe3) A teacher is in the church
(2–2–T: probe2) A baker is in the school
(1–1–F: probe5) A doctor is in the park
(1–2–F: probe8) A sailor is in the school
(2–1–F: probe7) A teacher is in the boat
(2–2–F: probe6) A baker is in the train

The first two digits in these indicate the fan (number of facts) associated with the person and the location. The letter indicates whether it is a target or a foil. The probe name indicates which chunk encodes it in the file on the disk.

The file on the disk also contains a set of productions to perform in a typical fan experiment. These productions parse the probe into a propositional representation and then to try to see if a similar representation can be found in memory. The critical production in that sequence for recognizing targets is:

RECOGNIZE-SUCCEED
    = goal >
    isa goal
    action recognize
    object = understanding
    result = answer

```
=understanding>
  isa comprehension
  subject  =person
  location  =location
=fact>
  isa fact
  subject  =person
  location  =location
=answer>
  isa recognition
==>
=answer>
  value positive
```

This production finds a fact in memory (= fact) that matches the understanding built up of the probe (= understanding). A trace of the critical activation quantities (Act =) and latencies (Lat =) in the matching of this production in the 1–1 fan case would be:

```
WME SUBGOAL2$137 Act = 4.431 Lat = 0.012
WME UNDERSTANDING$137 Act = 5.410 Lat = 0.004
WME FACT1 Act = 1.844 Lat = 0.158
WME ANSWER$137 Act= 3.738 Lat = 0.024
  Total Latency = 0.198
```

Recall from chapter 3 that the total time to match a production is the sum of the latencies for the individual wmes, or chunks. The latencies for the four wmes are included in the foregoing. The goal has a high level of activation and, so, is quickly matched. Because =goal mentions =understanding and =answer in its slots, these are also highly active and are matched quickly. The wme that has a long latency is fact1, which matches to =fact. It is only indirectly connected and depends on the level of activation of the elements =person and =location, which were given a total activation of .5 by the preceding parsing production.

If we look at the matching of this production in the case of a 2–2 probe we get a picture different only with respect to the matching of the critical fact wme:

```
WME SUBGOAL2$138 Act= 4.431 Lat= 0.012
WME UNDERSTANDING$138 Act= 5.266 Lat= 0.005
WME FACT8 Act= 1.642 Lat= 0.194
WME ANSWER$138 Act= 3.738 Lat= 0.024
  Total Latency = 0.235
```

It is less active (1.642 vs. 1.844) because of the higher fan and so takes longer to match (0.158 units vs. 0.194 units). It is worth reviewing how these activation levels get converted into latencies.

According to Equation 3.3, time to match a wme is:

$$T = Be^{-b(A + S)}$$

where S is the production strength and A is activation level of the wme or chunk. In this application, B and b are default set to 1, and S is set to 0, so this equation simply becomes:

$$T = e^{-A}$$

You may confirm that the latencies listed result from substituting the activation levels for the various wmes.

It is also useful to review how the activation of the FACT1 and FACT8 chunks is determined. In the initial data base, there are 80 chunks. A one-fan concept is involved in two chunks (the fact and the connection to the word). Thus, the concept *doctor is involved in the following two chunks:

```
doctor
   isa noun
   meaning *doctor
fact1
   isa fact
   subject *doctor
   location *bank
```

A two-fan concept is involved in three chunks—an extra one for the extra fact. The default strength of association of the links between element i and j is set according to the following rule:

$$\text{strength of association} = \log[\max \{p(j|i)/p(j),1.0\}]$$

In the case of an n-fan, fact $p(j|i) = 1/(n + 1)$, whereas for all j, $p(j) = 1/80$, because this is the size of the data base, and by default all wmes are treated as equally likely. Thus, we get:

$$\text{strength of association} = \log(80) - \log(n + 1)$$

which in the case of a one-fan fact yields 3.69, and in the case of a two-fan fact yields 3.28.

Both the person and the location contribute to the activation of the target fact. Both are weighted as sources of activation by .25. Thus, the actual activation of a one-fan fact is $(.25 + .25) * 3.69 = 1.84$; in the case of a two-fan fact, it is $(.25 + .25) * 3.28 = 1.64$.[8]

---

[8]The actual implementation constrains the sum of two sources to be .5, but allows the activation to be randomly distributed between the two sources. The reason for this is the treatment of the foils in that simulation. This embodies an interesting conjecture about fan experiments, which is too detailed to pursue here.

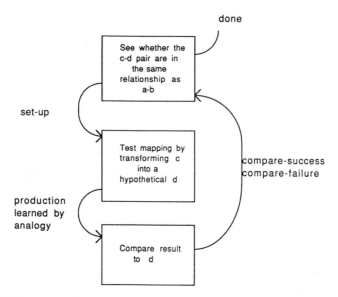

FIG. 12.3. The goal structure in the Sternberg example. The boxes illustrate the goals. The arrows are production rules in the simulation on the disk. The production learned by analogy maps the second goal onto the third goal.

12.5.3 Analogy

I use the Sternberg analogy problem discussed in chapter 4 (see Fig. 4.3) to illustrate analogy. The subject's task in that problem is to decide if a particular figure d satisfies the relationship "a is to b as c is to d." Chapter 4 discussed this in general terms to explain the mechanism of analogy. This subsection discusses it in more specific terms, particularly with respect to how one embeds analogy in an overall problem structure. The disk contains a file called Sternberg in the Examples folder, which simulates this analogy task. This subsection does not go into the level of detail of that file, but explains the basic logic of that model.[9]

Figure 12.3 illustrates the fundamental logic of the model and the role of the various productions in the Sternberg simulation. The system starts with the goal of checking whether the c–d pair is correct. To do this it chooses to map c (according to the a–b example) and see if the result matches d. Analogy creates a mapping that then has to be compared to d. If it matches, one has succeeded; if it does not, one has failed.

---

[9]The file "Learning Ch. 1 LISP," also in the Examples folder, contains an extensive example of the use of analogy.

In order for analogy to produce an appropriate mapping, the *a–b* pair must be encoded as starting with the goal of mapping *a* and resulting in a goal of comparing *b*, just as *c* and *d* are treated in Fig. 4.3. Thus, there are the following working-memory elements:

    goala
        isa test-mapping
        size tall
        weight thin
        color dark
        sex male
        achieved-by goalb

    goalb
        isa compare-features
        size tall
        weight thin
        color light
        sex female

The production that is learned by analogy is:

    = goal >
        isa test-mapping
        size   = size1
        weight = weight1
        color = color1
        sex   = sex1
    = color1
        isa attribute
        opposite = color2
    = sex 1
        isa attribute
        opposite = sex2
    = = >
    = goal >
        isa compare-features
        size   = size1
        weight = weight1
        color = color2
        sex   = sex2

Note that this production switches the goal from testing the mapping to the more specific goal of comparing features. The actual working memory representations on the disk are a little more complicated, as is the resulting production that is learned. These complications were necessary to deal with the details of fitting in with the overall control structure but the production here reflects the essential material.

12.6 CONCLUSION

This completes the discussion of the process of creating production rule models in ACT-R. As indicated, there is a basic ACT-R for writing models, and we understand fairly well the process of creating models in this "vanilla" version. Many of the issues of psychological interest reside in the embellishments of the core system, however, and for these, because we do not understand the modeling process very well, we work largely with yet-to-be-analyzed scientific intuitions. Also, there are no well-defined perimeters on exactly what variations of ACT-R can be explored. If users are willing to get down into the LISP underpinnings of ACT-R, they can create their own production systems. (This has already happened at Carnegie Mellon University, and we welcome such exploration. Our only request is that people indicate, in any published reports or dissemination of software, when what they have produced is a modification of the original ACT-R software.)

13

Reflections on the Theory

John R. Anderson
Carnegie Mellon University

13.1 THE STATUS OF THE ACT-R THEORY

I decided to write this book because I wanted to describe how well production rules accounted for skill acquisition. As discussed in the first chapter, as I progressed down this path I felt compelled to place this account within a coherent production-rule theory and wanted to make a runnable version of this theory available to users. This motivation, in conjunction with the existing rational theory of cognition, led to the ACT-R theory.

The foregoing chapters have provided evidence for the utility of production rules in understanding the performance, acquisition, and transfer of cognitive skills, and have shown how they can serve as the basis of intelligent tutoring systems for teaching skills. When one observes students learning a skill because of the instructional power of a production-rule analysis, the theory is most compelling. When one can see students (e.g., as I have seen my own sons) learn these skills one production at a time, the production rules become very real.

Our production rule analysis of skill acquisition continues. We are still working on a better understanding of the declarative origins of these rules. We need to improve our understanding of their origins in examples and determine whether there are non-example-based declarative origins, as well. The analogy process needs further work; its shortcomings will be apparent to anyone who uses the analogy component on the accompanying system. We are now studying more carefully the time course by which knowledge moves from declarative to procedural form. In the domain of tutoring, we are trying to find ways to develop more veridical student models.

The ACT-R theory is the best specified of the ACT theories. This is in no small part because of the discipline of trying to create a well-working simulation of the theory. It inherits most of the predictive successes of the ACT* theory and, due to the guidance of the rational analysis, acquires new successes thereby; some of these were recounted in Anderson (1990a) and some have been recounted here.

There are aspects of the rational analysis not represented in the current ACT-R. In particular, there is nothing that corresponds to the inductive components associated with categorical and causal inference. There are places within the theory for incorporating these components. The categorical theory is basically a theory of how various chunk types (isa links) are created and recognized. The causal theory is a theory of how the dependency (achieved-by) links, which facilitate analogy, are created. Thus, these are theories of how the declarative knowledge gets structured initially. A goal for the future is to incorporate them within ACT-R.

ACT-R lacks a theory of how productions might misapply. This was part of the partial matching theory of ACT*, which was that theory's greatest promise but also, in the final analysis, its greatest disappointment. There never was an efficient and workable version of partial matching in ACT*. A version of partial matching was implemented for the ACT* book (Anderson, 1983a) but it proved to be highly inefficient. It also gave bizarre results in a number of test areas. The topic was, therefore, deliberately avoided in ACT-R. Nevertheless, it is something that needs to be addressed if there is to be a complete theory of error in ACT-R. ACT-R can handle errors of omission (a production rule does not fire in time), but it has a problem with errors of commission (the wrong rule applies) as happens, for instance, in the Stroop task. We are optimistic that progress can be made on the partial matching issue as the ACT-R theory evolves.

As stated in the introduction, the intention was to have the implementation of the ACT-R production system proceed in neural-like terms. The use of activation-based processing is a step in this direction, but there are a great many details to fill in. Therefore, another direction for further research will be in possible neural-like implementations of ACT-R components.

One of the important features of this book is the availability of the implementation of the theory. You can try out the simulations, build your own, and provide us with feedback. We have been encouraged by how usable local researchers have found ACT-R. We hope this is not an illusion, but rather an indication that production-system implementations and computer power have reached a point of maturity where such modeling is generally feasible. This could prove to be an important avenue for disseminating the theory, and feedback from users could serve as an important source of ideas for advancing the theory.

13.2 INDICES TO THE THEORY

This chapter concludes with an appendix that is intended to serve as a multiple index to the ACT-R theory. This appendix lists the assumptions of the ACT-R theory, and describes their critical attributes. The purpose of each attribute is explained below:

Relationship to ACT*. Many of the assumptions behind the ACT-R theory are identical to those in ACT*. Others are quite similar. For each ACT-R assumption, I have identified what ACT* assumption it is related to and what the nature of that relationship is.

References. This contains a listing of the sections in which this assumption is discussed.

Empirical Claims and Evidence. Under this heading I describe what behavioral implications follow from the assumption. Some of these have the status of evidence for the theory, because there exist data confirming these implications. Others have the status of claims, because the experiments have not been done or the data are not clear. Presumably, there can be some debate as to what qualifies as evidence and what statements are just claims. For this reason, I have made no effort to distinguish between them, and list them all together.

Rational Analysis. This is concerned with indicating the relationship between the assumptions and the rational analysis that appeared in Anderson (1990a) and in subsequent publications. In some cases, the assumptions directly reflect the derivations in the rational analysis. In other cases, the issues noted are just more informal arguments for the adaptiveness of the assumptions.

Simulation Details. The disk accompanying this book contains information relevant to running the ACT-R simulation on an Apple Macintosh with its Commonlisp. That disk contains four files and folders. The first is a file that loads ACT-R. It can be evoked by double-clicking on it. The second is a folder containing documentation, including a manual written by Chris Lebiere and Nick Kushmerick and a beginner's primer written by Rich Lehrer. The third is a folder containing a set of examples of the programs referenced in the book. The fourth is a folder containing the code behind ACT-R. Under Simulation Details are pointers to the ACT-R simulation constructs that are particularly relevant to the assumption. Some of these are discussed in chapter 12. More information can be culled from the manual on the disk.

Neural Implementation.   Under this heading, I discuss how I conceive
that the assumption might be implemented in the brain. Much of this is speculation that did not find its way into the chapters. This speculation assumes a configuration of processors like that illustrated in Fig. 13.1, which shows declarative
memory and how it relates to the following abstract production:

```
= goal
  isa type1
  arg1  = variable1
  arg2  = variable2
= variable1
  isa type2
  arg1  = variable3
  arg2  = variable2
= = >
= new
  isa type3
  arg1  = variable2
  arg2  = variable3
```

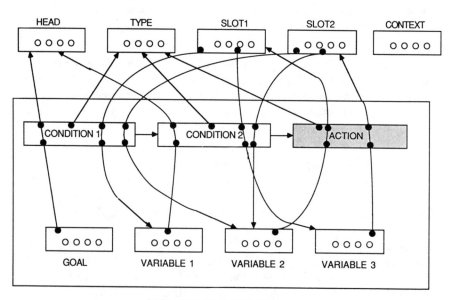

FIG. 13.1.   A possible set of neural connections that might implement a production rule.

Declarative memory is conceived of as a set of modules for representing a head (which is a unique identifier corresponding to a chunk), a type, values of various other slots, and context elements. Information is represented in each module by a pattern of activation over the neural elements that constitute that module. The patterns across the modules are interassociated, such that if some are active they tend to evoke others. For conceptual clarity, each slot is represented by a separate set of neural elements; as Smolensky (1990) notes, however, it is possible to generalize this concept so that the slot-value binding is represented as distributed across all the modules.

The production instantiation consists of a set of modules to hold the values of variables, plus three control elements (condition1, condition2, and action) to coordinate the matching and executing of the production rule. The variable modules hold patterns that correspond to their bindings. The production is seeded by reading into it the pattern corresponding to the goal element. This pattern and type1 are passed through condition1 and fill the head and type slot of declarative memory. If possible a pattern will complete the slot1 and slot2 modules in response to the patterns in the head, type, and context modules. The values from slot1 and slot2 are read back to fill variable1 and variable2. When this is complete, control passes to condition2, which fills the head module with variable1, the type module with type2, and the slot2 module with variable2. The pattern that fills in slot1 is read back as the value of variable3. The action slot then takes control and reads type3, variable2, and variable3 into declarative memory. Associations are then strengthened, which allows this pattern to be reproduced when its recall is needed.

The previous paragraph describes what happens with respect to a single production instantiation. There are multiple productions, and some of these productions may even have multiple instantiations. Each of these would have its own structure and would be in contention for access to declarative memory. Chapter 3 prescribed how this contention should be resolved in terms of which production chunks should be retrieved when. It remains to be worked out how this competition can be resolved by neural mechanisms that satisfy the ACT-R prescriptions.

The foregoing is a fairly direct way of reading the ACT-R architecture into a more detailed neural implementation. It is possible that there might be implementations that are equivalent in their detail but that do not so closely respect the structure of the ACT-R architecture. Even the scheme in Fig. 13.1 has an interesting deviation from ACT-R implementation: It only calculates a single instantiation per production. The neural realization of multiple instantiations of a single production has always been problematic. It is possible to imagine multiple duplicates of a production structure to handle multiple instantiations, but this would still imply only a specific number of instantiations. It does not seem physiologically realistic to suppose production rules can have unlimited numbers of simultaneous instantiations.

13.3 APPENDIX: ACT-R ASSUMPTIONS

Assumption 0: Technical Time Assumption

Time is continuous.

Relationship to ACT*.   Same as ACT* Assumption 0.

Reference.   Assumed throughout.

Empirical Claims and Evidence.   Not applicable.

Rational Justification.   Not applicable.

Simulation Details.   If one runs ACT-R with the flag "Rational Analysis" set to nil, one just gets a sequence of discrete cycles. Continuous time, which is the assumption of the theory, is only calculated when the flag is turned on. Then, the time for a production cycle to complete is the time elapsed until the system satisfices and selects a production. Timing options are discussed in Section 9 of the manual on the disk.

Neural Implementation.   Time necessary for network to propagate and settle.

Assumption 1: Procedural–Declarative Distinction

There is a production system component that operates on a declarative component. Both declarative and procedural representations are permanent.

Relationship to ACT*.   Same as ACT* Assumption 1.

Reference.   Section 2.2.

Empirical Claims and Evidence.   Only declarative knowledge is reportable and subject to associative priming. In contrast, only procedural knowledge is subject to retrieval asymmetries. Declarative knowledge is acquired by the direct encoding of experience, whereas procedural knowledge is acquired through practice. Damage in the hippocampal area only impacts on the ability to acquire declarative knowledge. Normal subjects can become highly skilled at a procedural task and show no improvement in their declarative access to the associated knowledge.

Rational Justification. The declarative representation allows one to quickly encode information from the environment in a form that is not committed to a particular use. On evidence that a particular use will be frequent, a procedural representation is built up that is optimized to that use.

Simulation Details. Productions are designated through use of the p command; declarative memory is created through the use of the SetWM command.

Neural Implementation. See discussion of declarative and procedural representations further on.

Assumption 2: Declarative Representation

Declarative representation can be decomposed into a set of chunks, where each chunk consists of a limited number of elements (about three) in specific relationships or slots. The elements of a chunk are themselves chunks. Complex structures are represented as hierarchies of chunks.

Relationship to ACT*. This is the same as ACT* Assumption 2, except that the term *chunk* was not used in ACT* but rather *cognitive unit*. The current representation is also of a more manifest schema-like structure, with schemas of different types having different slots to reflect their different relationships.

Reference. Section 2.3.

Empirical Claims and Evidence. Memory performance is best when information is organized into chunks of about three elements. Memory retrieval is best when test material is encoded according to the same relational structure as that used for study. Retrieval of large structures displays hierarchical organization reflecting chunk structure.

Rational Justification. A limited chunk size leads to optimal efficiency in encoding information (Servan-Schreiber, 1991) and in retrieval of information (Dirlam, 1972). Specifying elements by relational slots allows direct access through relational roles.

Simulation Details. A chunk type must be declared, with its associated slots, by WMEType command. Individual chunks are created in working memory by specifying a unique identifier, a type in an isa slot, and values for some subset of the other slots. There is no enforced limitation on chunk size.

Neural Implementation. A chunk is to be represented as a pattern of activation that associates the elements of the chunk and the context information. Specifying part of the pattern (e.g., some elements and their roles) allows other parts to be retrieved (i.e., other elements and their roles). These patterns are encoded in associations among modules of neurons in the cortex.

Assumption 3: Procedural Representation

Production rules are the basic units of skills. They are organized into condition-action pairs, in which the condition specifies a set of things that must be true of working memory, and the action specifies a set of things to add to working memory. These rules are specific to particular goals but have variables to allow them to apply in more than one situation.

Relationship to ACT*. Same as ACT* Assumption 8.

References. Section 2.4 and chapters 7 through 10.

Empirical Claims and Evidence. The learning of a complex cognitive skill can be understood in terms of relatively simple learning processes defined on the underlying production rules. The range of applicability of a skill can be understood in terms of the application conditions for the underlying rules. Skills acquired for one use will not generalize to another use because of condition-action asymmetry.

Rational Justification. The condition–action asymmetry allows rapid recognition of the applicability of the knowledge. Pattern recognition tests can be built that are specific to appropriate goals and working-memory configurations. The decomposition into relatively small production-rule units allows for recombination of the skill components so that there can be transfer to many situations.

Simulation Details. A production rule is specified as a sequence consisting of the p command, a unique production-rule identifier, a goal specification, a specification of any other condition tests, the separator ==>, and a sequence of additions to working memory and goal actions.

Neural Implementation. A production instantiation would be represented by a module for holding the variable bindings that define the production instantiation (Fig. 13.1). Multiple modules might exist to hold multiple instantiations in parallel. Part of the production-rule instantiation would be control elements for sequencing the matching of chunks in the condition and for broadcasting to declarative memory the chunks created in the action.

Assumption 4: Goal-Directed Processing

Goals are ordered on last-in-first-out (LIFO) goal stacks. The top goal is always a source of activation. Productions can push goals on the stack or pop goals off the stack. Goals can have specific utilities or values associated with them. Every production that fires must respond to some goal on some stack.

Relationship to ACT*. Same as ACT* Assumption 12.

References. Section 3.2.1 and chapter 6.

Empirical Claims and Evidence. Human behavior is goal directed. Momentary performance is determined by the number of goals that must be pushed on the stack, not by the depth of the stack.

Rational Justification. Goal specifications define the values that allow various courses of actions to be justified. Hierarchical goal structures reflect the dependency structure in the environment.

Simulation Details. Goals are pushed by the !push! command and popped by the !pop! command. Top goals on stacks are automatically assigned a value of 20 units, although this quantity can be changed by the SetG command. Multiple goal stacks are not implemented, and there is no way to respond to goals other than the top goal on the stack.

Neural Implementation. Goal stacks would be encoded by pairwise associations of goal chunks in declarative memory. Current goals would be activated in a goal module. Associated with a stack would have to be one mechanism for creating these associations when goals are pushed and one for retrieving past goals when a goal is popped. Hierarchical goal processing is implemented by the prefrontal cortex.

Assumption 5: Sources of Activation

The top elements on goal stacks and elements focused on from the environment are sources of activation. Environmental sources include the internal environment created by rehearsal processes. When a goal is popped, it is automatically removed as a source of activation. When elements are no longer focused on in the environment, they are also removed.

Relationship to ACT*. This is related to ACT* Assumptions 6 and 7. ACT* also allowed for each element on the action side of a production to be a temporary source of activation.

References. Sections 3.2.2 and 5.3.1.

Empirical Claims and Evidence. Rehearsal limitations produce memory span limitations. The rate of rehearsal determines the number of elements that can be kept active. Priming effects are a very short duration, because activation decays rapidly with intervening events.

Rational Justification. The goal and the elements in the current context are predictive of what memory chunks will be useful. Once an element is no longer in the environment, it is no longer predictive of what memory chunks will be useful.

Simulation Details. The goal is automatically included as a source of activation when it is the top goal. The goal is also automatically removed as a source of activation when it is no longer the top goal. Additional chunks can be made sources of activation through operation of the addactivationsource command. They must be removed through the operation of the removeactivationsource command. Thus, it is up to the simulator to specify the movement of attention over elements in the current context.

Neural Implementation. As in most connectionist models, elements being perceived are, naturally, sources of activation. The goal would have to be added as an internal source of activation. As in most connectionist models, when perceptual elements are removed, they are no longer sources of activation. Patterns representing these elements would be superimposed on each other in the context module within declarative memory.

Assumption 6: Activation in Declarative Memory

Chunks have, associated with them, activation levels that reflect the log odds that they will match a particular production instantiation. At any point in time, the base-level activation of a chunk is combined with activation from associated sources according to the formula:

$$A_i = B_i + \sum_j W_j S_{ji} \qquad (3.2)$$

where B_i is the base level activation (or strength) of the structure, W_j is the salience (on a scale of 0 to 1) of the source j, and S_{ji} are the strengths of association from elements j in the current context.

Relationship to ACT*. This is similar to ACT* Assumptions 3 and 5, but because activation levels reflect log odds, it is possible to have negative activation levels in ACT-R, whereas this was not allowed in ACT*. ACT* also lacked a place for base-level activation, and ACT* allowed for multi-link spread of activation. The change in these features was motivated by both rational analysis and empirical evidence. A final difference is that ACT* allowed for a continuous transition in activation level according to the differential equation:

$$\frac{dA_i(t)}{dt} = BN_i(t) - p^*A_i(t)$$

where $N_i(t)$ is the input to the node at time t and is defined as:

$$N_i(t) = C_i(t) + \sum_j S_{ji} A_j(t)$$

where S_{ji} is the relative strength of the connection from node j to i and $C_i(t)$ is 0 unless i is a source node. If i is a source node, $C_i(t)$ is a function of the strength of i. Something like this would seem to be a reasonable addition to the theory but it is not implemented in the simulation nor has it played a role in ACT-R predictions. With only one-link spread there is less need to be concerned with time transients.

References. Sections 3.2.2, 3.2.4, 5.3.1, and 5.4.

Empirical Claims and Evidence. Anderson and Milson (1989) showed that Equation 3.2 accounts for many phenomena of human memory, including fan effects, priming effects, and frequency effects.

Rational Justification. We want to order the declarative knowledge by the probability that it will lead to a successful instantiation. This allows us to maintain a large data base of knowledge without slowing down information processing. Equation 3.2 calculates log odds from log prior odds and log likelihood ratios.

Simulation Details. If the "Rational Analysis" flag is turned on, activation values are automatically associated with declarative chunks, and Equation 3.2 is automatically computed for each chunk.

Neural Implementation. The level of activation of a chunk would be represented by the strength of the signal encoding its representation in a neural module. This is a standard formula for activation combination. The W_j in Equation 3.2 would be represented by the strength of the signal for the jth element in the context module.

Assumption 7: Production Pattern Matching

The chunks in a production condition are matched sequentially, and total time to calculate an instantiation to production p is given by:

$$T_p = \sum_i Be^{-b(A_i + S_p)} \qquad (3.4)$$

where S_p is the strength of the production, A_i is the level of activation of the ith chunk matched in the condition, and b and B are constants.

Relationship to ACT*. This is related to ACT* Assumption 11, but there are substantial contrasts with the ACT* conception of pattern matching. In ACT-R chunks are matched sequentially, and matching is separated conceptually from production selection (ACT-R Assumption 11 further on). ACT* matched all conditions in parallel and embedded conflict resolution in pattern matching. ACT-R does, however, preserve many essential features of ACT*, such as controlling match time by production strength, level of declarative activation, and production complexity.

References. Sections 3.2 and 7.3.3.

Empirical Claims and Evidence. This predicts the multiplicative effects that exist between factors influencing production strength and factors influencing declarative strength. Along with the assumptions about strength growth (Assumptions 5 and 9), this predicts the power law of learning and the power law of forgetting.

Rational Justification. This formula allows for production instantiations to be computed in order of their probability of firing and, so, minimizes pattern matching costs.

Simulation Details. When the "Rational Analysis" flag is turned on, instantiation times will be printed out according to this formula.

Neural Implementation. Each condition element has to be sequentially matched, producing the summation in Equation 3.4. The resolution of the contention for access is both a function of the strength of the signal broadcast from the production (i.e., production strength) and the strength of the response in declarative memory (i.e., activation level).

Assumption 8: Production Selection

When productions are matched, they can have their utility evaluated according to the expression $PG - C$, where P is the expected probability that they will lead to the goal, G is the value of the goal, and C is the expected cost of the path. P is calculated as:

$$P = qr/(1 - (1 - q)f) \qquad (3.5)$$

where q is the probability the production will succeed, r is the probability of eventual success if the production succeeds, and f is how much prospects diminish if the production fails. C is calculated as:

$$C = a + b \qquad (3.6)$$

where a is the cost of the production and b is the expected future cost. The parameters r and b are estimated from the amount of effort so far and the difference between the current state and the goal state, respectively. A satisficing scheme operates such that a best production instantiation so far will be selected when it is estimated that it is not worth waiting for further instantiations.

Relationship to ACT*. This is related to ACT* Assumption 11, but there are substantial differences. It is a significant elaboration on ACT*, in that it separates the factors that control production-rule matching (ACT-R Assumption 7) from those that determine production-rule selection.

References. Sections 3.3, 5.3.2, 5.4, and 5.5.

Empirical Claims and Evidence. This is capable of producing the various speed–accuracy tradeoffs that have been observed. The emphasis on difference reduction produces a hillclimbing structure to problem solving. Combined with operator subgoaling, this produces means–ends analysis.

Rational Justification. This formulation identifies the production with the highest expected gain at the lowest expected cost.

Simulation Details. The calculation of P and C are determined from the parameters q, r, a, and b, which can be associated with a production by the Parameters command. The G parameter is set by the SetG function, and the threshold for satisficing is set by the :threshold keyword of SetG. The increment is set as a fraction of G. The default fraction is 5%.

Neural Implementation. The various factors going into the calculation of $PG - C$ for an instantiation achieve their effects by positive and inhibitory influences (see Fig. 3.4). Inhibitory relationships will also exist among production instantiations. The strength of the inhibitory influence of a production instantiation will be a function of the value $PG - C$. A production will fire when it surpasses threshold.

Assumption 9: Strength in Declarative Memory

Chunks have base levels of activation that reflect their log prior odds of matching to the chosen instantiation. Associations among chunks have strengths that reflect the log likelihood ratios of one chunk being a source if the other chunk is going to match to the chosen instantiation. The base level activation of a chunk is described by:

$$B_i = \log \sum_{j=1}^{n} t_j^{-d} + B \qquad (4.3)$$

where t_j is the time since the jth use of the item, and d and B are constants. The strength of association from chunk j to chunk i, S_{ji}, is defined as log R_{ji} where R_{ji} is defined as:

$$R_{ji} = \frac{a\ R^*_{ji} + F(C_j)\ E_{ji}}{a + F(C_j)} \qquad (4.5)$$

where a is a constant, R^*_{ji} is a prior estimate of the strength, $F(C_j)$ is the frequency with which C_j has occurred in the context, $E_{ji} = P_e\ (N_i|C_j)/P_e(N_i)$, $P_e(N_i|C_j)$, is the conditional probability of i matching to the chosen productions if j is in the context, and $P_e(N_i)$ is the unconditional probability of i matching.

Relationship to ACT*. This is related to ACT* Assumptions 4 and 9. ACT* assumed that chunk strength grew with each use, as in Equation 4.3, but it did not include a decay component. The associative strength between j and i was defined there only if one of i or j was a chunk containing the other.

References. Sections 3.2.2, 4.2, 5.3.1, 7.3.2, and 8.2.1.

Empirical Claims and Evidence. Equation 4.3 predicts retention and acquisition data. Equation 4.5 predicts the fan effect and priming effects.

Rational Justification. This allows the system to estimate the prior odds that a chunk will be matched and the likelihood ratio that a chunk j will be in the context if i is needed.

Simulation Details. Default association strengths are assigned to chunk associations that reflect R^*_{ji} unless specified otherwise by the SetIA command. If the "Associative Learning" flag is set, these will be changed with experience. Chunks are assigned a base level activation of 0 if the "Base Level Learning" flag is not set. If it is set to a decay parameter d, base level activations will be computed according to Equation 4.3.

Neural Implementation. There appears to be a significant role of the hippocampus in building up strength in declarative memory. Long-term potentiation appears to follow the predictions of Equation 4.3.

Assumption 10: Production Strength

Production strength is a measure of the log odds that an instantiation of the production will fire. Productions acquire strength according to the earlier Equation 4.3 under Assumption 9, where a use of a production is defined as a firing of a production instantiation.

Relationship to ACT*. The growth of strength in ACT*, described in ACT* Assumption 10, was linear with use. This did not account for the effects of the temporal pattern of practice on access to a rule.

References. Sections 4.5.1, 5.3.2, 5.5.3, 7.3.2, 7.5.2, 8.2.1, 9.2, and 9.3.

Empirical Claims and Evidence. Cognitive skills show the same practice and retention functions as do declarative structures.

Rational Justification. This makes productions available according to the log odds of their being the rule to match.

Simulation Details. Productions can be assigned strengths through the Parameters command. Strength will accumulate with experience if the "Strength Learning" flag is turned on.

Neural Implementations. Production strength helps resolve contention for access to declarative memory.

Assumption 11: Interpretive Application of Declarative Knowledge

Examples that are similar to the current problem situation can be retrieved. These examples can be analyzed into a goal and a response linked by an achieved-by relation. The current goal is mapped onto the example goal, and that mapping is used to map the example response into a response for the current problem.

Relationship to ACT*. This is related to ACT* Assumption 13. ACT* had a more general but less clearly defined conception of the declarative antecedents of productions.

References. Sections 4.3, 9.3, and chapter 7.

Empirical Claims and Evidence. There is evidence for retrieval of similar examples and problem solving by analogy. The mechanism predicts the computational costs of making an analogy.

Rational Justification. Analogy produces a solution to the current problem as a generalization of a solution to a past problem. This generalization has a high probability of succeeding, provided that the preconditions and categorical restrictions are satisfied.

Simulation Details. Analogy will be evoked under the following conditions:

1. No production applies to the current goal.
2. An example of similar type to the goal exists.
3. The example is attached to a response by an achieved-by slot.
4. A successful mapping can be computed.

Note that 1 is not a requirement under the theory.

Neural Implementation. One possibility would be to create a set of productions that computed analogies and then give these a standard neural implementation.

Assumption 12: Knowledge Compilation

Production rules are created, which embody the generalizations performed by analogy.

Relationship to ACT*. This is related to ACT* Assumption 13. ACT-R knowledge compilation is equivalent to the proceduralization process of ACT*. There is nothing that really corresponds to composition in ACT*, although the effect of composition can be obtained by compiling an analogy to an example that reflects the effect of a sequence of operations.

References. Sections 4.4, 9.3, and chapter 7.

Empirical Claims and Evidence. This produces the change in the nature of skilled performance and can sometimes produce first-trial discontinuities in the learning function.

Rational Justification. Conditional on the analogy succeeding, the generalization embodied in the analogy has a fairly high probability of being correct. Analogy computation is fairly expensive, so it makes sense to store the result of such an analogy as a production rule.

Simulation Details. A production of zero strength[1] is automatically compiled whenever an analogy takes place.

Neural Implementation. Creating new productions seems quite problematic, given the scheme sketched out in Fig. 13.1. It is conceivable that we could do away with compilation and just have strength speed up the analogy process. Then, a new production would just become equivalent to a fast analogy.

Assumption 13: Learning Production-Rule Utilities

The parameters a, b^* (underlying b), q, and r^* (underlying r) are all estimated by Bayesian methods as weighted combinations of prior and empirical quantities.

Relationship to ACT*. This is somewhat related to the ACT* tuning Assumption 14. ACT* did not separate out a measure of production-rule utility from the measure of production-rule probability. These were conflated in its tuning mechanisms.

References. Sections 4.5.2, 4.5.3, and 5.4.

Empirical Claims and Evidence. See Experiment 2 of chapter 5.

Rational Justification. This allows the system to identify the production rule of maximum expected utility.

Simulation Details. This can be evoked by turning on the "Parameters Learning" flag.

Neural Implementation. Standard neural learning techniques might well succeed in learning to map similarity and effort onto production evaluation. The parameters a, b^*, q, and r^* are really only part of the rational analysis, and there is no requirement that the brain explicitly calculate them.

---

[1]Note that strengths can be negative, and thus zero reflects an intermediate level of strength.

References

Aaronson, D., & Scarborough, H. S. (1977). Performance theories for sentence coding: Some quantitative models. *Journal of Verbal Learning and Verbal Behavior, 16,* 277–304.

Abelson, R. P. (1981). Psychological status of the script concept. *American Psychologist, 36,* 715–729.

Anderson, J. A., & Hinton, G. E. (1981). Models of information processing in the brain. In G. E. Hinton & J. A. Anderson (Eds.), *Parallel models of associative memory* (pp. 9–48). Hillsdale, NJ: Lawrence Erlbaum Associates.

Anderson, J. R. (1976). *Language, memory, and thought.* Hillsdale, NJ: Lawrence Erlbaum Associates.

Anderson, J. R. (1978). Arguments concerning representations for mental imagery. *Psychological Review, 85,* 249–277.

Anderson, J. R. (1981). Interference: The relationship between response latency and response accuracy. *Journal of Experimental Psychology: Human Learning and Memory, 7,* 326–343.

Anderson, J. R. (1982). Acquisition of cognitive skill. *Psychological Review, 89,* 369–403.

Anderson, J. R. (1983a). *The architecture of cognition.* Cambridge, MA: Harvard University Press.

Anderson, J. R. (1983b). A spreading activation theory of memory. *Journal of Verbal Learning and Verbal Behavior, 22,* 261–295.

Anderson, J. R. (1983c). Retrieval of information from long-term memory. *Science, 220,* 25–30.

Anderson, J. R. (1984). Spreading activation. In J. R. Anderson & S. M. Kosslyn (Eds.), *Essays on learning and memory* (pp. 61–90). San Francisco, CA: W. H. Freeman.

Anderson, J. R. (1986). Knowledge compilation: The general learning mechanism. In R. Michalski, J. Carbonell, & T. Mitchell (Eds.), *Machine learning II* (pp. 191–216). Los Altos, CA: Morgan Kaufmann.

Anderson, J. R. (1987a). Methodologies for the study of human knowledge. *The Behavioral and Brain Sciences, 10,* 467–505.

Anderson, J. R. (1987b). Skill acquisition: Compilation of weak-method problem solutions. *Psychological Review, 94,* 192–210.

Anderson, J. R. (1989a). The analogical origins of errors in problem solving. In D. Klahr & K. Kotovsky (Eds.), *Complex information processing* (pp. 343–372). Hillsdale, NJ: Lawrence Erlbaum Associates.

Anderson, J. R. (1989b). A rational analysis of human memory. In H. L. Roediger, III, & F. I. M. Craik (Eds.), *Varieties of memory and consciousness: Essays in honor of Endel Tulving* (pp. 195–210). Hillsdale, NJ: Lawrence Erlbaum Associates.

Anderson, J. R. (1989c). A theory of human knowledge. *Artificial Intelligence, 40*, 313–351.

Anderson, J. R. (1990a). *The adaptive character of thought.* Hillsdale, NJ: Lawrence Erlbaum Associates.

Anderson, J. R. (1990b). Analysis of student performance with the LISP tutor. In N. Fredericksen, R. Glaser, A. Lesgold, & M. Shaffo (Eds.), *Diagnostic monitoring of skill and knowledge acquisition* (pp. 27–50). Hillsdale, NJ: Lawrence Erlbaum Associates.

Anderson, J. R. (1990c). *Cognitive psychology and its implications* (3rd ed.). New York: W. H. Freeman.

Anderson, J. R. (1991). Is human cognition adaptive? *The Behavioral and Brain Sciences, 14*, 471–484.

Anderson, J. R., & Bower, G. (1973). *Human associative memory.* Washington, DC: Winston & Sons.

Anderson, J. R., Boyle, C. F., Corbett, A. T., & Lewis, M. W. (1990). Cognitive modeling and intelligent tutoring. *Artificial Intelligence, 42*, 7–49.

Anderson, J. R., Boyle, C. F., & Yost, G. (1985). The geometry tutor. *Proceedings of the IJCAI*, 1–7.

Anderson, J. R., Conrad, F. G., & Corbett, A. T. (1989). Skill acquisition and the LISP tutor. *Cognitive Science, 13*, 467–506.

Anderson, J. R., Corbett, A. T., Fincham, J. M., Hoffman, D., & Pelletier, R. (1992). General principles for an intelligent tutoring architecture. In V. Shute & W. Regian (Eds.), *Cognitive approaches to automated instruction* (pp. 81–106). Hillsdale, NJ: Lawrence Erlbaum Associates.

Anderson, J. R., Corbett, A. T., & Reiser, B. R. (1987). *Essential LISP.* Reading, MA: Addison-Wesley.

Anderson, J. R., Farrell, R., & Sauers, R. (1984). Learning to program in LISP. *Cognitive Science, 8*, 87–130.

Anderson, J. R., & Fincham, J. M. (1992). *Acquisition of procedural skill.* Unpublished manuscript.

Anderson, J. R., Greeno, J. G., Kline, P. K., & Neves, D. M. (1981). Acquisition of problem solving skill. In J. R. Anderson (Ed.), *Cognitive skills and their acquisition.* Hillsdale, NJ: Lawrence Erlbaum Associates.

Anderson, J. R., & Jefferies, R. (1985). Novice LISP errors: Undetected losses of information from working memory. *Human-Computer Interaction, 22*, 403–423.

Anderson, J. R., & Milson, R. (1989). Human memory: An adaptive perspective. *Psychological Review, 96*, 703–719.

Anderson, J. R., & Paulson, R. (1977). Representation and retention of verbatim information. *Journal of Verbal Learning and Verbal Behavior, 16*, 439–451.

Anderson, J. R., & Pelletier, R. (1991). A development system for model-tracing tutors. In *Proceedings of the International Conference of the Learning Sciences*, 1–8.

Anderson, J. R., & Reiser, B. J. (1985). The LISP tutor. *Byte, 10*, 159–175.

Anderson, J. R., & Schooler, L. J. (1991). Reflections of the environment in memory. *Psychological Science, 2*, 396–408.

Anderson, J. R., & Thompson, R. (1989). Use of analogy in a production system architecture. In S. Vosniadou & A. Ortony (Eds.), *Similarity and analogical reasoning* (pp. 267–297). Cambridge, England: Cambridge University Press.

Angell, J. R. (1908). The doctrine of formal discipline in the light of the principles of general psychology. *Educational Review, 36*, 1–14.

Angiolillo-Bent, J. S., & Rips, L. J. (1982). Order information in multiple element comparison. *Journal of Experimental Psychology: Human Perception and Performance, 8*, 392–406.

Anzai, Y., & Simon, H. A. (1979). The theory of learning by doing. *Psychological Review, 86*, 124–140.

Atkinson, R. C., & Shiffrin, R. M. (1968). Human memory: A proposed system and its control processes. In K. Spence & J. Spence (Eds.), *The psychology of learning and motivation* (Vol. 2, pp. 89–105). New York: Academic Press.

Ausubel, D. P. (1968). *Educational psychology: A cognitive view.* New York: Holt, Rinehart & Winston.

Barnes, C. A. (1979). Memory deficits associated with senescence: A neurophysiological and behavioral study in the rat. *Journal of Comparative Physiology, 43*, 74–104.

Barnes, C. A., & McNaughton, B. L. (1980). Spatial and hippocampal synaptic plasticity in senescent and middle-aged rats. In O. Stein (Ed.), *Psychobiology of aging: Problems and perspectives* (pp. 253–272). Amsterdam: Elsevier Press.

Baylor, G. (1971). *A treatise on the mind's eye: An empirical investigation of the visual mental imagery.* Unpublished doctoral dissertation, Carnegie Mellon University, Pittsburgh, PA.

Bell, C. G., & Newell, A. (1971). *Computer structures: Readings and examples.* New York: McGraw-Hill.

Berger, J. O. (1985). *Statistical decision theory and Bayesian analyses.* New York: Springer-Verlag.

Berry, D. C., & Broadbent, D. E. (1984). On the relationship between task performance and associated verbalizable knowledge. *Quarterly Journal of Experimental Psychology, 36A,* 209–231.

Bhuiyan, S., Greer, J. E., & McCalla, G. I. (1992). Learning recursion through the use of a mental model-based programming environment. In C. Frasson, G. Gauthier, & G. McCalla (Eds.), *Intelligent tutoring systems: Second International Conference Proceedings* (pp. 50–57). New York: Springer-Verlag.

Bloom, B. S. (1984). The 2-sigma problem: The search for methods of group instruction as effective as one-to-one tutoring. *Educational Researcher, 13,* 4–16.

Bobrow, D. G., & Winograd, T. (1977). An overview of KRL, a knowledge representation language. *Cognitive Science, 1,* 3–46.

Bonar, J. G., & Cunningham, R. (1988). Bridge: Tutoring the programming process. In J. Psotka, L. D. Massey, & S. A. Mutter (Eds.), *Intelligent tutoring systems: Lessons learned* (pp. 409–434). Hillsdale, NJ: Lawrence Erlbaum Associates.

Boring, E. G. (1953). A history of introspection. *Psychological Bulletin, 50,* 169–189.

Bovair, S., Kieras, D. E., & Polson, P. G. (1990). The acquisition and performance of text-editing skill: A cognitive complexity analysis. *Human Computer Interaction, 5,* 1–48.

Bower, G. H., Clark, M. C., Lesgold, A. M., & Winzenz, D. (1969). Hierarchical retrieval schemes in recall of categorical word lists. *Journal of Verbal Learning and Verbal Behavior, 8,* 323–343.

Broadbent, D. E. (1975). The magical number seven after fifteen years. In R. A. Kennedy & A. Wilkes (Eds.), *Studies in long-term memory.* New York: Wiley.

Broadbent, D. E. (1989). Lasting representations and temporary processes. In H. L. Roediger, III, & F. I. M. Craik (Eds.), *Varieties of memory and consciousness: Essays in honor of Endel Tulving* (pp. 211–228). Hillsdale, NJ: Lawrence Erlbaum Associates.

Broadbent, D. E., Fitzgerald, P., & Broadbent, M. H. P. (1986). Implicit and explicit knowledge in the control of complex systems. *British Journal of Psychology, 77,* 33–50.

Brown, J. S. (1983). Learning-by-doing revisited for electronic learning environments. In M. A. White (Ed.), *The future of electronic learning.* Hillsdale, NJ: Lawrence Erlbaum Associates.

Brown, J. S. (1985a). Idea amplifiers: New kinds of electronic learning. *Educational Horizons, 63,* 108–112.

Brown, J. S. (1985b). Process versus product: A perspective on tools for communal and information electronic learning. *Journal of Educational Computing Research, 1,* 179–201. (Original work published 1983)

Brown, J. S., & Burton, R. R. (1978a). Diagnostic models for procedural bugs in basic mathematical skills. *Cognitive Science, 2,* 155–191.

Brown, J. S., & Burton, R. R. (1978b). A paradigmatic example of an artificially intelligent instructional system. *International Journal of Man–Machine Studies, 10,* 323–339.

Brown, J. S., Burton, R. R., & de Kleer, J. (1982). Pedagogical, natural language, and knowledge engineering techniques in SOPHIE I, II, and III. In D. H. Sleeman & J. S. Brown (Eds.), *Intelligent tutoring systems* (pp. 227–282). London: Academic Press.

Brown, J. S., & VanLehn, K. (1980). Repair theory: A generative theory of bugs in procedural skills. *Cognitive Science, 4,* 397–426.

Brownston, L., Farrell, R., Kant, E., & Martin, N. (1985). *Programming expert systems in OPS5.* Reading, MA: Addison-Wesley.

Burton, R. R. (1982). Diagnosing bugs in a simple procedural skill. In D. H. Sleeman & J. S. Brown (Eds.), *Intelligent tutoring systems* (pp. 157–184). London: Academic Press.

Burton, R. R., & Brown, J. S. (1982). An investigation of computer coaching for information learning activities. In D. H. Sleeman & J. S. Brown (Eds.), *Intelligent tutoring systems* (pp. 79–98). London: Academic Press.

Butters, N., Wolfe, J., Martone, M., Gramholm, E., & Cermak, L. S. (1985). Memory disorders associated with Huntington's disease: Verbal recall, verbal recognition and procedural memory. *Neuropsychologia, 23*, 729–743.

Carbonell, J. R. (1970). AI in CAI: An artificial intelligence approach to computer-assisted instruction. *IEEE Transactions on Man–Machine Systems, 11*, 190–202.

Carbonell, J. R. (1985). *Derivational analogy: A theory of reconstructive problem solving and expertise acquisition* (Tech. Rep. No. 85-115). Pittsburgh, PA: Carnegie Mellon University, Computer Science Department.

Card, S. K., Moran, T. P., & Newell, A. (Eds.). (1983). *The psychology of human–computer interaction*. Hillsdale, NJ: Lawrence Erlbaum Associates.

Chase, W. G. (1982). *Spatial representations of taxi drivers* (Tech. Rep. No. UPITT/LRDC/ONR/KBC-6). Pittsburgh, PA: Carnegie Mellon University.

Chase, W. G., & Ericsson, K. A. (1982). Skill and working memory. In G. H. Bower (Ed.), *The psychology of learning and motivation* (Vol. 16, pp. 1–58). New York: Academic Press.

Chi, M. T. H., Bassok, M., Lewis, M., Reimann, P., & Glaser, R. (1989). Self-explanations: How students study and use examples in learning to solve problems. *Cognitive Science, 13*, 145–182.

Chi, M. T. H., Feltovich, P. J., & Glaser, R. (1981). Categorization and representation of physics problems by experts and novices. *Cognitive Science, 5*, 121–152.

Clancey, W. J. (1982). Tutoring rules for guiding a case method dialogue. In D. H. Sleeman & J. S. Brown (Eds.), *Intelligent tutoring systems* (pp. 201–226). London: Academic Press.

Clancey, W. J. (1984). Methodology for building an intelligent tutoring system. In W. Kintsch, P. G. Polson, & J. R. Miller (Eds.), *Methods and tactics in cognitive science* (pp. 51–83). Hillsdale, NJ: Lawrence Erlbaum Associates.

Clements, D. H., & Gullo, D. F. (1984). Effects of computer programming on young children's cognition. *Journal of Educational Psychology, 76*, 1051–1058.

Cohen, N. J., Eichenbaum, H., Deacedo, B. S., & Corkin, S. (1985). Different memory systems underlying acquisition of procedural and declarative knowledge. In D. S. Olton, E. Gamzu, & S. Corkin (Eds.), *Memory dysfunctions: An integration of animal and human research from preclinical and clinical perspectives*. Annals of the New York Academy of Sciences, *444*, 54–71.

Cohen, N. J., & Squire, L. R. (1980). Preserved learning and retention of pattern analyzing skills in amnesia: Dissociation of knowing how and knowing that. *Science, 210*, 207–210.

Collins, A., & Brown, J. S. (1987). The computer as a tool for learning through reflection. In H. Mandl & A. M. Lesgold (Eds.), *Learning issues for intelligent tutoring systems*. New York: Springer-Verlag.

Collins, A., Brown, J. S., & Newman, S. (1989). Cognitive apprenticeship: Teaching students the craft of reading, writing, and mathematics. In L. B. Resnick (Ed.), *Knowing, learning, and instruction: Essays in honor of Robert Glaser*. Hillsdale, NJ: Lawrence Erlbaum Associates.

Collins, A., Warnock, E. H., & Passafiume, J. (1975). Analysis and synthesis of tutorial dialogues. In G. H. Bower (Ed.), *The psychology of learning and motivation* (Vol. 9). New York: Academic Press.

Cooper, T. A., & Wogrin, N. (1988). *Rule-based programming with OPS*. San Mateo, CA: Morgan Kaufmann.

Corbett, A. T., & Anderson, J. R. (1989). Feedback timing and student control in the LISP Intelligent Tutoring System. *Proceedings of the Fourth International Conference on AI and Education*, 64–72.

Corbett, A. T., & Anderson, J. R. (1990). The effect of feedback control on learning to program with the LISP tutor. *Proceedings of the 12th Annual Conference of the Cognitive Science Society,* 796–803.

Corbett, A. T., & Anderson, J. R. (1992). Student modeling and mastery learning in a computer-based programming tutor. In C. Frasson, G. Gauthier, & G. McCalla (Eds.), *Intelligent tutoring systems: Second international conference proceedings* (pp. 413–420). New York: Springer-Verlag.

Corbett, A. T., Anderson, J. R., & Fincham, J. M. (1991). Menu selection vs. typing: Effects on learning in an intelligent programming tutor. In L. Birnbaum (Ed.), *Proceedings of the International Conference of the Learning Sciences* (pp. 107–112). Charlottesville, VA: Association for the Advancement of Computing in Education.

Corkin, S. (1968). Acquisition of motor skill after bilateral medial temporal excision. *Neuropsychologia, 6,* 255–265.

Craik, F. I. M., & Lockhart, R. S. (1972). Levels of processing: A framework for memory research. *Journal of Verbal Learning and Verbal Behavior, 11,* 671–684.

Dalbey, J., & Linn, M. C. (1986). Cognitive consequences of programming: Augmentations to basic instructions. *Journal of Educational Computer Research, 2,* 75–93.

Dirlam, D. K. (1972). Most efficient chunk size. *Cognitive Psychology, 3,* 355–359.

du Boulay, B., Patel, M., & Taylor, C. (1992). Programming environments for novices. In E. Lemut (Ed.), *Cognitive models and intelligent environments for learning programming: NATO advanced research workshop proceedings.* Genova, Italy: University of Genova.

Dulany, D. E., Carlson, R. A., & Dewey, G. I. (1984). A case of syntactical learning and judgment: How conscious and how abstract? *Journal of Experimental Psychology: General, 113,* 541–555.

Dyer, F. N. (1973). The Stroop phenomenon and its use in the study of perceptual, cognitive, and response processes. *Memory & Cognition, 1,* 106–120.

Egan, D. E., & Greeno, J. (1974). Theory of rule induction: Knowledge acquired in concept learning, serial pattern learning, and problem solving. In L. W. Gregg (Ed.), *Knowledge and cognition* (pp. 43–104). Hillsdale, NJ: Lawrence Erlbaum Associates.

Ericsson, K. A., & Simon, H. A. (1980). Verbal reports as data. *Psychological Review, 87,* 215–251.

Ericsson, K. A., & Simon, H. A. (1984). *Protocol analysis: Verbal reports as data.* Cambridge, MA: MIT Press.

Farley, M. (1974). *VIPS: A visual imagery and perception system: The results of a protocol analysis.* Unpublished doctoral dissertation, Carnegie Mellon University, Pittsburgh, PA.

Feldman, J. (1959). *An analysis of predictive behavior in a two-choice situation.* Unpublished doctoral dissertation, Carnegie Institute of Technology, Pittsburgh, PA.

Feldman, J. (1963). Simulation of behavior in the binary choice experiment. In E. A. Feigenbaum & J. Feldman (Eds.), *Computers and thought* (pp. 329–346). New York: McGraw-Hill.

Fong, G. T., Krantz, D. H., & Nisbett, R. E. (1986). The effects of statistical training on thinking about everyday problems. *Cognitive Psychology, 18,* 253–292.

Forgy, C. L. (1981). *OPS5 user's manual* (Tech. Rep.). Pittsburgh, PA: Carnegie Mellon University, Department of Computer Science.

Forgy, C. L. (1984). *The OPS83 report* (Tech. Rep.). Pittsburgh, PA: Carnegie Mellon University, Department of Computer Science.

Fox, B. A. (1988). *Cognitive and interactional aspects of correction in tutoring* (Tech. Rep. No. 88-2). Boulder: University of Colorado, Institute of Cognitive Science.

Frasson, G., Gauthier, G., & McCalla, G. I. (Eds.). (1992). *Intelligent tutoring systems: Second International Conference Proceedings.* New York: Springer-Verlag.

Frijda, N. J. (1967). Problems of computer simulation. *Behavioral Science, 122,* 59–81.

Gagné, E. D. (1985). *The cognitive psychology of school learning.* Boston: Little, Brown.

Gagné, R. M., & Briggs, L. J. (1979). *Principles of instructional design* (2nd ed.). New York: Holt, Rinehart & Winston.

Gagné, R. M., & Smith, E. C. (1962). A study of the effects of verbalization on problem solving. *Journal of Experimental Psychology: Human Learning and Memory, 3,* 305–315.

Genesereth, M. R. (1977). An automated consultant for MACSYMA. *Proceedings of the Fifth International Joint Conference on Artificial Intelligence*. Cambridge, MA, 789.

Gentner, D. (1983). Structure-mapping: A theoretical framework for analogy. *Cognitive Science, 7*, 155–170.

Gick, M. L., & Holyoak, K. J. (1980). Analogical problem solving. *Cognitive Psychology, 12*, 306–355.

Gick, M. L., & Holyoak, K. J. (1983). Schema induction and analogical transfer. *Cognitive Psychology, 15*, 1–38.

Gillund, G., & Shiffrin, R. M. (1984). A retrieval model for both recognition and recall. *Psychological Review, 91*, 1–67.

Goldberg, E., & Bilder, R. M. (1987). The frontal lobes and hierarchical organization of cognitive control. In E. Perecman (Ed.), *The frontal lobes revisited* (pp. 159–187). New York: IRBN Press.

Goldenson, D. R. (1989a). The impact of structure editing on introductory computer science education: The results so far. *SIGCSE Bulletin, 21*, 26–29.

Goldenson, D. R. (1989b). Teaching introductory programming methods using structure editing: Some empirical results. In W. C. Ryan (Ed.), *Proceedings of the National Educational Computing Conference 1989* (pp. 194–203). Eugene, OR: University of Oregon, International Council on Computers in Education.

Goldstein, I. P. (1979). The genetic graph: A representation for the evolution of procedural knowledge. *International Journal of Man-Machine Studies, 11*, 51–77.

Gomez, L. M., Egan, D. E., & Bowers, C. (in press). Learning to use a text editor: Some learner characteristics that predict success. *Human-Computer Interaction, 2*, 1–23.

Gray, W. D., & Atwood, M. E. (in press). Transfer, adaptation, and use of intelligent tutoring technology: The case of Grace. In M. Farr & J. Psotka (Eds.), *Intelligent computer tutors: Real world applications*. New York: Taylor & Francis.

Hayes-Roth, B., & Hayes-Roth, F. (1979). A cognitive model of planning. *Cognitive Science, 3*, 275–310.

Hirst, W., Phelps, E. A., Johnson, M. K., & Volpe, B. T. (1988). Amnesia and second language learning. *Brain & Cognition, 8*, 105–116.

Hoffer, A. (1981). Geometry is more than proof. *Mathematics Teacher*, 11–18.

Hollan, J. D., Hutchins, E. L., & Weitzman, L. (1984). STEAMER: An interactive inspectable simulation-based training system. *AI Magazine, 5*, 15–27.

Horn, J. L., & Stankov, L. (1982). Auditory and visual intelligence. *Intelligence, 6*, 165–185.

Hull, C. L. (1952). *A behavior system*. New Haven, CT: Yale University Press.

Huppert, F. A., & Piercy, M. (1978). The role of trace strength in recency and frequency judgments by amnesic and control subjects. *Quarterly Journal of Experimental Psychology, 30*, 346–354.

Ijiri, Y., & Simon, H. A. (1977). *Skew distributions and the sizes of business firms*. Amsterdam: North Holland.

James, W. (1890). *The principles of psychology*. New York: Holt.

Johnson, N. F. (1970). The role of chunking and organization in process of recall. In G. H. Bower (Ed.), *Psychology of learning and motivation* (Vol. 4). New York: Academic Press.

Johnson, W. B. (1988). Intelligent tutoring systems: If they are such good ideas, why aren't there more of them? Paper presented at the *Tenth Interservice/Industry Training Systems Conference*, Orlando, FL.

Johnson, W. L., & Soloway, E. M. (1984). PROUST: Knowledge-based program debugging. *Proceedings of the Seventh International Software Engineering Conference*, Orlando, FL, 369–380.

Karat, J. (1982). A model of problem solving with incomplete constraint knowledge. *Cognitive Psychology, 14*, 538–559.

Katz, I. R. (1988). *Transfer of knowledge in programming*. Unpublished doctoral dissertation, Carnegie Mellon University, Pittsburgh, PA.

Kessler, C. M. (1988). *Transfer of programming skills in novice LISP learners*. Unpublished doctoral dissertation, Carnegie Mellon University, Pittsburgh, PA.

Kessler, C. M., & Anderson, J. R. (1986). A model of novice debugging in LISP. In E. Soloway & S. Iyengar (Eds.), *Empirical studies in programmers* (pp. 198-212). Norwood, NJ: Ablex.

Kieras, D. (1985). The why, when, and how of cognitive simulation: A tutorial. *Behavioral Research Methods, Instruments, and Computers, 17,* 279-285.

Kieras, D., & Bovair, S. (1984). The role of a mental model in learning to operate a device. *Cognitive Science, 8,* 255-273.

Kieras, D., & Bovair, S. (1986). The acquisition of procedures from text: A production-system analysis of transfer of training. *Journal of Memory and Language, 25,* 255-273.

Klahr, D., & Carver, S. M. (1988). Cognitive objectives in a LOGO debugging curriculum: Instruction, learning, and transfer. *Cognitive Psychology, 20,* 362-404.

Klahr, D., Chase, W. G., & Lovelace, E. A. (1983). Structure and process in alphabetic retrieval. *Journal of Experimental Psychology: Learning, Memory, and Cognition, 9,* 462-477.

Klahr, D., Langley, P., & Neches, R. (Eds.). (1987). *Production system models of learning and development.* Cambridge, MA: MIT Press.

Knopman, D. S., & Nissen, M. J. (1987). Implicit learning in patients with probable Alzheimer's disease. *Neurology, 37,* 784-788.

Koedinger, K. R., & Anderson, J. R. (1990). The role of abstract planning in geometry expertise. *Cognitive Science, 14,* 511-550.

Koedinger, K. R., & Anderson, J. R. (1991). Interaction of deductive and inductive reasoning strategies in geometry novices. In *Proceedings of the 14th Annual Conference of the Cognitive Science Society,* 780-784.

Köhler, W. (1927). *The mentality of apes.* New York: Harcourt, Brace.

Kotovsky, K., & Fallside, D. (1988). Representation and transfer in problem solving. In D. Klahr & K. Kotovsky (Eds.), *Complex information processing* (pp. 69-108). Hillsdale, NJ: Lawrence Erlbaum Associates.

Kotovsky, K., & Kushmerick, N. (1991). Processing constraints and problem difficulty: A model. *Proceedings of the 13th Annual Conference of the Cognitive Science Society,* 790-795.

Kotovsky, K., Hayes, J. R., & Simon, H. A. (1985). Why are some problems hard? Evidence from Tower of Hanoi. *Cognitive Psychology, 17,* 248-294.

Kurland, D. M., Pea, R., Clement, C., & Mawby, R. (1986). A study of the development of programming ability and thinking skills in high-school students. *Journal of Educational Computer Research, 2,* 429-458.

Laird, J. E., Newell, A., & Rosenbloom, P. S. (1987). Soar: An architecture for general intelligence. *Artificial Intelligence, 33,* 1-64.

Langley, P., & Ohlsson, S. (1984). Automated cognitive modeling. In *Proceedings of the Fourth National Conference of the American Association for Artificial Intelligence,* pp. 193-197. Austin, TX.

Larkin, J. H. (1981). Enriching formal knowledge: A model for learning to solve textbook physics problems. In J. R. Anderson (Ed.), *Cognitive skills and their acquisition* (pp. 311-334). Hillsdale, NJ: Lawrence Erlbaum Associates.

Larkin, J. H., & Chabay, R. W. (Eds.). (1992). *Computer assisted instruction and intelligent tutoring systems: Shared issues and complementary approaches.* Hillsdale, NJ: Lawrence Erlbaum Associates.

Lave, J., & Wenger, E. (1990). *Situated learning: Legitimate peripheral participation.* Palo Alto, CA: Institute for Research in Learning.

Leinhardt, G., & Greeno, J. G. (1986). The cognitive skill of teaching. *Journal of Educational Psychology, 78,* 75-95.

Lepper, M. R., & Chabay, R. W. (1988). Socializing the intelligent tutor: Bringing empathy to computer tutors. In H. Mandl & A. Lesgold (Eds.), *Learning issues for intelligent tutoring systems* (pp. 242-257). New York: Springer-Verlag.

Lewis, M. W. (1989). *Developing and evaluating the CMU algebra tutor: Tension between theoretically driven and pragmatically driven design.* Paper presented at the annual meeting of the American Educational Research Association, San Francisco, CA.

Luchins, A. S. (1942). Mechanization in problem solving. *Psychological Monographs, 54*, (Whole No. 248).

Maier, N. R. F. (1931). Reasoning in humans: II. The solution of a problem and its appearance in consciousness. *Journal of Comparative Psychology, 21*, 181–194.

MacLeod, C. M., & Dunbar, K. (1988). Training and Stroop-like interferences: Evidence for a continuum of automaticity. *Journal of Experimental Psychology: Learning, Memory, and Cognition, 14*, 126–135.

Mandinach, E. B., & Linn, M. C. (1987). Cognitive consequences of programming: Achievements of experienced and talented programmers. *Journal of Educational Computing Research, 3*, 53–57.

Marescaux, P., Dejean, K., & Karnas, G. (1990). *Acquisition of specific or general knowledge at the control of a dynamic simulated system: An evaluation through a static situations questionnaire and a transfer control task* (Report No. 2PR2GK). Brussels, Belgium: KAUDYTE Project.

Marr, D. (1982). *Vision*. San Francisco: W. H. Freeman.

McCloskey, M. (1991). Networks and theories: The place of connectionism in cognitive science. *Psychological Science, 2*, 387–395.

McDermott, J. (1982). R1: A rule-based configurer of computer systems. *Artificial Intelligence, 19*, 39–88.

McDermott, J., & Forgy, C. L. (1978). Production system conflict resolution strategies. In D. A. Waterman & F. Hayes-Roth (Eds.), *Pattern-directed inference systems* (pp. 177–199). Orlando, FL: Academic Press.

McKendree, J. E. (1990). Effective feedback content for tutoring complex skills. *Human-Computer Interaction, 5*, 381–414.

McKendree, J. E., & Anderson, J. R. (1987). Frequency and practice effects on the composition of knowledge in LISP evaluation. In J. M. Carroll (Ed.), *Cognitive aspects of human–computer interaction* (pp. 236–259). Cambridge, MA: MIT Press.

Merrill, D. C., Reiser, B. J., Beekelaar, R., & Hamid, A. (1992). Making processes visible: Scaffolding learning with reasoning-congruent representations. In C. Frasson, G. Gauthier, & G. McCalla (Eds.), *Intelligent tutoring systems: Second international conference proceedings* (pp. 103–110). New York: Springer-Verlag.

Merrill, D. C., Reiser, B. J., Ranney, M., & Trafton, J. G. (in press). Effective tutoring techniques: A comparison of human tutors and intelligent tutoring systems. *The Journal of the Learning Sciences*.

Milberg, W., Alexander, M. P., Charness, N., McGlinchey-Berroth, R., & Barrett, A. (1988). Complex arithmetic skill in amnesia: Evidence for a dissociation between compilation and production. *Brain & Cognition, 8*, 77–90.

Miller, G. A. (1956). The magical number seven, plus or minus two: Some limits on our capacity for processing information. *Psychological Review, 63*, 81–97.

Miller, M. L. (1979). A structured planning and debugging environment for elementary programming. *International Journal of Man–Machine Studies, 11*, 79–95.

Moran, T. P. (1973). *The symbolic imagery hypothesis: An empirical investigation of human behavior via a production system simulation of human behavior in a visualization task*. Unpublished doctoral dissertation, Carnegie Mellon University, Pittsburgh, PA.

Neches, R. T. (1982). Simulation systems for cognitive psychology. *Behavior Research Methods and Instrumentation, 14*, 77–91.

Neves, D. M. (1977). *An experimental analysis of strategies of the Tower of Hanoi puzzle* (C.I.P. Working Paper No. 362). Pittsburgh, PA: Carnegie Mellon University.

Neves, D. M., & Anderson, J. R. (1981). Knowledge compilation: Mechanisms for the automatization of cognitive skills. In J. R. Anderson (Ed.), *Cognitive skills and their acquisition* (pp. 57–84). Hillsdale, NJ: Lawrence Erlbaum Associates.

Newell, A. (1972). A theoretical exploration of mechanisms for coding the stimulus. In A. W. Melton & E. Martin (Eds.), *Coding processes in human memory* (pp. 373–434). Washington, DC: Winston.

Newell, A. (1973). Production systems: Models of control structures. In W. G. Chase (Ed.), *Visual information processing*. New York: Academic Press.

Newell, A. (1991). *Unified theories of cognition*. Cambridge, MA: Cambridge University Press.

Newell, A., & Rosenbloom, P. S. (1981). Mechanisms of skill acquisition and the law of practice. In J. R. Anderson (Ed.), *Cognitive skills and their acquisition* (pp. 1-56). Hillsdale, NJ: Lawrence Erlbaum Associates.

Newell, A., & Simon, H. A. (1972). *Human problem solving*. Englewood Cliffs, NJ: Prentice-Hall.

Nisbett, R. E., & Schachter, S. (1966). Cognitive manipulation of pain. *Journal of Experimental Social Psychology, 2*, 227-236.

Nisbett, R. E., & Wilson, T. D. (1977). Telling more than we can know: Verbal reports on mental processes. *Psychological Review, 84*, 231-259.

Nissen, M. J., & Bullemer, P. (1987). Attentional requirements of learning: Evidence from performance measures. *Cognitive Psychology, 19*, 1-32.

Nissen, M. J., Knopman, D. S., & Schacter, D. L. (1987). Neuro-chemical dissociation of memory systems. *Neurology, 37*, 789-794.

Norman, D. A. (1973). Memory, knowledge, and the answering of questions. In R. L. Solso (Ed.), *Contemporary issues in cognitive psychology* (pp. 135-166). Washington, DC: Winston.

Norman, D. A. (1981). Categorization of action slips. *Psychological Review, 88*, 1-15.

Ohlsson, S. (1973). *PSS reference manual* (Tech. Rep. No. 4.) Stockholm, Sweden: University of Stockholm, Department of Psychology.

Ohlsson, S. (1988). Computer simulation and its impact on educational research and practice. *International Journal of Educational Research, 12*, 5-34.

Ohlsson, S. (1990). Trace analysis and spatial reasoning: An example of intensive cognitive diagnosis and its implications for testing. In N. Frederiksen, R. Glaser, A. Lesgold, & M. C. Shafto (Eds.), *Diagnostic monitoring of skill and knowledge acquisition* (pp. 251-296). Hillsdale, NJ: Lawrence Erlbaum Associates.

Ohlsson, S., & Rees, E. (1991). The function of conceptual understanding in the learning of arithmetic procedures. *Cognition & Instruction, 8*, 103-129.

Pachella, R. G. (1974). The interpretation of reaction time in information-processing research. In B. H. Kantowitz (Ed.), *Human information processing: Tutorials in performance and cognition* (pp. 41-82). Hillsdale, NJ: Lawrence Erlbaum Associates.

Paivio, A. (1971). *Imagery and verbal processes*. New York: Holt, Rinehart & Winston.

Palumbo, D. B., (1990). Programming languages/problem-solving research: A review of relevant issues. *Review of Educational Research, 60*, 65-89.

Payne, S. J., & Squibb, H. R. (1990). Algebra mal-rules and cognitive accounts for error. *Cognitive Science, 14*, 445-481.

Peck, V. A., & John, B. E. (1992). Browser-Soar: A computational model of a highly interactive task. *Proceedings of CHI 1992* (Monterey, CA, May 3–May 7, 1992) ACM, New York, 1992, pp. 165-172.

Pennington, N., & Nicolich, R. (1991). Transfer of training between programming subtasks: Is knowledge really use specific? In J. Koenemann-Belliveau, T. G. Moher, & S. P. Robertson (Eds.), *Proceedings of the Fourth Workshop on Empirical Studies of Programmers* (pp. 156-176). Norwood, NJ: Ablex.

Phelps, E. A. (1989). *Cognitive skill learning in amnesics*. Unpublished doctoral dissertation, Princeton University, Princeton, NJ.

Pillsbury, W. B. (1908). The effects of training on memory. *Educational Review, 36*, 15-27.

Pirolli, P. L., & Anderson, J. R. (1985). The role of practice in fact retrieval. *Journal of Experimental Psychology: Learning, Memory, and Cognition, 11*, 136-153.

Polson, P., & Kieras, D. E. (1985). A quantitative model of learning and performance of text editing knowledge. In L. Bormann & B. Curtis (Eds.), *Proceedings of CHI '85 Human Factors in Computing Systems Conference*. New York: Association for Computing Machinery.

Polson, P. G., Muncher, E., & Kieras, D. E. (1987). *Transfer of skills between inconsistent editors* (MCC Tech. Rep. No. ACA-HI-395-87). Austin, TX: Microelectronics and Computer Technology Corporation.

Post, E. L. (1943). Formal reductions of the general combinatorial decision problem. *American Journal of Mathematics, 65,* 197–268.

Postman, L. (1971). Transfer, interference, and forgetting. In L. W. Kling & L. A. Riggs (Eds.), *Experimental psychology* (pp. 1019–1032). New York: Holt, Rinehart & Winston.

Ratterman, M. J., & Gentner, D. (1987). Analogy and similarity: Determinants of accessibility and inferential soundness. In *Proceedings of the Ninth Annual Conference of the Cognitive Science Society* (pp. 22–34). Hillsdale, NJ: Lawrence Erlbaum Associates.

Reder, L. M., Charney, D. H., & Morgan, K. I. (1986). The role of elaborations in learning a skill from an instructional text. *Memory & Cognition, 14,* 64–78.

Reed, A. V. (1973). Speed–accuracy tradeoff in recognition memory. *Science, 181,* 574–576.

Reed, S. K. (1987). A structure-mapping model for word problems. *Journal of Experimental Psychology: Learning, Memory, and Cognition, 13,* 124–139.

Reiser, B. J., Kimberg, D. Y., Lovett, M. C., & Ranney, M. (1992). Knowledge representation and explanation in GIL, an intelligent tutor for programming. In J. H. Larkin & R. W. Chabay (Eds.), *Computer assisted instruction and intelligent tutoring systems: Shared issues and complementary approaches* (pp. 111–150). Hillsdale, NJ: Lawrence Erlbaum Associates.

Roediger, H. L., & Blaxton, T. A. (1987). Effects of varying modality, surface features and retention interval on priming in word fragment completion. *Memory & Cognition, 15,* 379–388.

Ross, B. H. (1984). Remindings and their effects in learning a cognitive skill. *Cognitive Psychology, 16,* 371–416.

Ross, B. H. (1987). This is like that: The use of earlier problems and the separation of similarity effects. *Journal of Experimental Psychology: Learning, Memory, and Cognition, 13,* 629–639.

Ross, B. H. (1989). Distinguishing types of superficial similarities: Effects on the access and use of earlier problems. *Journal of Experimental Psychology: Learning, Memory, and Cognition, 15,* 456–468.

Ruiz, D. (1987). Learning and problem solving: What is learned while solving the Tower of Hanoi? (Doctoral dissertation, Stanford University, 1986). *Dissertation Abstracts International, 42,* 3438B.

Ruiz, D., & Newell, A. (1989). Strategy-change in the Tower of Hanoi: A Soar model. In *Proceedings of the 11th Annual Conference of the Cognitive Science Society* (pp. 521–529). Hillsdale, NJ: Lawrence Erlbaum Associates.

Rumelhart, D. E., & McClelland, J. L. (1986). *Parallel distributed processing: Explorations in the microstructure of cognition* (Vol. 1). Cambridge, MA: MIT Press/Bradford Books.

Rumelhart, D. E., & Ortony, A. (1976). The representation of knowledge in memory. In R. C. Anderson, R. J. Spiro, & W. E. Montague (Eds.), *Semantic factors in cognition* (pp. 99–136). Hillsdale, NJ: Lawrence Erlbaum Associates.

Rumelhart, D. E., Smolensky, P., McClelland, J. L., & Hinton, G. E. (1986). Schematic and sequential thought processes in PDP models. In J. L. McClelland & D. E. Rumelhart (Eds.), *Parallel distributed processing* (Vol. 2, pp. 7–57). Cambridge, MA: MIT Press.

Ryan, J. (1969). Grouping and short-term memory: Different means and patterns of grouping. *Quarterly Journal of Experimental Psychology, 21,* 137–147.

Ryle, G. (1949). *Concept of the mind.* London: Hutchinson.

Salomon, G., & Perkins, D. N. (1987). Transfer of cognitive skills from programming: When and how? *Journal of Educational Computer Research, 3,* 149–169.

Santa, J. L. (1977). Spatial transformations of words and pictures. *Journal of Experimental Psychology: Human Learning and Memory, 3,* 418–427.

Sauers, R., & Farrell, R. (1982). *GRAPES user's manual* (Tech. Rep.). Carnegie Mellon University, Department of Psychology.

Schacter, D. L. (1987). Implicit memory: History and current status. *Journal of Experimental Psychology: Learning, Memory, and Cognition, 13,* 501–518.

Schank, R. C., & Abelson, R. P. (1977). *Scripts, plans, goals, and understanding: An inquiry into human knowledge structures*. Hillsdale, NJ: Lawrence Erlbaum Associates.

Scheines, R., & Sieg, W. (in press). An experimental comparison of alternative proof construction environments. *Proceedings of the Fifth International Conference on Computers and Philosophy*.

Schneider, W. (1988). Sensitivity analysis in connectionist modeling. *Behavior Research and Methods, Instruments, & Computers, 20*, 282–288.

Schoenfeld, A. H. (1985). *Mathematical problem solving*. New York: Academic Press.

Schofield, J. W., & Evan-Rhodes, D. (1989). Artificial intelligence in the classroom: The impact of a computer-based tutor on teachers and students. *Proceedings of the Fourth International Conference on AI and Education*, 238–243.

Scholtz, J., & Wiedenbeck, S. (1989). *Learning second and subsequent programming languages: A problem of transfer* (Tech. Rep. #80). Department of Computer Science and Engineering, University of Nebraska.

Self, J. A. (1988). Bypassing the intractable problem of student modelling. *Proceedings of the International Conference on Intelligent Tutoring Systems*, Montreal.

Servan-Schreiber, E. (1991). *The competitive chunking theory: Models of perception, learning, and memory*. Unpublished doctoral dissertation, Carnegie Mellon University, Pittsburgh, PA.

Servan-Schreiber, E., & Anderson, J. R. (1990). Chunking as a mechanism of implicit learning. *Journal of Experimental Psychology: Learning, Memory, and Cognition, 16*, 592–608.

Shepard, L. A. (1991). Psychometricians' beliefs about learning. *Educational Researcher, 20*, 2–16.

Simon, H. A. (1955). A behavioral model of rational choice. *Quarterly Journal of Economics, 69*, 99–118.

Simon, H. A. (1975). The functional equivalence of problem solving skills. *Cognitive Psychology, 7*, 268–288.

Singley, M. K. (1986). *Developing models of skill acquisition in the context of intelligent tutoring systems*. Unpublished doctoral dissertation, Carnegie Mellon University, Pittsburgh, PA.

Singley, M. K., & Anderson, J. R. (1985). The transfer of text-editing skill. *International Journal of Man–Machine Studies, 22*, 403–423.

Singley, M. K., & Anderson, J. R. (1987). A keystroke analysis of learning and transfer in text editing. *Human–Computer Interaction, 3*, 223–274.

Singley, M. K., & Anderson, J. R. (1989). *The transfer of cognitive skill*. Cambridge, MA: Harvard University Press.

Singley, M. K., Anderson, J. R., Gevins, J. S., & Hoffman, D. (1989). The algebra word problem tutor. *Artificial Intelligence and Education*, 267–275.

Sleeman, D. H. (1982). Assessing aspects of competence in basic algebra. In D. H. Sleeman & J. S. Brown (Eds.), *Intelligent tutoring systems* (pp. 185–200). London: Academic Press.

Sleeman, D., Kelly, A. E., Martinak, R., Ward, R. D., & Moore, J. L. (1989). Studies of diagnosis and remediation with high-school algebra students. *Cognitive Science, 13*, 551–568.

Smolensky, P. (1986). Information processing in dynamical systems: Foundations of harmony theory. In D. E. Rumelhart & J. L. McClelland (Eds.), *Parallel distributed processing: Explorations in the microstructure of cognition* (Vol. 1, pp. 194–281). Cambridge, MA: MIT Press/Bradford Books.

Smolensky, P. (1990). Tensor product variable binding and the representation of symbolic structures in connectionist systems. *Artificial Intelligence, 46*, 159–216.

Snow, R. E., & Lohman, D. F. (1984). Toward a theory of cognitive aptitude for learning from instruction. *Journal of Educational Psychology, 76*, 347–376.

Squire, L. R. (1987). *Memory and brain*. New York: Oxford University Press.

Sternberg, R. J. (1977). *Intelligence, information processing, and analogical reasoning*. Hillsdale, NJ: Lawrence Erlbaum Associates.

Sternberg, R. J., & Gardner, M. K. (1983). Unities in inductive reasoning. *Journal of Experimental Psychology: General, 112*, 80–116.

Stigler, J. W., & Perry, M. (1990). Mathematics learning in Japanese, Chinese, and American classrooms. In J. W. Stigler, R. A. Shweder, & G. Herdt (Eds.), *Cultural psychology* (pp. 328–356). New York: Cambridge University Press.

Swan, K. (1989). *LOGO programming and the teaching and learning of problem solving.* Unpublished doctoral dissertation, Teachers College, Columbia University, New York.

Thagard, P., Holyoak, K. J., Nelson, G., & Gochfeld, D. (1990). Analog retrieval by constraint satisfaction. *Artificial Intelligence, 46,* 259–310.

Thorndike, E. L. (1922). *The psychology of arithmetic.* New York: Macmillan.

Thorndike, E. L. (1906). *Principles of teaching.* New York: A. G. Seiler.

Thorndike, E. L., & Woodworth, R. S. (1901). The influence of improvement in one mental function upon the efficiency of other functions. *Psychological Review, 8,* 247–261.

Titchener, E. B. (1912). Prolegomena to a study of introspection. *American Journal of Psychology, 23,* 427–448.

Touretzky, D. S., & Hinton, G. E. (1988). A distributed connectionist production system. *Cognitive Science, 12,* 423–466.

Towne, D. M., Munro, A., Pizzini, Q. A., & Surmon, D. S. (1987). Simulation composition tools with integrated semantics. *Abstracts of the Third International Conference on Artificial Intelligence and Education* (p. 54). University of Pittsburgh, Learning Research and Development Center, Pittsburgh, PA.

Townsend, J. T. (1974). Issues and models concerning the processing of a finite number of inputs. In B. H. Kantowitz (Ed.), *Human information processing: Tutorials in performance and cognition* (pp. 133–186). Hillsdale, NJ: Lawrence Erlbaum Associates.

Trafton, J. G., & Reiser, B. J. (1991). Providing natural representations to facilitate novices' understanding in a new domain: Forward and backward reasoning in programming. *Proceedings of the 13th Annual Conference of the Cognitive Science Society,* 923–927.

VanLehn, K. (1989). Learning events in the acquisition of three skills. *Proceedings of the 11th Annual Conference of the Cognitive Science Society,* 434–441.

VanLehn, K. (1990). *Mind bugs: The origins of procedural misconceptions.* Cambridge, MA: MIT Press.

Vosberg, D. (1977). *On the equivalence of parallel and serial models of information processing.* Paper presented at the 10th Mathematical Psychology Meetings, Los Angeles, CA.

Waterman, D. A., & Newell, A. (1971). Protocol analysis as a task for artificial intelligence. *Artificial Intelligence, 2,* 285–318.

Watson, J. B. (1930). *Behaviorism.* Chicago, IL: University of Chicago Press.

Wellington, D. B., Nissen, M. J., & Bullemer, P. (1989). On the development of procedural knowledge. *Journal of Experimental Psychology: Learning, Memory, and Cognition, 15,* 1047–1060.

Wenger, E. (1987). *Artificial intelligence and tutoring systems: Computational and cognitive approaches to the communication of knowledge.* Los Altos, CA: Morgan Kaufmann.

Wertheimer, R. (1990). The Geometry Proof Tutor: An "intelligent" computer-based tutor in the classroom. *Mathematics Teacher,* 308–313.

Wickelgren, W. A. (1964). Size of rehearsal group and short-term memory. *Journal of Experimental Psychology, 68,* 413–419.

Winograd, T. (1975). Frame representations and the declarative–procedural controversy. In D. Bobrow & A. Collins (Eds.), *Representations and understanding* (pp. 185–210). New York: Academic Press.

Winston, P. H., Binford, T. O., Katz, B., & Lowry, M. (1983). Learning physical descriptions from functional definitions, examples, and precedents. *Proceedings of the American Association of Artificial Intelligence,* Washington, DC.

Wixted, J. T., & Ebbesen, E. B. (1991). On the form of forgetting. *Psychological Science, 2,* 409–415.

Woodrow, H. (1927). The effect of the type of training upon transference. *Journal of Educational Psychology, 18,* 159–172.

Woolf, B. P., & McDonald, D. D. (1984). Building a computer tutor: Design issues. *IEEE Computer, 17*, 61–73.

Wu, Q. (1992). *Knowledge transfer among programming languages*. Unpublished doctoral dissertation, Carnegie Mellon University, Pittsburgh, PA.

Wu, Q., & Anderson, J. R. (1992). *Problem-solving transfer among programming languages*. Manuscript submitted for publication.

Young, S. R. (1985). Programming simulations of cognitive processes: An example of building macrostructures. *Behavior Research Methods, Instruments, and Computers, 17*, 286–293.

Young, R. M., & O'Shea, T. (1981). Errors in children's subtraction. *Cognitive Science, 5*, 153–177.

Author Index

Subject Index

A

Abstraction of productions, 7

Activation, 13, 20-21, 48-56, 63-65, 70-71, 83, 100-101, 272-275, 287-289

  base-level activation, 50-51, 71-76

  associative strengths, 51, 70-71, 76-77

ACT*, 3, 8-9, 13-15, 26, 47, 50, 51, 54, 69, 87-88, 90, 93, 184, 280, 281, 284-295

ACT-R specifications, 281-295

Addition, model of, 4-7, 29-30, 38-43

Algorithm level, 10

Amnesia, 22-25

Analogy, 78-85, 183, 238-239, 276-278, 293-294

  see also knowledge compilation

Architectures—see cognitive architectures

Associative priming—see priming

Asymmetry of productions, 7, 21-22, 196-203

C

Calculus, 196-203

Chunks, 25-31, 285-286—see also activation

configural structure, 27-28

hierarchical organization, 28-29

notation, 29-31

size, 26-27

storage, 70-71

Cognitive architectures, 3-4

  production systems, 4-10

Compilation—see knowledge compilation

Composition of productions, 26, 87-88

Computer programming, 205-233

  see also LISP learning

Computer simulation

  developing a basic production-rule model, 266-268

  evaluation, 105-106

  in ACT-R, 8, 27, 38-43, 46, 49, 50, 55, 71, 76, 80, 82, 83-84, 90, 91, 99, 103, 132, 150, 267-278, 280-281, 284-295

  navigation, 99-119

  source of ideas, 257-266

  Tower of Hanoi, 123-142

Conflict resolution, 7, 15, 45-67, 93-119, 268-272

  in the geometry tutor, 167-168

  see also activation, production evaluation

Connectionism, 3, 10, 20, 50, 91, 119

  see also neural-style computation

P

Pascal—see computer programming
Pattern matching, 7, 47–56, 63–65, 290
Power-law forgetting, 71–76
Power-law learning, 52, 71–76, 91
  see also learning curves
Priming, 21, 24, 52
Probability of success of a production, 58–59,
  65–67, 90–91, 113–115
Problem-solving, 59, 93–94
  see also analogy, computer pro-
    gramming, eight puzzle, goal struc-
    tures, LISP learning, navigation task,
    production evaluation, Tower of
    Hanoi, transfer
Procedural-declarative distinction, 9, 18–25,
  284–285
see also interpretive application, knowledge
    compilation
  definition, 19–20
  dissociations, 22–25
Procedural memory—see productions
Production evaluation, 56–63, 101–102,
  268–272, 290–291, 295
  see also strategy change
  cost, 58–59, 65–67, 90–91, 113–115,
    271–272
  probability of success, 58–59, 65–67,
    90–91, 113–115, 271–272
  satisficing, 60–63, 101–102
Production-rule modeling—see computer
  simulation
Production systems
  alternative systems, 8–9
  evidence, 9–10
  features, 4–8
Production, 31–43, 286
  see also production evaluation
  abstraction, 7, 35–37
  asymmetry, 7, 35–37
  goal structuring, 7, 35–37
  learning, 85–91
  modularity, 7, 32–35
  notation, 38–43
  strength, 52–54, 63–65, 90
Prolog—see computer programming
Protocols, 259–262
  see also reportability
PUPS production system, 8, 82

R

Rational analysis, 13–14, 47, 63–67, 70, 77,
  78, 82–83, 86, 93, 279–295
  of memory activation, 50–55, 71–77
  of production evaluation, 56–63
Reportability, 19–20, 21
  see also, protocols
Representation, 17–43
Retention, 22, 71–76, 232

S

Satisficing, 60–63, 101–102
Short-term memory, 2–3
Skill acquisition—see geometry learning,
  knowledge compilation, learning, LISP
  learning, strategy change, transfer
Soar, 8–9, 18–20, 46, 87, 118–119, 161
Spreading activation
  see activation
Stimulus-response bonds, 35
Strategy change, 111–117
Strength, 13
  declarative memory, 51, 70–71, 76–77,
    100–101, 154–155, 174–175, 275,
    292–293
  productions, 52–54, 63–65, 90, 101, 117,
    154–155, 174–176, 293

T

Task analysis, 32, 258–259
Text editing, 185–196
Theories, 2–3
  see also identifiability
Tower of Hanoi task, 23, 121–142, 261–262,
  265–266
  ACT-R implementation, 268–271
  isomorphs, 137–141
Transfer, 37–38, 183–233
  calculus, 196–203
  declarative transfer, 200–203, 228–232
  identical elements theory, 184–196
  negative transfer, 191–193
  programming, 205–233
  text-editing, 185–196
  use-specificity, 196–203